Re-Thinking
E-Learning
Research

Studies in the
Postmodern Theory of Education

Joe L. Kincheloe and Shirley R. Steinberg
General Editors

Vol. 333

PETER LANG
New York • Washington, D.C./Baltimore • Bern
Frankfurt am Main • Berlin • Brussels • Vienna • Oxford

NORM FRIESEN

Re-Thinking
E-Learning
Research

Foundations, Methods, and Practices

PETER LANG
New York • Washington, D.C./Baltimore • Bern
Frankfurt am Main • Berlin • Brussels • Vienna • Oxford

Library of Congress Cataloging-in-Publication Data

Friesen, Norm.
Re-thinking e-learning research: foundations, methods, and practices /
Norm Friesen.
p. cm. — (Counterpoints: studies in the postmodern theory of education; v. 333)
Includes bibliographical references and index.
1. Computer-assisted instruction—Research.
2. Internet in education—Research. 3. Educational technology—
Psychological aspects—Research. I. Title
LB1028.5.F76 371.33'44678—dc22 2008043864
ISBN 978-1-4331-0136-6 (hardcover)
ISBN 978-1-4331-0135-9 (paperback)
ISSN 1058-1634

Bibliographic information published by **Die Deutsche Bibliothek**.
Die Deutsche Bibliothek lists this publication in the "Deutsche
Nationalbibliografie"; detailed bibliographic data is available
on the Internet at http://dnb.ddb.de/.

The paper in this book meets the guidelines for permanence and durability
of the Committee on Production Guidelines for Book Longevity
of the Council of Library Resources.

© 2009 Peter Lang Publishing, Inc., New York
29 Broadway, 18th floor, New York, NY 10006
www.peterlang.com

Printed in the United States of America

Contents

Foreword

Andrew Feenberg

In 1982 I was part of a team at the Western Behavioral Sciences Institute that created one of the first e-learning programs. We attracted professors from leading universities, excited about gaining access to a computer network and business and government leaders interested in experiencing the new technology and able to afford the high cost of this early experiment. Our equipment was primitive by contemporary standards and enabled us to do no more than exchange messages online. The faculty elaborated a pedagogy based on discussion with and between the students. Gradually, other faculty at other institutions initiated similar experiments. But it was only in the late 1990s that university administrations and software companies showed an interest. Their involvement led to a huge expansion of access to online education, but their agenda was quite different from ours. While we were mainly intrigued by the educational potential of online discussion, they seemed more interested in automating higher education on the Internet. These divergent agendas emerging at the very origins of e-learning as a recognized field typify the field of educational technology.

In nearly every country in the world except the United States, education is the single most costly item in the state budget. Yet there are grave doubts about the effectiveness of all this expense. It is widely believed that achievement has declined as educational opportunity has increased. Many researchers and political and corporate leaders continue to hope that technology can meet the challenge of mass education. After all, technology has vastly revolutionized production, distribution, and many services. Why not in education as well? Studies are conducted to ground this hope in numbers with the aim of justifying expensive investments today by the promise of future cost savings. Meanwhile, teachers propose other solutions, such as smaller class sizes, and these proposals are supported by other studies.

These debates over the problems of education would be more likely to lead to a conclusion if the various policy alternatives could be judged by the same standard. Funding and administrative agencies demand quantitative results. But professional teachers often feel that their knowledge is ignored by such research. Different methods are privileged by these different actors and no "meta-method" exists to judge between them.

The issue is often formulated in terms of the distinction between quantitative and qualitative research. Qualitative methods are rooted in experience. They can articulate the informal knowledge acquired by teachers in the course of teaching and the commonsense understanding of students. Much of this knowledge concerns what "works" in the classroom. Some of it is also contextual and has to do with institutional features of the educational system. Starting out from this basic experiential knowledge, social scientists elaborate more or less rigorous methodological approaches. But qualitative methods are contested for their lack of experimental grounding.

Quantitative research is modeled on the natural-scientific method and seeks to tease out causal connections from statistical correlations. Like the natural scientist, the researcher sees himself or herself as completely independent of the object of research and various checks are incorporated into studies to eliminate subjective bias. In the best case, research would supersede professional judgment in education, as it has to a great extent in medicine. However, the results in education will never carry conviction to the same degree as controlled double-blind studies of many thousands or even tens of thousands of experimental subjects in medicine. Inconclusive studies give rise to the researchers' worst nightmare, the phenomenon known as "no significant difference," which appears to show that different practices and technologies have no impact on outcomes. This has very practical consequences.

Education is not a pill, and relationships between cause and effect are notoriously difficult to establish. Methodological conflicts and disagreements over strategies for improving education are intertwined in ways that block consensus. We have no choice but to learn to live without certainties. Many different perspectives must be brought to bear on the problems of mass education and many different solutions to those problems need to be experimented. The book you are reading is a plea for such methodological pluralism in the study of e-learning.

Education is complex and reveals different aspects from different points of view. Qualitative methods are too often overlooked and undervalued, but they can inform the study of technology in education, sharpening awareness of achievements and problems. Methodological self-awareness may refute assumptions that seem obvious but cannot stand up to informed scrutiny. Correctives to flawed quantitative studies can be developed.

Since teachers have access to research results, these flow into the field and influence practice for better or for worse. This is especially true of the qualitative methods described here, which are often more accessible and open to commonsensical application and adoption. These methods can help teachers make their tacit understanding of their work explicit and so subject to criticism and refinement.

Thus a survey such as this one has a double purpose: to inform researchers of the variety of available methods, and to enable teachers to appreciate the contributions of research to their practice. The latter is particularly important in the field of e-learning, which has yet to establish a uniform culture guiding the expectations of teachers and students.

When we first explored the potential of computer-mediated communication in the early 1980s, I wrote that this new form of communication was uniquely reflexive because so many of its codes were still uncertain. At the time I thought that by the first decade of the twenty-first century the field would have settled into a familiar pattern. But rapid changes in technology and usages have refuted my expectations. E-learning is an example of a domain of communicative practice that is still in flux nearly thirty years after its earliest emergence. This book can contribute to the realization of its potentials.

Acknowledgments

An overview like the one provided in this book can emerge only through extensive dialogue with friends and colleagues, across disciplines, research orientations, and national boundaries. The author therefore has many specific contributions to acknowledge and many individuals to thank.

For many lively discussions and exchanges of ideas on matters of e-learning research generally and issues of culture, narrative, genre, and media in particular, a considerable debt of gratitude is owed to Liam Rourke and Theo Hug. For a recent and rich postdoctoral experience that contributed much to the treatment of critical theory and critical-historical research in this book, I thank Andrew Feenberg and members of his Applied Communication Lab at Simon Fraser University. Darryl Cressman and Edward Hamilton are two students at this research center who deserve special mention, not only for their considerable assistance in gathering conversational data utilized in chapter seven of this book, but especially for helping me to gain a better understanding of my own field from a critical-theoretical perspective. The critique of cognitivism and the introduction to conversational analysis and discursive psychology in this book benefitted from the advice of W.M. Roth, and from guidance provided by psychologists Jack Martin, Tom Strong, and Henderikus Stam. Finally, the hermeneutic-phenomenological emphasis of the final chapters owes much to the continued support and guidance of Max van Manen. This section also reflects the ongoing influence and encouragement of my Scandinavian (and other) peers in phenomenological research, Tone Saevi and Carina Henriksson. The outstanding assistance of Johanne Provençal with issues of editing and strategies of organization and emphasis for this publication also deserves special notice.

Thanks are also due to a number of organizations whose assistance has been critical in making this book possible: the support of the Social Sciences and Humanities Research Council of Canada (in the form of a Postdoctoral Fellowship and Standard Research Grant), the Infrastructure Fund of the Canada Foundation for Innovation, the Canada Research Chair Program, as well as Thompson Rivers University, and my new colleagues and friends at this young and growing institution.

Finally, I owe a much greater debt of gratitude to those who "lived" through the process of writing this book with me. For the unfailing support and patience of my wife, Barbara Simler, I am indebted beyond all repayment.

Material in various chapters appears elsewhere. Chapter 2 is based on an article, Chronicles of Change: The Narrative Turn and E-Learning Research appearing in *E-Learning* (vol. 5, no. 3); a version of chapter 3 appears in the *International Journal of Computer Mediated Communication* under the title Genre and CSCL: The Form and Rhetoric of the Online Posting. A version of chapter 5 appears in *Mind, Culture and Activity* (vol. 16) in an article entitled Discursive Psychology and Educational Technology: Beyond the Cognitive Revolution. Finally, chapters 4 and 6 appear in *AI & Society* (vol. 23), and a version of chapter 8 has appeared in *Ubiquity* (vol. 9, no. 22; www.acm.org/ubiquity /volume_9/v9i22_ friesen.html).

Chapter One

Introduction:
Re-Thinking E-Learning Research

In the rapidly changing world of the Internet and the Web, theory and research frequently struggle to catch up with technological, social, and economic developments. Since the mid-1990s, for example, myriad business models and even an entire "new economy" associated with the Internet have risen to prominence and fallen into disrepute. The same period has also witnessed the rise of wikis, blogs, and other social software as new means of collaborative authorship and dissemination, of advocacy and social action. In the wake of such developments it becomes a significant challenge to interpret, differentiate, and disentangle hype and backlash, design and accident, as well as past certainties and future possibilities. In the social sciences generally, Internet and Web studies have emerged to address this situation by developing and adapting ethnographic, social-psychological, linguistic, critical, and other methodologies for this new virtual world. These fledgling fields provide valuable interdisciplinary contexts for investigating new online manifestations of identity, language use, and other cultural, commercial, and technical forms, from Aggregators through Facebook to YouTube.

In education, a similar proliferation of novel practices, applications, and forms—from bulletin boards to Webcasts and from online educational games to open educational resources—have come to be addressed under the rubric of "e-learning." This is also a relatively new field for both practice and research. Its disciplinary cornerstones and precursors include instructional technology and design, distance education, and educational psychology. E-learning combines insights from these fields together with an emphasis on Internet and Web technologies in general. But so far, research in this field has gravitated toward many of the same methods and philosophical frameworks used to investigate and design earlier and quite different instructional technologies and practices. Above all, this research is marked by studies that reaffirm assumptions about the nature of technology, of human activity, and the interaction of humans and technology that have long been cast into doubt in other fields of research. Technical progress, for example, is seen as single-handedly "impacting" education; human action is seen as fundamentally rational and rule-bound, while phenomena such as education and communication are understood according to models that are predominantly functional or technical in nature. These understandings have been contradicted by the complex unpredictability of technical, social, economic, and educational continuities and transformations, which continue to defy reductive explanation or predictive calculation. The challenge remains, then, for research in e-learning to be re-thought, to catch up with new developments in theory, and to reflect rapidly developing social and technical practices and configurations.

Re-Thinking E-Learning Research takes up this challenge by introducing and illustrating a number of research frameworks and methodologies relevant to e-learning. These include methods of narrative, content, genre, and discourse analysis, of hermeneutic-phenomenological investigation, and also, of critical and historical inquiry. These frameworks and investigations stand as examples of a few possibilities taken from the rich palette of methodological opportunities that can begin to address the ever richer and expanding subject matter proper to e-learning. Almost every chapter in this book both describes and applies a particular "alternative" research method to a common or emerging e-learning technology, practice, or phenomenon. Examples of these pairings of method and subject matter include narrative research into the adaptation of blogs in a classroom setting, the discursive-psychological analysis of student conversations with artificially intelligent agents, a genre analysis of an online discussion, and a phenomenological study of online mathematics puzzles. Nearly every chapter in this book, then, offers a discussion of technologies familiar to a wide range of students, teachers, and researchers in e-learning, and of methods that can readily be used in their investigation.

The subjects and methods discussed and illustrated in this book present important and timely examples and contextualizations intended for both master's- and Ph.D.-level students in educational technology, instructional design, and distance education programs. Students who are seeking to learn about qualitative and alternative methodological possibilities and approaches available for their research will be wellserved by this book. This text will also be of interest to those researching, teaching, and studying technology and education from a variety of theoretical and academic perspectives, including curriculum studies, the history and philosophy of education, media and education, as well as Internet and new media studies. It will also be valuable to reflective practitioners or teachers who are working with new technologies of various kinds, and are interested in ways of thinking about technologies in educational contexts that avoid either reduction or hyperbole. This book, finally, could also be useful as a textbook for courses in educational technology and media, instructional design and distance education. This is especially the case in courses with a focus on research methods where there is an understood need to present students with a balance of both quantitative and qualitative, post-positivist and "naturalistic" approaches (Lincoln & Guba, 1985).

Defining E-Learning as Research and Practice

This introductory chapter provides more than just an overview of the contents of this book. It also presents an argument for re-thinking the way that e-learning is typically researched and outlines a "rethought," alternative approach to this kind of research. The chapter begins by examining and synthesizing dominant understandings or definitions of "e-learning" and of "e-learning research." It then looks at the challenges and inconclusive results that have been produced thus far through these understandings of e-learning and its investigation. It advocates the adoption of an approach to e-learning that it refers to as "multivocal": one that affirms a multiplicity of knowledge types or forms, rather than understanding knowledge in exclusively technical or natural-scientific terms. This chapter concludes by showing how this multivocal knowledge can be mapped out, and indicates how this multivocality is realized in the individual chapters of this book.

The term "e-learning" was first used in the mid-1990s as a shortened form of "Electronic learning" (OED, 2007). Since that time, of course, the term has been used to describe not only a kind of learning, but also practices in education, teaching, design, and research. Looking at the way "e-learning" has been used in the titles of various books and articles indicates that it has come to represent a useful shorthand for a range of different orientations to research and to the use of technologies in education and learning. Often the precise way that the term e-learning is used is dependent on an author's particular purposes or specific research agenda. For example, in *E-Learning and the Science of Instruction,* instructional designer Ruth Colvin Clark and cognitive psychologist Richard E. Mayer (2003) describe e-learning essentially in terms of multimedia technologies and theories of individual learning and cognitive processing: "E-Learning," they explain, "should promote psychological engagement between the learner and the lesson content in ways that help learners to select, integrate, and retrieve new knowledge" (p. 151). In a book titled *E-Learning in the 21st Century,* distance education specialists D.R. Garrison and Terry Anderson (2003) speak of e-learning principally in terms of its "unique ability to bring together a community of learners, unrestricted by time or place" (p. 12). Instead of seeing a single learner engaged with content as the paradigmatic e-learning scenario, Garrison and Anderson understand e-learning primarily in terms of what they call a "collaborative constructivist" framework of learning and communal inquiry.

Despite these very different characterizations of e-learning—as predominantly individual on the one hand, and predominantly communal on the other—attempts at defining e-learning for general use have shown considerable consistency and agreement. "E-learning," as educational technologist Rob Koper writes (2007), "can be defined as the use of information and communication technologies (ICTs) to facilitate and enhance learning and teaching" (p. 356). Other sources similarly indicate that e-learning designates "learning conducted via electronic media [especially], on the Internet" (OED, 2007). As educational technologist William Horton (2006) writes, e-learning "marshals computer and network technologies to the task of education" (p. 1). E-learning, then, designates the intersection of education, teaching, and learning with information and communication technologies. In addition, it gives special emphasis to technologies and practices associated specifically with the Internet and the Web. The utility and flexibility of this general definition is illustrated by its ability to embrace the emphases of Garrison and Anderson on "bringing together communities of learners" and of Mayer and Clark on "psychological engagement between the learner and the lesson content": both refer to the conjunction of computer and especially Internet technologies with a particular conception of learning or education.

Designating the intersection of online technologies with learning and education, e-learning as a field is intrinsically interdisciplinary. It involves disciplines proper to technologies and technical design as well as fields related to the study of education, curriculum, and learning itself. E-learning, however, is not the first field of practice and research to take both technology *and* education simultaneously as its principal focus. It is preceded in this by at least two other disciplines, *educational technology* and *distance education*. Educational technology, which also goes by the name of instructional technology — and "computer-based instruction" and "programmed instruction" before it — has concentrated on the integration of media and other technical artifacts into classrooms and other teaching and learning settings. Distance education, as the name itself implies, focuses on the systematic provision of education over distance and on the use of print, televisual, electronic, and other media for this purpose. The significance of distance education and educational technology for e-learning is also indicated by some of the definitions and orientations cited above and the disciplinary backgrounds of those who have authored them. For example, Garrison and Anderson, who characterize e-learning in terms of learning communities, are experts in distance education; and Koper and Horton, who provide definitions of e-learning more generally, are experts in educational technology. These connections are illustrative of the intellectual and practical continuities that link e-learning with these more established fields of study. They also suggest that e-learning, like any other field of endeavor, does not arise completely sui generis or without precedent, but that it inherits many of the strengths and also the limitations of the disciplines and disciplinary configurations from which it emerged.

At the same time, the interdisciplinary reach of e-learning extends well beyond educational technology and distance education. Because e-learning involves education, learning, and teaching, the interdisciplinary makeup of this field also includes the related disciplines of psychology and instructional design. Again the connection of these fields to e-learning can be illustrated in terms of the specializations of some of the experts cited above. Richard E. Mayer and Ruth Colvin Clark, who define e-learning as the engagement of individual learners with multimedia, are writing from the perspectives of cognitive psychology and instructional design, respectively. This is illustrative of the close connection of cognitive psychology and instructional design to e-learning as a discipline. As in the case of distance education and educational technology, e-learning is in many ways constituted through the intellectual and practical legacy that it shares with these psychological and design fields. The individual characteristics of psychology and instructional design are as a result related to e-learning, too, and are therefore worth defining, however briefly.

Psychology, of course, refers to the systematic study of mental processes, behavior, and of human activity. Of all the disciplines with an immediate connection to e-learning, psychology is unique in that it has both practical and applied dimensions, in addition to well-developed theoretical and philosophical aspects or sub-disciplines. Both of the practical and theoretical dimensions of psychology are given significant attention in this book. Instructional design, on the other hand, has been described as a form of "applied...psychology in the best sense of the term" (Dick, 1987, p. 183). It is concerned with the design and development of instructional materials and activities to meet learning needs. Instructional design as a field generally investigates the instructional use of technologies and media through the application of systems science to organizational and educational processes.

E-learning can thus be defined as a field that emerges at the confluence of educational psychology and instructional design, of educational technology and distance education, and of recent technological developments related to the Internet and the Web. This way of defining e-learning generally is closely associated with specific ways of understanding e-learning research in particular. To use the words of educational technologist Rob Koper (whose definition of e-learning was quoted earlier), this research tends not to be "theory-oriented," but rather "technology-oriented" in character. E-learning research, Koper (2007) explains, is not focused on "predicting or understanding events [in] the world as it exists" (p. 356); it instead seeks to "*change the world as it exists*" (p. 356; emphasis added). E-learning or technology-oriented research, in other words, attempts "to develop new technological knowledge, methods, and artifacts" for practical ends or purposes (p. 356). It is this applied, practical, and technological research that Koper (2007) says is ideally suited to e-learning. E-learning is seen in this way as developing new technological knowledge, methods, and artifacts specifically with the aim of improving "learning, training and teaching" (p. 356). Koper sees this as occurring in a number of particular ways:

- By making [learning, training, and teaching] more *accessible* to everyone at any place and at any time
- By making [learning, training, and teaching] more *effective* by facilitating the implementation of advanced pedagogical and organizational approaches, [and]
- By making [learning, training, and teaching] more *efficient* by providing advanced (partly automated) support mechanisms for learners and teachers to perform their various tasks. (p. 356; emphases in original)

E-learning research, in other words, is seen as harnessing predictive, technological knowledge "about the world as it exists" in order to change and improve this world—making technologies and techniques more effective, efficient, and better. Speaking in terms of the various disciplines and definitions discussed above, one can say that the point of e-learning research is to take the practical and theoretical knowledge of psychology, instructional design, distance education, and educational technology, and adapt it to the effective, efficient, and inclusive design of Internet, Web, and other advanced technologies for education. According to this definition, where a new technological innovation appears that could allow for gains in efficiency, effectiveness, or accessibility, it would be the task of e-learning research to investigate and optimize the results of its application.

E-Learning Research: Ripe for Re-Thinking?

Although this way of defining research in e-learning appears quite direct and simple, and presents a clear, pragmatic path for both development and research, a more in-depth look at the nature and implications of this definition reveals serious problems. These problems are of two kinds: First, this definition of e-learning research does not begin to address some practical and contextual aspects that are indispensable to understanding e-learning as the use of ICTs in learning and teaching. These are presented by human, cultural contexts in which learning, teaching, and ICT use take place, and include questions such as teaching and learning practices, personal and institutional decision making, and the conventions and cultures in which all of these things take place. A second problem is presented by past experience with the kind of "technology-" and improvement-"oriented" research described by Koper—namely, the inconclusive results or statistically insignificant measures that this kind of research has tended to produce. These two problems are considered here in order to underscore the need for new methodological possibilities and alternatives in this area of research.

First, education is generally a collective and organized undertaking, be it school-level education, job retraining, or university-level specialization. (Even if it is undertaken informally or independently, it is made possible and contextualized by others' organized efforts.) This means that the deployment of technologies in e-learning settings of whatever kind is necessarily *not just* a technical or scientific problem. It is also necessarily collective, institutional, and even political in character. As such, it is and should be subject to examination and discussion that is of social and critical relevance, directed at issues of equity and social justice. Although social-critical research is of a very different kind than the natural-scientifically based technological research defined by Koper, it too holds out the promise of practical, "world-chang[ing]" results that Koper promises for e-learning research. A fairly obvious example of this type of research and of its possible results is provided by the issue of the digital divide, both within wealthy and technologically advanced countries as well as in parts of the world that are less privileged. The accessibility, effectiveness, and efficiency of e-learning programs and technologies can, of course, be closely tied to the digital divide issue. And such a divide needs to be dealt with not only as a technical problem, but also as one that is sociopolitical and economic in nature. Consequently, it is a major issue for learning that can be addressed as much through research contributing to advocacy and policy change as through technological improvements or adaptations.

As a corollary to the importance of advocacy and policy in education, e-learning research must also take into account *practice*, specifically the practices of teaching and learning. Practices of these kinds are not always anticipated in the technical design and improvement of ICTs in learning, and do not always occur right at or directly through a technological interface. As the study of the use of new technologies in teaching and learning, e-learning research consequently also needs to focus on what students and teachers are actually *doing* with technology in often complex circumstances and how they may be *adapting* it in unforeseen ways to their own educational practices and priorities. These obvious but complex questions are all too easily overlooked in design and development processes, and, for example, in task-oriented usability tests. At the same time, these questions can be very directly and explicitly addressed in the form of case study research, as is illustrated in chapters two and three of this book. Such studies do not measure the efficiency or effectiveness of a technological intervention or task completion per se. What they *do* investigate is a range of challenges and opportunities afforded through the use of particular Internet technologies in specific educational contexts. Given the rapid and ongoing changes in technologies and practices, this kind of approach has much to contribute to e-learning.

In the context of these dynamics of change, it is possible to argue that an expansion of e-learning research approaches and questions could be quite radical. Consider the question of the nature of learning and education itself. Basic questions related to education—such as student experience, teaching processes and practices, and even processes of thought and expression—are affected and reconfigured under the technical and social conditions and circumstances associated with the use of ICTs in teaching and learning. One example of these kinds of basic questions is that of common student experiences such as communication and interaction. These come to have meanings on the Web and in technological settings that are quite different from the significance that they might have in the "traditional" classroom. Although students are said to interact, discuss, and chat in both settings, the actual experience of, say, a threaded discussion forum can be quite different from a seminar meeting: one unfolds through written expression over days or weeks, and the other occurs through the spoken word over minutes or hours. The redefinition of seminar or classroom experiences in terms of interactive and even artificially intelligent Web technologies is examined in the second and third parts of this book. This explication and investigation shows that the educational significance of basic pedagogical experiences and processes is hardly self-evident and that research can benefit from a re-evaluation of some of the most fundamental terms constitutive of learning, education, and student experience.

The second problem in e-learning research as a technology-oriented activity is presented by previous research undertaken by its disciplinary precursors, educational technology and distance education. For decades, research studies in these fields have attempted to utilize natural-scientific and technical means of both effecting and measuring improvements in techniques and technologies. According to some (e.g., Schulmeister, 1997), this emphasis on the measurement of improvements has dominated research in these established fields. At the same time, this kind of research and development has not produced the results that were expected. It has not led to a coherent, progressive set of findings and insights that have been associated with gradual increases in student learning, performance, and educational productivity. Instead, studies of these kinds — seeking to measure the effect of the introduction of a new media or other technological innovation in education — have been associated with what is called the "no significant difference" phenomenon. The phrase refers to the innumerable quasi-experimental "media comparison" studies that show the introduction of a new medium or technology in education as producing only statistically insignificant differences in student outcomes. These studies have shown, in other words, that technology-based courses, when compared to those taught in the classroom, do not

result in a statistically significant difference in student performance or educational efficiency. From print-based correspondence to
courses taught via radio, television, and the Web, the use of new
media in each case was *not* found to result in a statistically significant improvement in educational efficiency. When compared with
more traditional classroom settings, any differences in student performance attributable to technological innovations tend to fall
within acceptable margins of error or statistical insignificance. In a
book-length survey of the phenomenon, Russell (1999) examines
more than 350 studies conducted over 75 years, all of which consistently arrive at the result of no significant difference. Although this
is not a predetermined outcome for all studies of this kind, one can
generally expect to conclude (as does a more recent report cited by
Russell) that, "no significant differences [are] found in outcomes
for students in...two [technologically different] modes of instruction."

The general response of educational technology and distance
education to this disappointing or at least inconclusive finding has
been to urge a redoubling of existing efforts and to demand increased scientific rigor and precision. In the conclusion of one report that attempts a rigorous analysis of many such media
comparison studies, Lou, Bernard, and Abrami (2006) urge that in
the future, such "studies should...strive for [more] rigorous control
of...methodological factors, such as instructor equivalence, instructional materials equivalence, and time on task differences" (p. 168).
Similarly, Ungerleider and Burns (2002) conclude their own review
of this type of research by saying that "[t]here are simply too few
studies of sufficiently rigorous design to permit informed policy
choices...concerning the use and implementation of ICTs" (p. 17).
Still others have advocated more radical solutions: characterizing
educational technology in particular as being largely "pseudo-
scientific" in nature, Reeves (1995) has argued for a "moratorium"
on "efforts to find out how instructional technology can effect
learning through empirical research." While this book supports the
views of scholars like Reeves that past and current circumstances
of e-learning research could be better, it advocates not a halt, but

rather an expansion of research frameworks and approaches in e-learning.

E-Learning Research as a Multivocal Enterprise

The expansion and inclusion of different approaches, under-standings, or voices that this book advocates and demonstrates is interdisciplinary and multidisciplinary in character. It is *inter*disci-plinary in that it seeks to combine and explore the *inter*connections between new and different approaches from different fields and specializations; it is *multi*disciplinary in that it simultaneously tries to respect the *multi*plicity of differences that can separate one re-search approach from another. One programmatic characterization of e-learning research that will serve as a kind of working definition for this book emphasizes both of these aspects of e-learning research:

> As a research area, e-learning is both multi- and inter-disciplinary, covers a vast range of research topics, from those that focus on technologies through to wider socio-cultural research questions...[as these extend] across peda-gogical, technical and organisational boundaries. (Conole & Oliver, 2007, pp. 3, 5)

This basic definition, provided in an edited collection entitled *Con-temporary Perspectives in E-Learning Research*, highlights a number of elements central in re-thinking e-learning research. First, it identifies e-learning as interdisciplinary, not simply in the sense of linking edu-cational efficiencies with technological ones, but in a much deeper and expansive sense: one that extends well beyond technology to en-compass not only psychology and technical and instructional design but, as the authors add, also to wider "socio-cultural research ques-tions," and matters of "professional roles and identities, organiza-tional structures and associated strategy and policy" (Conole & Oliver, 2007, p. 3). This interdisciplinarity also goes far beyond any attempt to combine or meld a number of disciplines into a single, con-sistent, and unitary purpose. Instead, e-learning research, as Conole and Oliver define it, encompasses a multiplicity of "separate voices, each with its own potentially productive tale to tell..." (p. 5). This re-thinking of e-learning research, in other words, is not about the construction of a single, "authoritative" perspective, account, or knowledge form. It is instead about the combination of many different and not always consistent "voices" and points of view that represent a range of disciplinary and methodological possibilities.

In addition to being designated "multivocal," the type of research that is explored in this book could just as easily be called "multi-epistemological," referring to a plurality of "method[s] or grounds of knowledge" (OED, 2007). There are many ways of conceptualizing the multiplicity or plurality of knowledge forms, but one that is widely referenced and also central to this book is outlined below (Table 1.1). It describes both human knowledge and human interests as "technical," "practical," and "emancipatory," and is the principal way in which the multivocality of knowledge is understood here. This understanding of knowledge is commonly associated with a theoretical framework and approach to research known as "critical theory," described in detail in chapter eight. Knowledge is understood in this context as taking the form of instrumental, causal explanation, of practical, lingusitic understanding, and of emancipatory, critical reflection.

Table 1.1: Three kinds of human interest and knowledge as identified by critical theorist Jürgen Habermas

Interest	Knowledge	Medium	Science
Technical	Instrumental (causal explanation)	Work	Empirical, analytical, or natural sciences
Practical	Practical (understanding)	Language	Hermeneutic or "interpretive" sciences
Emancipatory	Emancipatory (reflection)	Power	Critical sciences

Source: From Carr and Kemmis (1986, p. 136)

Instrumental knowledge corresponds to human interests and activities that are associated with work, labor or production, and with the natural sciences. This corresponds directly to the type of technology-oriented research and knowledge that Koper (2007) describes as the proper focus of e-learning research. This type of research, as Koper explains, is directed at the development of "new technological knowledge, methods, and artifacts" for the sake of practical efficiency (p. 356).

Practical knowledge is concerned with the meaning and coordination of everyday activities. It serves to establish "a common identity (or mutual understanding) between persons" in everyday domestic, workplace and social settings (Ingram & Simon-Ingram, 1991, p. xxx). It is the kind of knowledge used in conversing at the water cooler, making dinner arrangements, or discussing the events of one's day. Despite its practical and commonplace character, this kind of knowledge — and the way it is generated and validated — is not simple or one-dimensional. Formally speaking, this type of knowledge is developed and validated through interpretive or hermeneutic methods. Hermeneutics, or the "science of interpretation," involves a kind of progressive, cyclical inquiry that takes into account both the individualized parts and the contextualized whole. Hermeneutic knowledge of this kind has proven to be invaluable to branches of psychology and sociology focusing on the complexity and unpredictability of both human interactions and institutional change. Given the importance of interactions and institutions to education and learning, this kind of practical knowledge should also be indispensable in re-thinking e-learning research. This kind of practical knowledge, therefore, plays a correspondingly central role in this book. It is especially important for the second chapter of this book, which introduces the methodology of hermeneutics in the context of narrative forms and accounts. It also plays a central role in the sixth and seventh chapters, which introduce and apply hermeneutic or interpretive phenomenology to the study of student experiences of technology, specifically in the context of mathematics education.

The third knowledge form and corresponding human interest is *emancipatory*. This type of knowledge is articulated in terms of politics, ideology, and the dynamics of social power. Epistemological validity in this context is not understood as something unchanging and certain, but rather, as the expression of a struggle between contradictory interests, influences, and social groups. This type of knowledge is central to the final two chapters of the book, which look at the political or ideological character of some of the basic "truths" or presuppositions of e-learning and its institutional, post–Cold War history.

This way of understanding epistemological multiplicity, it should be noted, does not ascribe any kind of special or exclusive status to one knowledge form; all three forms of knowledge and corresponding human interests are seen as being equally important. Also, this multiplicity of knowledge and methods does not imply, as is sometimes said, that simply "anything goes": it does not mean that any finding or account is as valid as the next. As the different chapters and sections of this book demonstrate, each method brings with it different potentialities, strengths, and limitations. Each also brings with it particular ways of judging and validating the knowledge it produces.

Outline of the Book

As indicated earlier, the chapters and various methodological orientations presented in this book are organized into four principal sections or parts. The first of these deals with methods, frameworks, and understandings related to questions of *culture* in e-learning. Like any human activity, e-learning possesses important cultural dimensions and these are explored in terms of the specific cultural categories of *narrative* and *genre*. Referring to the work of psychologist Jerome Bruner, the first chapter in this section introduces *narrative* as an epistemology or way of knowing that provides a valuable set of alternatives to more "logical" and scientific epistemologies. This chapter presents narrative inquiry as a research method by focusing on the case of an instructor's narrative account of the introduction of blogging into a writing class. Through its use of techniques of interviewing and interpretation, this chapter illustrates the potential of narrative epistemology and narrative case study research for e-learning.

The next chapter does something similar by operationalizing the cultural category of *genre*. Referring to "kind," "sort," or "style," genre can provide a useful means of understanding the various electronic forms, formats, and conventions that have proliferated and become commonplace on the Internet and in e-learning. This third chapter illustrates how it is possible to undertake a kind of "genre analysis" in e-learning by examining the form and style of online discussions. It combines this examination with a content analysis of an online discussion transcript. The results of this inquiry show how formal or generic continuity—rather than processes of "critical discourse" or "communal inquiry"—can serve as a basis for understanding how students orient themselves in online discussion forums.

The second section (constituting chapters four and five) focuses on the role of psychology in e-learning research and practice. Chapter four differs slightly from those that precede it in that it does not introduce and apply a particular method to a given e-learning context or technology. Instead, it undertakes a historical examination of the role of technological innovations as metaphors for mind and learning, and investigates the connection of these metaphors to ways of doing research in e-learning. Computer and networked technology are shown to play two different roles in this research: as metaphors or models for understanding human thought and learning, and also as vital means of supporting these processes. These two roles are argued to have a circular or self-referential relationship that renders them problematic. The role of ICTs as defining both the challenges and the solutions associated with e-learning research represents a kind of epistemological and practical conflict of interest. "[H]aving conceived of thinking as a kind of machinery," as Andrew Feenberg (2002) puts it, "machinery in fact turns out to be the perfect image of the process of thought" (p. 97).

This argument serves as the basis for the introduction and application of an alternative psychological methodology in chapter five. This alternative is sometimes characterized in computer design and psychology communities as coming *after* cognitivist psychology. It is seen as being part of a *"post-cognitivist* turn" that breaks with understandings of the mind as a knowledge-representation and information-processing device. This alternative psychology focuses on the recording and rigorous analysis of everyday conversation and discourse and is therefore also often referred to as "discursive psychology." "Discourse" in this sense takes the place of cognitive processes as psychology's central focus. Discourse or "talk-in-interaction" is seen as the means through which people construct their social and psychological worlds, "produc[ing] versions of reality and of cognition...in the course of their [everyday] practices" (Potter, 2000, p. 35). This chapter looks specifically at the way that these versions of reality and of cognition are produced in examples of "chatbot" conversations—text-based interactions with "artificial" interlocutors or agents. Through this analysis, this chapter shows how discursive-psychological methods and heuristics can be applied to interactions both between humans and between humans and computers.

The third section of the book focuses on another methodology—hermeneutic phenomenology—by first devoting a chapter (chapter six) to the introduction of its philosophical and theoretical underpinnings. The "phenomenon" that hermeneutic phenomenology takes as its principal subject matter is nothing less than lived human experience and its meanings. This chapter shows how certain traditions of hermeneutic-phenomenological research allow for the development of rich and unconventional ways of understanding and investigating the "lived experience" of human interaction with complex interfaces and computer technologies. The vocabulary through which these understandings and investigations are articulated, involving terms and concepts such as "handiness," "invisibility," and "breakdown," is derived from studies and descriptions of experience itself, rather than from the language of technical organization and operation. Along with these terms and concepts, chapter six describes different methods for drawing out experiential data from interviewees and research participants. It also shows how to develop these data in the form of self-contained quasi-fictional accounts and how to interpret these accounts through techniques of reflective writing. In doing so, this chapter provides a number of examples of such descriptive experiential accounts, and it discusses how they are illustrative of various principles of hermeneutic phenomenology, both as a philosophy and a methodology.

This study of lived experience is taken a step further in chapter seven, which presents a hermeneutic-phenomenological study of children's experiences of a particular puzzle or "manipulative" used in mathematics education. This is the "Tower of Hanoi" puzzle, which is well known in computer science and in psychological studies of problem-solving performance. The chapter shows how the experience of engaging with this puzzle can be both highly engaging and emotionally charged. As such, the experience of working with the puzzle appears to be only indirectly related to the process of leading the student from concrete involvement to disembodied mathematical abstraction (as it is described in cognitivist research in development and mathematics learning). Instead, the experiential characteristics associated with this puzzle are remarkably similar to those described and celebrated by mathematicians as constitutive of what is at the "core" of mathematical experience and discovery. This study concludes by making the case that the unexpected, experiential meaning and value of this puzzle has ramifications for understanding student experience generally: that the vicissitudes of this experience can be obscured rather than illuminated through preconceived administrative and technological categories and abstractions. The chapter also presents the argument that important aspects of technological and educational experience overall can be brought to light by using tools and methods that are descriptive, simulative, and even countertheoretical in nature.

The fourth section of the book focuses on the study of politics and history in e-learning. Even though the field of e-learning research and practice is relatively new and closely associated with technology, it has its own distinct political and developmental history. Chapter eight looks at the politics of e-learning by first explaining and then deploying some of the methods associated with *critical theory*. It takes up again the question of multiple knowledge forms and human interests and focuses specifically on emancipatory and critical interests as knowledge. One methodology that is especially important to this emancipatory knowledge is "immanent" or "ideology" critique, which seeks to show how competing and conflicting knowledge claims underlie the most final or authoritative "truths" in a given subject area. The chapter applies the method of ideology critique to a number of commonplace claims in e-learning discourse. These include the claim that technology represents a kind of prime mover or "destiny" that single-handedly "impacts" society, culture, and education. In this way, chapter eight shows that technological forms and uses can be viewed as a "scene of struggle," rather than as a fait accompli for e-learning. The chapter also makes the more general case that knowledge generally—whether it pertains to e-learning technologies or any other subject—is always something that has multiple interests and is therefore prone to contradiction and conflict.

Chapter nine develops this general ideological frame of reference further by looking at how historical and political interests have been encoded in e-learning research and development over the past decade or more. This chapter employs two particular methods of ideological and historical analysis, one emphasizing linguistic devices and the second, the design and appropriation of technologies. The first of these methods is a kind of "discursive analysis" that focuses specifically on metaphor and other aspects of language. It examines the ways in which a particular official or specialized discourse is used to construct a particular political, ideological world. The chapter examines a particular discourse within which the development of monolithic technological solutions to complex human problems—such as ideological struggle or education itself—is made to appear unavoidable. The second method of analysis examines technological artifacts and their design in terms of what is described as their "technical code." This refers to the way in which political values or ideologies are "encoded" into the design of technical devices. An examination of the technical codes of the Internet and other technologies shows that these technologies bring with them significant evidence of their origins in the U.S. military-industrial complex. Chapter nine uses these two methods of analysis to show how the codes and priorities reflective of the U.S. military-industrial complex (as they relate to American empire or imperialism) can be traced to certain conceptions of e-learning. This chapter also argues that the codes and patterns evident in e-learning technology designs are not unchangeable and that they can be re-coded to be expressive of other values and priorities.

The concluding chapter picks up where this introduction leaves off: it gives additional consideration to research in e-learning as a multivocal enterprise, and contrasts this to recent attempts to define research and practice in this field in terms of a single, unified "natural" science of learning. Drawing from arguments presented throughout the book, the conclusion shows how understandings of the "learning sciences" can lead to a repetition of the problematic findings and patterns of past research. The final chapter argues for a reconceptualization of e-learning as an inter- and cross-disciplinary endeavor — one that simultaneously offers multiple approaches to a field that is itself rife with possibility.

PART I: CULTURAL RESEARCH

Chapter Two

Narrative: The Storied Multiplicity of E-Learning Research

Introduction

"Narrative" and "genre" are terms that are most often used in literary and cultural contexts: in speaking of novels (noting their setting or climax, for example); in poems (classifying them, say, as epic or lyric); or in movies (discerning an action movie from a comedy or a romance). Narrative and genre are terms whose definitions date back to as early as Aristotle's *Poetics* (350 BCE), where they were used to analyze and classify the poetry and drama of the day. In the context of contemporary research, however, narrative and genre can *also* be understood as methodological categories or frameworks in their own right. They have been applied in a variety of fields and research contexts, including studies of computer-mediated communication (e.g., Mor & Noss, 2004; Yukawa, 2005b) and of software interface design (e.g., Wolff, Mulholland, Zdrahal, & Joiner, 2007). Narrative in particular has been invoked as a category relevant to the design of human-computer interfaces (Laurel, 1993) and has been used as a paradigm in psychology and epistemology (e.g., Bruner, 1990; Kirkman, 2002). It has also been used to study the expression of teacher's professional identities (e.g., Clandinin & Connelly, 2000) and even in understanding processes of "legitimation" across entire societies and cultures (e.g., Lyotard, 1984).

This chapter, which focuses specifically on narrative (genre is taken up in the chapter that follows), describes and operationalizes narrative as an epistemology and method. It does so by taking the reader through a number of stages:

1. Defining narrative: The discussion opens by presenting psychologist Jerome Bruner's understanding of narrative as both a mode of cognition and a mode of inquiry—a dual emphasis that is central to understanding narrative as a research method. This part of the chapter provides an overview of Bruner's basic "criteria" and "operating principles" for narrative as a way of knowing.

2. Gathering and analyzing narrative data: The chapter then presents a first-person narrative, and describes its elicitation in an "active interview" context. This narrative account provides an example of the way in which narrative has been used as a research method in education generally. Specifically, the narrative tells a revealing story of technology and the teacher as agents of educational change.

3. Considering other e-learning narratives: In concluding, the chapter highlights how the depiction of teacher and technology differ in the first-person narrative and in more common but less explicitly "narrative" accounts in e-learning research. In doing so, the chapter makes significant reference to Jean-Francois Lyotard's notion of "meta-narratives" in order to illustrate one final way in which narrative can be used as an analytic tool. The chapter presents the argument that an overarching narrative of technical progress still informs much research e-learning, and that attention to this meta-narrative needs to be balanced by attention to multiple "micro-narratives," which sometimes tell rather different stories.

In all, this chapter shows how narrative interpenetrates and even saturates—in many different ways and forms—both the substance of e-learning and also its investigation. At the same time, though, it attempts to give a voice to at least one example of a kind of position and story that is generally not heard in e-learning research.

Narrative as an Epistemic Mode and as Method

Jerome Bruner, well-known as a pioneer in cognitivism, devoted much of his early research career to the study of the mind as a logical information-processing device. In the late 1940s, Bruner was studying the internal, mental processes of inference, hypothesis generation, and above all, *categorization* that enable human beings to function, as he says, "in a world of more or less ambiguously organized sensory stimulation" (Bruner & Goodman, 1947, p. 35). Thinking of perception in terms of data and their processing and storage, Bruner (1986) theorized that it was *categorization* that allowed the ambiguity of these perceptual data to be sorted and organized by the mind into discrete entities, such as chairs, tables, people, letters on a page. Bruner later referred to the epistemological mode involved in these processes as the "logico-scientific" mode—one that "attempts to fulfill the ideal of a formal, mathematical system of description and explanation" (p.

12). "At a gross level, the logico-scientific mode," Bruner explains, "deals in general causes, and in their establishment, and empirical truth. Its language is regulated by requirements of consistency and non-contradiction" (p. 13). Individual, empirically verified "truths," Bruner (1991) explains further, are gradually accumulated through the use of "logical and scientific procedures" to form "constructs" (p. 4). And these constructs—which can also be referred to as theories or "paradigms"—are further refined in accordance with logical and mathematical rules and scientific principles. Because of the "practical power inherent in the use of logic, mathematics and empirical science," Bruner explains, learning and development generally have come to be conceptualized as activities that reproduce these processes of knowledge construction and verification (p. 4). In this way, the logico-scientific mode is privileged not only in many approaches to research and innovation, but also in cognitive theories of mind and learning.

But Bruner later came to see that logical operations such as hypothesis generation, inference, and categorization were only half of the story, so to speak. Instead of maintaining that only one way of knowing or establishing truth is valid or valuable, Bruner came to recognize the multiplicity of knowledge forms. The "logico-scientific mode," Bruner (1986) later asserts, is only one of *two* very different and indispensable ways of "ordering experience and constructing reality" (p. 11). Logico-scientific knowledge, in other words, is insufficient on its own for developing a full understanding of the mind and of learning. For Bruner, there is a second, neglected way of thinking and knowing. "This knowledge form or epistemic mode," as Bruner (1991) describes, "is so familiar and ubiquitous that it is likely to be overlooked, in much the same way as we suppose that the fish will be the last to discover water" (p. 4). Of course, this second, all-too-familiar epistemic mode or way of knowing is *narrative*; an "account of a series of events, facts...given in order and with the establishing of connections between them" (OED, 2007).

Bruner spent the latter part of his career exploring and drawing attention to the nature and implications of narrative as both a cognitive mode and as a means of inquiry. Bruner's understanding of narrative as a way of knowing and a way of researching encompasses both thinking and communication in narrative form, and also, reading, hearing, and interpreting of narratives: both are part of a broad epistemology for Bruner. In characterizing narrative as a way of knowing, Bruner (1986) generally begins by describing it in sharp contrast to the logico-scientific mode:

> Each of the[se two] ways of knowing...has operating principles of its own and its own criteria of well-formedness. They differ radically in their procedures for verification. A good story and a well-formed argument are different natural kinds. Both can be used as a means of convincing another. Yet what they convince *of* is fundamentally different: arguments convince one of their truth, stories of their lifelikeness. (p. 11; emphasis in original)

Narratives, in other words, generally do not depend on *literal* truth to be accepted as valid or "well-formed." Thinking especially of examples of fictional accounts, the "truth" of a narrative can be judged in terms of persuasive suggestion and convincing evocation. These narrative "operating principles" are put to use in place of the use of logical verification, causal explanation, or empirical corroboration. It is a question, as Bruner (1990) explains, of the "believability" of these accounts, rather than their "testability" or "falsifiability" (p. 122).

Writing in 1937, critical theorist Walter Benjamin (1968a) puts this in slightly different terms. He opposes what he calls the "art of storytelling" to the provision of explanation and information:

> it is half the art of storytelling to keep a story free from explanation as one reproduces it. [...] The most extraordinary things, marvelous things, are related with the greatest accuracy, but the psychological connection of the events is not forced on the reader. It is left up to him to interpret things the way he understands them, and thus the narrative achieves an amplitude that information lacks. (p. 89)

Storytelling or narrative, as Benjamin says, is a matter of interpretation or "making connections" between events and their psychological meaning. In doing so, he says, it is able to achieve a force and energy that "information," with its emphasis on explicit explanation, cannot match.

One further difference between narrative on the one hand, and information and explanation on the other, is presented by their treatment of the general and particular. Unlike the categorizing and hypothesizing functions of the logico-scientific mode, narrative does not dissolve the particular into general categories, seeking to "transcend the particular by...reaching...higher and higher...for abstraction" (Bruner, 1986, p. 13). Narrative is not about making sense of particular things or specific sensory stimuli by classifying them according to universal, abstract categories such as "chair," "table," or "person." Instead, narratives verily revel in the incidental, in particularity and specificity. Fictional films and television shows, for example, are not literally about abstract categories or relationships, about people as a general category, or about a theoretical conflict or principle. Instead, they are about very *particular* characters, circumstances, and actions: the more specific and unique the characters, events, and circumstances, the more vivid and engaging the narrative account.

Accordingly, the narrative epistemological mode is *not* subject to methods of experimental repeatability or confirmation that are foundational to "logico-scientific" inquiry and knowing. Events and other phenomena described in narratives do not unfold according to fixed rules of causal necessity, and the actions described in them are not principally a question of indifferent calculation and objective fact. Narratives are instead formed through the actions and motivations of their characters; and these acts and motives have much more to do with characters' desires, plans, and intentions than any physical laws of change and motion. Action and intention are also closely intertwined with moral opinion and judgment. And this includes the moral responses of the story's characters and listeners and readers. "Narrative is built upon concern for the human condition" (1986, p. 14), according to Bruner, making it "necessarily normative" (1991, p. 15). It is a question, in other words, of values and mores rather than facts and figures.

All of this further implies that reading, hearing, and interpreting a story is also not a matter of knowing and predicting events with unfailing certainty. It is instead a question of more tentative knowledge that sometimes involves feelings of empathy or antipathy for characters and their plans and hopes. In speaking of the interpretation of characters' motivations in narration, Bruner (1991) refers to "intentions" and "intentional states":

> The loose link between intentional states and subsequent action is the reason why narrative accounts cannot provide causal explanations. What they supply instead is the basis for *interpreting* why a character acted as he or she did. Interpretation is concerned with the "reasons" for things happening, rather than strictly with their "causes"... (p. 7; emphasis in original)

The methods and principles for undertaking interpretation as a systematic and evidence-based activity are generally referred to as *hermeneutics*. This term designates a set of methods or a kind of "science of the text" that has been developed in the twentieth century in the early work of Martin Heidegger and of his student, Hans-Georg Gadamer. Especially in Gadamer's *Truth and Method*, hermeneutics is described as a dialogical process through which understanding is gradually negotiated between reader and text. Unlike the isolation and accumulation of verified "truths" characteristic of the logico-scientific mode, this dialogical process is marked by its iterative or cyclical progression. A hermeneutic understanding entails an ongoing movement from any one part of a narrative or text to the story as a whole. For example, to understand why Hamlet asks the question, "to be or not to be," a reader might look to any one of a number of other points in Shakespeare's play, then back to Hamlet's famous soliloquy, and back again to other statements and actions elsewhere in the text. Speaking in terms that would again encompass both the composition and interpretation of narrative, Bruner (1991) explains,

> The accounts of protagonists and events that constitute a narrative are selected and shaped in terms of a [larger] story or plot that "contains" them... But that whole cannot be constructed without reference to such appropriate parts. This puzzling part-whole textual interdependence in narrative is, of course, an illustration of the defining property of [what is known as] the *hermeneutic circle*. (p. 8; emphasis added)

Hermeneutics generally and the hermeneutic circle in particular are integral to the kinds of qualitative research featured in this book. Hermeneutics, with its emphasis on the circular, and dialogical nature of knowledge and understanding provides methodological alternatives to quantitative, logico-scientific modes of understanding and research. As will be discussed in detail in chapter eight, hermeneutics provides alternative criteria to those of "testability" and "falsifiability," "reliability" and "validity" that are so central to logico-scientific ways of knowing and of conducting research.

Another important characteristic of a narrative is that it presents to readers or listeners a series of events that, as Bruner (1991) describes, constitute a "breach" or "violation" in "canonicity" or in the "canonical script" (p. 11). This refers to the fact that a narrative or story revolves around something going wrong, and needing to be corrected. It is when something goes wrong or when something out of the ordinary happens in the course of a day that we are provided with a story when we get home. As Bruner explains, "…to be worth telling, a tale must show how an implicit canonical script has been breached, violated, or deviated from in a manner to do violence to [the underlying] 'legitimacy' of the canonical script" (p. 11).

A "breach in canonicity" or departure from what is expected or normal is a part of a larger narrative structure or sequence of events referred to as *plot*. Typical progressions of developments, events, or actions that constitute a plot have been studied in literary (Abrams, 1999, pp. 226–227), linguistic (Labov, 1972), and other narrative analyses (e.g., Sheehan & Rode, 1999). These analyses have led to the identification of five plot components or stages, which recur in nearly any kind of narrative account:

1. An "exposition" (Abrams, 1999, p. 226) or "orientation" (Labov, 1972, p. 369) in which readers are oriented to a particular setting, background, or situation;

2. A "crisis" (Abrams, 1999, p. 227) or "complicating action" (Labov, 1972, p. 369), corresponding to Bruner's "breach in canonicity" in which a development of some kind "complicates or disrupts the otherwise predictable evolution of the original situation" (Sheehan & Rode, 1999, p. 338);

3. An "evaluation," "establishing the point or the meaning of the story" (Chase, 2005, p. 655), and including commentary on the meaning or consequences of the crisis or complicating action;

4. A "denouement" (Abrams, 1999, p. 227), "conclusion" (Sheehan & Rode, 1999), "result," or "resolution" (Labov, 1972, p. 369) in which "the action or intrigue ends in success or failure…the mystery is solved, or the misunderstanding cleared away" (Abrams, 1993, p. 139); and

5. A "coda," a "device" used especially in more informal narratives "to indicate closure," by bringing "the listener [back] to the present mo-

ment" in time (Chase, 2005, p. 655; Labov, 1972, p. 369). Examples of coda in everyday stories might include phrases such as "I hope I never see anything like that again," "And they all lived happily ever after" or "And that was that" (Labov, 1972, p. 369).

These five stages or components, despite their relatively unassuming character, are remarkably pervasive and ubiquitous. Narrative researchers in various fields have identified these same five stages in spoken and written communication of almost any length or kind— from anecdotes told on inner-city streets (Labov, 1972) to elaborate theoretical texts produced by philosophers and scientists (e.g., see Fisher, 1994; Sheehan & Rode, 1999).

Applied Narrative and the Qualitative Interview

Despite or perhaps precisely *because* of the fact that people tend to inhabit narrative in the way that fish inhabit water, narrative ways of knowing and organizing information have been long neglected in cognitive and constructivist psychologies and also in other areas of research related to e-learning. As Bruner (1986) observes, "we know a very great deal about the [logico-scientific] mode of thinking..." with narrative remaining decidedly "the less understood of the pair" (pp. 13, 15). As mentioned above, however, narrative has recently been investigated and applied in a wide range of contexts and areas of study. Outside of psychology, narrative analyses and interpretations have been applied in social sciences generally (e.g., Polkinghorne, 1988), in history (e.g., White, 1973), and in literary, cultural, and film studies (often under the rubric "narratology"; see Abrams, 1999). These and other "narrative" developments have been so significant that reference is being made to a "narrative turn" in social science and humanities research overall (Riessman, 2002, p. 696; Chase, 2005, p. 651).

As a part of this narrative turn, the methods and heuristics associated with narrative research have been applied specifically in education as a way of exploring the values, politics, and practices of students and teachers as individuals, and as a way of understanding their identities in educational and personal terms. In their landmark text on narrative research in education, Clandinin and Connelly (1988) speak of an individual teacher's narrative as providing a kind of "personal curriculum," as fostering a pedagogically relevant understanding of the self and of one's practices as a teacher: "Constructing a narrative account of oneself, or of someone else, is difficult, rewarding work. [...] It is rewarding because it is curricular and educational. It is a way of making educational meaning of our lives as we continue with the daily grind" (p. 24).

Narrative methods have also been valued in educational contexts for their ability to highlight individualized, contextual knowledge of pedagogical practices—knowledge that has proven elusive in other methods of inquiry into educational technology (e.g., Cuban, 1986, pp. 2–6) and in educational research generally (Shabani Varaki, 2007). Speaking as a teacher and teacher-educator, Kathy Carter (1995) emphasizes how narrative is able to provide

> a way of grasping the richness and indeterminacy of our experiences as teachers and the complexity of our understandings of what teaching is and how others can be prepared to engage in this profession. Furthermore, with the vigorous emphasis on cognition in teaching, story [has come] to represent a way of knowing and thinking that is particularly suited to explicating teachers' practical understandings, i.e., the knowledge that arises from action. (p. 326)

With its power to highlight aspects of practical and contextual action, narrative, in other words, presents a valuable counterweight to more logico-scientific cognitive emphases.

The means by which a researcher is able to access the elusive "richness and indeterminacy" of teachers' concrete experience is, unsurprisingly, by asking teachers about their experience both inside and outside of the classroom in terms that are as particular and unabstracted as possible. In narrative research these kinds of questions are asked in the context of an interview—but one that is quite different from a question-and-answer session typical of surveys and more structured interview techniques. At the same time, this kind of unstructured interview plays an important role in a number of e-learning research methods that are outlined and illustrated in this book. Referred to as the "active," "in-depth," or the "qualitative" interview, this technique—like hermeneutics generally—"is based in conversation," with its purpose being "to derive interpretation, not facts or laws, from respondent talk" (Warren, 2002, p. 83). Rubin and Rubin (2005) explain,

> Qualitative interviews and ordinary conversations share much in common. As in normal conversations, questions and answers follow each other in a logical fashion as people take turns talking. Researchers listen to each answer and determine the next question based on what was said. Interviewers do not work out three or four questions in advance and ask them regardless of the answers given. [The qualitative] interview, like an ordinary conversation, is invented new each time it occurs. (p. 12)

By thus undertaking the interview in terms of what one author refers to as a "guided conversation" (Warren, 2002, p. 85), the conventional "interviewer-interviewee relationship" (Chase, 2005, p. 660) is transformed. The relationship changes from that of researcher-interviewer and subject-interviewee to a relationship between conversational partners, with the interviewee as narrator and the interviewer as listener. As Chase explains,

> To think of an interviewee as a narrator is to make a conceptual shift away from the idea that interviewees have answers to researchers' questions and toward the idea that interviewees are narrators with stories to tell and voices of their own. (p. 660)

Although these kinds of "open-ended" interviews are generally unscripted, it is possible to identify a number of question *types* that often follow in sequence in this type of data gathering. According to Warren (2002), there are "*main questions* that begin and guide the conversation, *probe* to clarify answers or request further examples, and *follow-up questions* that pursue implications of answers to main questions" (pp. 86–87; emphasis added). But the key is not so much progressing through categories of questions as it is to remain "flexible and attentive to the variety of meanings that may emerge as the interview progresses" (p. 87).

There are of course a number of ways of sampling or selecting "narrators" for such conversational interviews. These include (1) "convenience sampling" (where one or more informants are chosen in an expedient, unstructured way); (2) "snowball sampling" (where existing informants are asked to recruit new ones "through the grapevine"); and (3) "*a priori* sampling" (where informants are selected according to criteria inherent in the research design itself [Warren, 2002, p. 87]). In the narrative interview described below, the narrator or informant was selected both on the basis of convenience sampling and on a priori design considerations: Lisa, a name used pseudonymously to identify an English as a Second Language (ESL) instructor at a small university, was a participant who was willing and able to participate in the research. And it had already been established through informal contact with the researcher that Lisa had a story to tell.

As is often the situation in narrative interview research, the inquiry described here represents a kind of case study (e.g., Riessman, 2002, p. 697), focusing on a single narrative rather than on multiple narrators or accounts. Lisa's story effectively provides a "case" that can be documented and analyzed. Both the case approach and narrative research direct the researcher's attention to the particular, situated, and concrete. This particularity is recognized as being valuable for research on its own. The narrative and the "case" are valuable in inquiry not because their particularities can ultimately be generalized to similar cases to "prove" something about them as a universal category. Instead, they are valuable simply because they can help researchers and practitioners learn more about the phenomenon in question. To quote psychologist Hans Eysenck, "Sometimes we simply have to keep our eyes open and look carefully at individual cases—not in the hope of proving anything but rather in the hope of [simply] learning something" (as cited in Flyvbjerg, 2001, p. 73).

Lisa's Narrative

The "active," "in-depth," or the "qualitative" interview methods described above were used to elicit an account of an e-learning innovation in Lisa's ESL classroom. The interview began with an unrecorded and loosely scripted discussion during which the extended and informal nature of the intended interview itself was described. As the interviewer, I also indicated my own specific interest in the incident that Lisa had mentioned informally in an earlier conversation and that I was hoping to find out more about through this interview. (Note that although Lisa was informed of the narrative nature of the interview and of the research associated with it, she was not prompted to fit her responses into any kind of explicit narrative framework.) My intention, in short, was to continue conversations that I had held with her earlier; and the record of the interview itself begins with my question: "So tell me, what was the course?"

Lisa responded not only simply by identifying the course but also by articulating her goals as the teacher of the course:

> Level three is paragraph composition, basically. And [it is also an] introduction to what essay structure is. So it's a lot of sentence structure, a lot of grammar, a lot of writing, drafts, outlines, and working through rewrites and revisions. My focus as a writing teacher has always been just the writing process, not necessarily all the grammar and mechanics—they're important—but I really like to focus on the writing process and to teach the students that the bottom line is that the writing process never ends and you should always be looking at what [you write] as a work in progress.

This initial response, despite its relative brevity, illustrates a number of important characteristics of personal narratives and their analysis. First, Lisa can be understood as articulating particular, situated knowledge arising from her actions and experience in an ESL writing classroom. To use Clandinin and Connelly's term, this knowledge is expressed in terms of a "personal curriculum" to which Lisa, as a teacher of the course in question, gives expression. She describes the course in terms of her own "focus as a writing teacher" and in terms of her emphasis on writing as an ongoing "work in progress." Lisa's words are also expressive of what, in narrative terms, is referred to as "voice"—a particular person speaking with her own words and from her own particular perspective. "Voice," as Chase (2005) explains, "draws our attention to what the narrator communicates and how he or she communicates it as well as to the subject unique or social locations from which he or she speaks" (p. 657). Of course, in articulating her narrative, Lisa speaks with a "voice" or articulates a position that is closely related to her professional identity as an ESL teacher. It is from this position that she affirms her pedagogical priorities. It is also from the position and identity of an ESL teacher—and its particular history and concerns—that she continues to articulate her story.

Lisa goes on to explain that in the course, students would typically look at and peer review each other's work, hand it in to me, and

I would have a look at it and hand it back. It was quite the cycle of "reworkings." In this characterization and in the passage quoted above, Lisa is also effectively providing the listener with the first element of plot: She *orients* the listener, proving information related to her story's *setting, background,* or *situation.* The setting, in this case, is a (presumably) conventional ESL course and classroom, with Lisa's individual emphasis on writing as an ongoing process.

But soon after Lisa orients the listener or reader to the setting of her story, a complication or "breach in cannonicity" arises. As Lisa explains, this particular class had been arranged to take place, through random chance, in a computer lab rather than in a regular classroom. This presented a disruption in the "canonical script" that had guided the way that Lisa had taught this ESL course. As Lisa explains, the course had "traditionally" been taught as "a pencil and paper type of writing course. It was all pencil and paper and handwriting..." It is the presence of the computer and Internet technologies, then, that represents a complication or breach in this canonical classroom setting and correspondingly, in Lisa's narrative.

As Lisa's account goes on to make clear, the problems that were soon to arise from this complication were significant to her as a teacher: "Students weren't listening; students were being distracted by the computers. They were turning them on and 'MSNing'... [M]any of them [wore] glasses, so [I] could see a blue glow in the[ir] lenses!" This presented a serious practical and pedagogical problem that needed to be addressed: "So I was saying okay, how long is this going to go on, because this is ridiculous too, I mean, I can't keep doing this." The presence of computer and Internet technologies represents a kind of crisis in the plot of Lisa's story. It "complicate[d] or disrupt[ed] the otherwise predictable evolution of the original situation" (Sheehan & Rode, 1999, p. 338) of a paper-and-pencil ESL writing course.

Lisa's account soon presents the possibility of a turning point, however. Lisa describes how, in the context of a graduate-level course in e-learning that she herself was taking at the time, she learned of Web-logs or blogs and of their educational potential:

> Then I started [learning] about the concept of blogs and using them as a
> writing source and using technology somehow. So I got to thinking well

okay...many things: [My ESL students] love the computers, they want to use the computers, in the future and in their academic courses they're going to have to come up with typed, computer-generated writing samples and so scaffolding them into that type of computer use and getting them online with Word might help them. It would help me read their writing because they could edit them easily or if they've got them on a memory stick then it would keep their hands on the computers with my rules.

The computer and Internet technology that initially presented a challenge now present a pedagogical opportunity. Lisa articulates this in terms of a wide range of factors, which include (1) her own identity, subject position, or "personal curriculum" as a teacher (she wants her students to be engaged but also wants "her rules" to be respected); (2) her priorities in the curriculum writing course (she wants to provide her students with meaningful learning tasks involving computer-generated writing, knowing that they will later have to "come up with typed, computer-generated writing samples" of their own); and (3) her student's own preferences (she recognizes that students "want to use the computers," and that they would be grateful if they were allowed to do so).

In narrative terms, the problem, crisis, or conflict appears to be moving toward a kind of solution or resolution. Lisa explains how this unfolded through the creation of a public blog for the class as a whole:

We all had a class blog which was this one blog that everybody wrote to, so that was a challenge. [...] Everybody signed their first names to their work. I had them go in and look at each other's work and make comments. They commented on content and grammar mistakes and anything like that and they did that very well. Sometimes [they contributed] just social things about ice cream parties and things, you know, so they'd be, *hey you did that on the weekend, why don't we get together next time,* or something.

To paraphrase, Lisa responded to the crisis presented by technology in her classroom by integrating a single class blog and by integrating it with the particular writing assignments that were a critical part of the way she taught the course. She provided specific ways in which students could identify themselves in their postings on this blog and encouraged them to make constructive comments on others' contributions.

With her description of her students' active contribution to the course blog, Lisa's story moves toward its "denouement," "conclusion," or "result"—in which its "complication" or "action" is resolved, ending either "in success or failure." In the case of Lisa's story, the conclusion can be deemed a success. This is indicated not only by her description, above, of the way that the students actually utilized her class blog; it is also indicated by Lisa's reflections on the ultimate results of adapting technology in this way to the writing classroom.

> It got me connected with them in another way, as well, as I was reading [their postings] and making comments to them. I don't know, it just changed the level of the class as far as, well, I noticed an attitude change in them from the very beginning of the course to the very end of the course and the way they felt about themselves as writers [...] The community that this created, that was one of the key things, was that people were helping each other, loaning paper out to print things off...staying back and helping each other, and being late for next classes together so that they could get through it and get something printed off; if there was a challenge, helping each other cut and paste, helping each other get pictures when they wanted some.

These kinds of reflections can be understood as corresponding to a narrative's evaluation—in which commentary is provided on "the meaning or consequences of the crisis or complicating action." It is worth noting that Lisa does not speak of the resolution of the technological complication in terms of measured student outcomes—the final success or failure of students in the course. Instead, she reflects on changes in the identity of her students and her relationship with them. It is their "attitude," their work as a "community," and "the way they felt about themselves as writers" that are of primary importance in terms of her teaching and use of technology. The principal contribution of technology in this course is what it led to in terms of her student's work together, their motivation, and their desire to write and to help one another.

In this sense, the kind of knowledge or lessons that can be derived from this particular narrative for research and practice in e-learning are situated, practical, and in some ways, personal in nature. Lisa's story can be said to inform e-learning research by providing valuable knowledge about the use of computer and Internet technology in the case of her classroom and others like it. To use more logico-scientific language, Lisa's narrative suggests that the careful integration of blogs into a writing-intensive course can result in increased student participation, and also in new forms of student participation, such as peer comments on writing, and informal, extracurricular writing in the target language of instruction.

Lisa's narrative also suggests that the use of blogs and related technologies (Word processing programs and computer hardware more generally) can be adapted in such a way as to complement and support her particular priorities as an ESL writing instructor: These technologies actually allowed the students to carry out the tasks of writing, rewriting, and checking not through the circulation of hand-written assignment sheets, but as online postings that all students (and also the larger public) could view and comment on. The situational particularity of the knowledge to be gained from this story is further heightened by Lisa's description of how her use of blogging in her ESL classroom has since changed and continues to change. And it is not surprising that her description of these changes is articulated in terms of how it affects both her as a teacher and her students communally:

> This year I did it different so everyone has their own blog. It's very different now, but community-wise they went through that one blog and that's where everybody was, so they could look at each other's postings.

A similar emphasis is evident in what can be interpreted as the *coda* of Lisa's narrative. In bringing her account into connection with the present and drawing it to its final conclusion, Lisa explains that although her course is no longer assigned to a computer lab, she has deliberately sought out such a lab environment, at least periodically, for her new students to use:

> I booked a computer lab one afternoon just as a bit of a break to have them look at their blogs and work on the final draft, and just to get them into a different environment. It was interesting...I was walking around, and they were *so* on task that all you could hear was keyboards. They were just—. I just stood there and watched them work, really.

This coda in Lisa's first-person narrative brings the narrative account to a conclusion and relates it to her present moment by again emphasizing her ongoing concern with her students' attitudes and their engagement in their writing tasks.

Conclusion: The Storied Multiplicity of E-Learning Research

As mentioned earlier, the story of Lisa's use of Web-logs is retold and analyzed here not so much in the hope of "proving" or establishing any generalizable truths about computer or Internet technologies. Instead, to refer again to Eysenck's comment about learning from case studies, the particular "case" constituted by Lisa's narrative has been presented in the hope of *learning* something about these technologies, about their educational contextualization, and to compare this knowledge with the ways that technology and its educational contextualization is already understood in the research. Of course, there are many potential lessons to be learned from the case presented by Lisa's adaptation of technology: As a case study in the integration of technology into classroom settings, Lisa's narrative illustrates the value of blogs for presenting writing collectively in the class and also to a wider, public audience. This account also provides evidence of the potential of blogs and other relatively new kinds of "social software" for fostering communication and cohesion among a class of students. In addition, it indicates the *ambivalence* of computer and Internet technology in a classroom setting, in the sense that these technologies, at least at the beginning of Lisa's story, have the potential to serve either as an enormous help or hindrance to both students and teacher. This multiplicity of lessons is consistent with the interpretive, hermeneutic nature of narrative generally: Narratives support not one but multiple interpretations and reward repeated interpretation and analysis.

One lesson that will be given special attention to in the concluding part of this chapter relates back to Bruner's distinction between narrative and logico-scientific epistemologies or ways of knowing. Lisa's story, of course, provides a way of understanding change and transformation associated with educational use of computer and Internet technologies in explicitly *narrative* terms. As such, it can be compared to "accounts" developed from more logico-scientific perspectives—those emphasizing the importance of causality, testability, and generalizable "truth." A common example of this kind of research in e-learning is found in experimentally designed "media comparison studies," which were described in the introduction. In such studies, a new medium or technology—such as online course components or laptop computers (see Johnson, 2002; TCER, 2007)—is introduced into an otherwise conventional educational setting in order to isolate and measure the "impact" of these technologies, specifically on student achievement. As was explained, studies designed and implemented in this way are seen as sufficiently important and widespread in e-learning to be themselves the subject of critical and synthesizing research (e.g., Kember, 2003; Lou, Bernard, & Abrami, 2006; Zhao, Lei, Chun Lai, & Tan, 2005) and ongoing controversy (e.g., Oblinger & Hawkins, 2006).

In both types of accounts—Lisa's narrative and the logico-scientific media comparison study—one could argue that computer and Internet technologies play a leading, catalytic role. In Lisa's story, the unexpected or initially uninvited presence of these technologies in the normally nontechnological setting of an ESL classroom presents an initial "breach in canonicity." In media comparison studies, technology is introduced as a clearly defined and isolated experimental "treatment" or "intervention" in classrooms that are seen as being otherwise free of conspicuous technologies.

In both kinds of research accounts, the introduction of technology presents a kind of "crisis" condition that drives the literal or figurative story toward its resolution or outcome. But significant differences between these accounts appear in terms of the resolution and evaluation that follow this crisis. Lisa responds to the challenge presented by technology by considering its manifold possibilities and by negotiating and working toward its effective use in the classroom. This takes place first over a matter of weeks and later, over a number of semesters.

Logico-scientific accounts in which technology is introduced in the form of an isolated experimental treatment—often for a single semester or a shorter period of time—have produced rather different results. As mentioned in the introduction, these studies have gained notoriety for the particular finding of no significant difference that they have produced through many and varied iterations. This final result is associated with what has come to be known as the "no significant difference phenomenon." This phrase, of course, refers to hundreds of media comparison studies that have attempted to measure student achievement and report that the introduction of technology or media did *not* make a statistically significant difference in terms of this metric.

Again to use narrative terms, the divergence of logico-scientific accounts and Lisa's narrative can be understood in terms of the assigned roles and conceptualizations of both teacher and technology. In Lisa's narrative, she is both the narrator and the protagonist. Although the availability of computer technology creates a crisis in her story, it is ultimately Lisa herself who drives the action of the story forward and who is implicated in its outcome: She is motivated by her priorities and principles as a teacher, and she is responsive to her classroom circumstances and her students' needs and preferences. As a result, it is also Lisa who consciously decides on a course of action that addresses all of these factors. In quasi-experimental media comparison accounts, the only "figurative" protagonist is the technology: It is the introduction of technology as an experimental variable that is seen as causing change or driving the figurative "action" of these accounts forward. And it is technology that is expected, single-handedly, to determine the resolution of what has been set in motion—in terms of statistically significant improvements in student outcomes. Actions of individual teachers, students, and others who might contribute in one way or another to the final outcome in these accounts are not so much marginalized or overlooked as they are deliberately and systematically excluded. This is evident in the manner in which "media comparison studies" identify and attempt to control what are called "confounding variables." Examples of such confounding variables would include the priorities and acts of individual agency or initiative on the part of teachers that are not anticipated. Teachers' and students' unforeseen adaptations of the technology to their priorities, abilities, and interests could also fall into this category; ideally, they would also be controlled or kept to a minimum. All of this is done in the name of reliability and generalizability, in order

that such logico-scientific accounts can be compared to and even combined with other, similar accounts in the form of meta-analyses. The
end result is ultimately envisaged as a single, common body of research or "knowledge" that should accumulate over time, leading to
ever more firmly established truth about the impact of technology in
the classroom, and in learning overall.

This combined, accumulated knowledge of multiple logico-
scientific accounts can itself be understood in narrative terms. The
narrative vocabulary for such an understanding is provided by
French philosopher Jean-François Lyotard (1984), who developed the
notion of the meta-narrative. As the name suggests, a meta-narrative
represents the integration of a number of lesser accounts or stories into a cumulative narrative whole. As indicated briefly in the outset of
this chapter, the "meta" or "master" narrative corresponds to grand,
overarching stories or accounts that entire societies and cultures can
be said to "tell" themselves, or to generate and reproduce. According
to Lyotard, meta-narratives are an integral part of the "legitimation"
or internal justification of a society and culture; they represent an attempt to explain or account for a universal collective enterprise in all
of its parts, or as a single whole or "totality":

> metanarratives are understood as totalizing stories about history and the
> goals of the human race that ground and legitimize knowledges and cultural
> practices. The two metanarratives that Lyotard sees as having been most
> important in the past are (1) history as progressing towards social enlight-
> enment and emancipation, and (2) knowledge as progressing towards to-
> talization. (Woodward, 2006)

The progression of scientific and technical knowledge to eventually form a complete and all-encompassing whole can be said to be
one of the figurative "stories" that researchers, students, and other
members of society tell themselves and others as a means of explaining and justifying their own goals and activities. In the context of such
an all-explaining and all-justifying meta-narrative of technical and
historical progress, individual scientific accounts of various kinds—
including those of quasi-experimental analyses of the effects of technologies on student outcomes—can be seen to represent figurative
sub-plots or secondary developments. They contribute to a body of

scientific knowledge that is itself striving to become more complete or total, working to complement and reinforce the progression and development that is central to the overarching meta-narrative.

The specific result of the "no significant difference" phenomenon produced repeatedly by media comparison studies, however, renders the relation between such studies and the larger totalizing meta-narratives of progress and enlightenment problematic: In repeatedly arriving at the same conclusion, especially one that shows that technology does not lead to improvement and progress, these studies make the accumulation of knowledge seem circular rather than cumulative or progressive. This is registered in many of the varying and contradictory contemporary interpretations of the "no significant difference phenomenon" result in e-learning: Some indicate that this repeated result is associated with a lack of rigor in e-learning research, thereby making such studies unusable for decision making in policy and practice (e.g., Lou, Bernard, & Abrami, 2006; Ungerlieder & Burns, 2002). Others insist that the result of no significant difference *does* contribute to meta-narratives of progress, simply because it indicates that technology is not *detrimental* to educational development and improvement and that it may be less expensive than more labor-intensive forms of amelioration (Russell, 1999). Still others say that the "no significant difference phenomenon" result and the kind of research associated with it is too narrow in its focus and needs to be complimented with other research methods and emphases (e.g., Oblinger & Hawkins, 2006).

In this context, Lisa's story is significant, because it stands as an example of a type of narrative that Lyotard invokes in diametric opposition to the single monolithic meta-narrative of historical progress. This narrative type has been labeled *micro-narratives* or *mini-narratives*. These are stories that are "provisional, contingent, temporary, and relative" (Barry, 2002, p. 87), and they are referred to in the *plural* because multiple, provisional stories of these kinds are seen as existing simultaneously and as being closely interwoven, rather than being subsumed to a single narrative or account. Such micro-narratives, like Lisa's and possibly like many other teacher-narratives or "personal curricula," are local and situated rather than universal and absolute.

But to suggest that examples of educational research can be understood as micro-narratives is not simply to affirm or celebrate plurality or idiosyncrasy for its own sake. To emphasize the potential of micro-narratives is instead to recognize that these narrative forms present a mode of understanding and inquiry that posses its own criteria and operating principles and that may be more sensitive or better attuned to the heterogeneous and local nature of classroom teaching and learning. To understand educational research in this way is also to regard it in a manner consistent with the Lyotard's own description of our current historical situation, which he famously defines as a "postmodern condition":

> Simplifying to the extreme, I define [the] postmodern as incredulity towards metanarratives... The [meta]narrative function is losing its functions, its great hero, its great dangers, its great voyages, its great goal. It is being dispersed in clouds of narrative language elements... Each of us lives at the intersection of many of these. (Lyotard, 1984, p. xxiv)

Lyotard is in some sense describing here what this book intends to provide: Given the difficulties of providing answers and findings concerning technology and education that are consistent with the "grand narratives" of historical and technical progress, this book in a sense presents to its readers a series of micro-narratives. These multiple, intersecting stories and narrative elements bring different perspectives on and accounts of the significance of technology in education.

Chapter Three

Genre in E-Learning: From Postal Practices to Electronic Epistolarity

Introduction

Narrative, as shown in the previous chapter, can be applied to a wide range of phenomena taken up in e-learning enquiry—from cognition and comprehension to studies of individual and collective values and identities. In fact, the more narrative is explored and utilized for research and analysis, the more possibilities for enquiry it appears to open up. For example, narrative can contribute to investigation of how an individual thinks and who an individual is, and it can even be used to understand the basis or "legitimacy" of the culture or civilization in which an individual lives and learns.

Similarly, "genre" can also play an important and far-reaching role in e-learning research. Genre can be defined as a "kind; sort; style" or more specifically as "a type of literary work characterized by a particular form, style, or purpose" (OED, 2007). Traditional examples of *fictional* genres include the novel, novella, and short story. Applied to the Web, the term can be used to designate digital "kinds" or "forms" such as e-mail messages, FAQs, home pages, blog entries. The analysis of these and other genre categories can include enquiry into the elements of their content and form, their evolution over time, as well as their functions in the communities or organizations in which they are used. As a result, it is perhaps no surprise that the "genre perspective" (Yates & Orlikowski, 1992, p. 318) has been utilized as a means of analysis in industry (e.g., Spinuzzi, 2003), in the academy (e.g., Ylönen, 2001), in different areas of cultural production (e.g., Berger, 1992), and of course, in the study of literature and film (e.g., Altman, 1982, 1999).

This chapter explores and applies genre as a methodological resource by undertaking the following:

1. Introducing the concept of "genre": This chapter provides an overview of the way genre is used as a category and framework for research, especially in research in e-learning and with the varied forms and contents of the Internet and Web.

2. Applying the work of a number of genre theorists: This chapter will explore how the particular genre of the Internet "posting" (in both e-mail and online discussion contexts) compares to the form and content of letter-based (or "epistolary") communication genres. Given the fundamental comparability of letter and electronic epistolary forms, the chapter proposes or hypothesizes that the characterizations of the dynamics of epistolary communication are applicable to online discussions in educational contexts.

3. Testing this hypothesis through the use of content analysis: Through a quantitatively oriented method that is frequently used in analyses of online discussions and communications media generally, this chapter illustrates a "mixed methods" approach to e-learning enquiry, combining content analysis with genre analysis to examine and measure the degree to which epistolary characteristics can be found in online discussion.

4. Identifying implications of the epistolary genre in e-learning: The chapter concludes by considering how this kind of research can inform more complete understandings of online discussion and its significance and utility in educational contexts.

Genres and Technologies of Communication

Like narrative, genre as a concept first emerges in Aristotle's *Poetics* in 350 BCE, where it is used as a means of differentiating comedy, tragedy, and other contemporaneous forms of drama and poetry. Some of these same basic categories of genre are still commonly used, of course, to recognize and interpret cultural forms such as television shows, movies, or books. These categories differentiate one kind or type from another on the basis of intersecting factors that are both practical and wide-ranging: A movie's genre classification, for example, helps to identify its potential audience, its expected content or atmosphere, or even its purpose or ostensible function. To consider watching a film labeled as a "horror" or a "thriller" is to have certain expectations about the *contents* of the film (e.g., violence, threats, intrigue) and about the *style* or even emotions associated with the film (e.g., horror or thrills). Or to consider watching an animated film, a western, or a popular documentary is to think of these cultural products in terms of their intended or typical audience (animated movies are generally for families or children), their setting ("westerns" are generally set in "the West" and in the past), or function (the function of a documentary is to inform or persuade rather than "simply" enter-tain). Yet, as these popular film designations illustrate, types of mov-ies and the audiences associated with them change and multiply over time: The classic western has spawned spaghetti westerns and more recently, the "revisionist" western (e.g., *Dances with Wolves, Brokeback Mountain;* see Tucker, 2005), with each permutation having its own implications for content, mood, and audience.

Much of the power of genre as a concept is derived from the way that it configures communicative processes or acts. As some genre theorists emphasize, the term "genre" designates a "fusion" or an "in-tersection" of a number of dimensions or aspects of communicative practices and situations: "...a genre is not any one thing," Kwaśnik and Crowston (2005) assert, "but rather an intersection of several phenomena in a context of use" (p. 76). These intersecting phenomena include not only form, style, and purpose, but also content, audience, as well as the issue of "social acceptance": "A genre is a genre," Kwaśnik and Crowston explain, only "to the extent that it is recog-nized as such within a given...community. In fact," these authors con-tinue, "successful membership in any number of social contexts requires a fluency in the genres in use in that context" (p. 77). Effec-tive membership in a blogging community, for example, requires flu-ency not only in the content or issues with which the community is overtly concerned (e.g., politics, gardening, e-learning), but also in the form and purpose of blog postings, RSS feeds, and other features or genre types associated with blogging. These issues of fluency, recog-nition, and familiarity further imply that the combination of form, purpose, and content in a particular genre is not simply a matter of pure function or efficiency, but that it is very much a matter of con-vention, tradition, or—as one author puts it—of "comfort": "Genres are a comfort zone of a patterned sign system that both an audience and an industry can read with relative ease" (Burnett & Marshall, 2003, pp. 90–91). Other genre researchers make a similar point when they emphasize the importance of the uniform and recurrent nature of genre: "Genres are typified communicative actions characterized by similar substance and form and taken in response to recurrent situations" (Yates & Orlikowski, 1992, p. 299). An example of how genres "typify" communication in recurrent situations is provided by the genre of the personal homepage on the Web: It has been said to have arisen as a means of addressing the recurrent situation or need to provide "personalized information...that is self-selected and maintained, and viewable by anyone with a web browser" (Dillon & Gushrowrowski, 2000, p. 203). As such, studies of the form and content of the personal homepage genre show that it is characterized by elements of form and content such as the e-mail address of the person it introduces, tables of contents, and welcome messages (p. 203). The personal homepage, then, is arguably "the first uniquely digital genre" (p. 203) arising on the Web in response to the recurrent situation or need to provide a kind of online *carte de visite* or to cultivate a virtual Web "presence."

Of course, the Internet and the Web also present innumerable examples of genre as defined by form, content, function, audience, and expectation. These digital contexts also provide as well as examples of the modification and multiplication of generic forms. Many of these changing and proliferating forms have their origins in the world of ink and paper, but that have been reproduced and reinterpreted in the digital, networked, and hypertextual realm. "Digital genres," as Dillon and Gushrowski (2000) explain, "borrow heavily from the paper world even though [digital and networked] media optimally support different forms, structures and interactions" (p. 202). Despite the functional differences separating paper and online media, innumerable forms and forums for communication on the Internet and the Web take their name, format, and other characteristics from their counterparts offline. Web *pages*, discussion *posts,* and Web-*log* (blog) *entries*, for example, all make meaningful reference to genres in the print or even preprint era. The Internet or "bulletin board" posting or post, for example, originally derives from to the literal hitching posts used by early express delivery services to swap horses (Wagner, 2004, p. 154). And like these "posts" of bygone eras, postings in Internet discussion forums and other online contexts are characterized by forms of identification (e.g., "addresses" of various kinds) and salutations whose basic patterns have remained remarkably consistent over decades and even centuries. The Internet and Web provide some of the most illustrative examples of how genres maintain aspects of continuity as conditions change around them, but also, how genres change over long periods of time and how generic forms have a tendency to proliferate. Older, more familiar and wide-ranging "meta-genres" readily give rise to new and derivative forms or "sub-genres." Starting as a "log" with chronological "entries," the meta-genre of the Web log, for example, can be seen as giving rise to a variety of sub-types such as the audio blog, the video blog or vlog, the photoblog, the legal blog—sometimes cleverly referred to as a "blawg" (Blog, 2008). Similarly, the familiar form of the letter has also served as a meta-genre in the world of print, pen, and paper. It has given rise not only to a range of epistolary "forms" (e.g., business, love letters, and even postcards), but also serving as the basis for the "epistolary novel," a sub-genre of the novel constituted by an exchange of letters between two or more characters.

The typified actions and recurrent situations that are the specific focus of this chapter are associated with a relatively small set of generic forms or categories designated by the term "posting" or "post": "A message displayed on a mailing list, newsgroup, or other online forum to which it has been sent. Also: [*sic*] the action of sending such a message" (OED, 2007). This form is ultimately derived from the aforementioned meta-genre of the letter—evolving through the epistolary sub-genres of the business letter and memo. In terms of e-learning practice and enquiry, the genre of the "posting" has played an important role—both directly and indirectly—in a wide range of research and practice. Of course, in its more traditional and general sense, the "post"—and the practices and possibilities associated with it—is central to distance education, an important disciplinary precursor to e-learning. Distance education in many ways began with the technology of the post, and its early popularity coincided with the rise of modern national postal systems. Even today, many distance education providers and open universities rely on postal services as a technology or medium for the delivery of course materials and other contents.

Educational research into the present-day Internet "post," however, stresses very different issues and concerns. It often takes the form of investigations of online "communities of inquiry" (e.g., Garrison, Anderson, & Archer, 2000), of forums for "computer supported collaborative learning" (e.g., Weinberger & Fischer, 2005), or of "environments" specifically designed for "knowledge building" (e.g., Scar-damalia & Bereiter, 2003), to name but a few examples. Much of this research proceeds from the argument that the educational value of the Internet posting—and the systems that enable its composition, or-ganization, and dissemination—can be understood principally in terms of its characteristics or functions as a communication medium or technology. In the case of the Internet posting, the medium in ques-tion is both written and asynchronous. It involves, in other words, the exchange of text-based messages over the course of hours and days. This is often contrasted to spoken or conversational exchanges or "discussion" that unfolds over seconds or minutes, and generally leaves behind no record for reference or reflection. By comparison, technical or mediatic characteristics of the Internet posting are said to encourage "higher-order cognitive learning" as well as "discipline and rigour in...thinking and communicating" (Garrison, Anderson, & Archer, 2000, p. 90). Genre and the histories and categorizations that it brings with it, however, tell a different story of the posting. This story is one where factors such as comfort, familiarity, and tradition play a role that is at least as important as a medium's technical capa-bilities, and in which the conventional, social dimensions of epistolary communication are also important.

Electronic Epistolarity

As mentioned above, the letter represents a kind of meta-genre that encompasses a multiplicity of epistolary sub-genres such as the love letter, the business letter, the "Dear John" letter, or letters of reference, acknowledgment, invitation, and so on. As a well-established and well-developed category or "typificiation," the letter exemplifies a familiar or recognizable fusion of form and content that is characteris-tic of genres generally. In their examination of the letter as a paper-based precursor to a range of digital genres, Kwaśnik and Crowston (2005) explain:

> From studying non-digital genres we know that the role of content and form inform each other. For example, if we are presented with only the empty framework of the format of a letter (heading, salutation, body, and closing) most people can identify the genre. Similarly, if we are presented with the

content without the form—just the text—we can still recognize it as a letter.
(p. 78)

This familiarity extends also to the genre of the e-mail message, as well as to the online posting. The posting in its contemporary form and meaning evolved out of changes in written commercial communication over the course of some 120 years—from the middle of the nineteenth century to the development of the Internet in the 1960s and 1970s. In an extensive historical analysis of this evolution, Yates and Orlikowski identify the development of the online posting or e-mail as starting with the formal business letter. Although the formal business letter already presents content elements similar to those of the e-mail (e.g., "addresses" and a "signature"), Yates and Orlikowski also emphasize the role of an intermediate stage or genre in the evolution from business letter to e-mail message. As indicated earlier, this genre is the business memorandum or "memo." The memo, they explain, introduces the more "direct but noncolloquial" language that is taken for granted in much online communication today. The memo also includes the regularized "To, From, Subject, and Date fields" that are also a familiar part of the digital genre of the online message or post. Yates and Orlikowski identify further similarities. They point out that, like the paper memo before them, many "electronic mail messages are used to document internal [organizational] events or outcomes for future reference, often with subject matter restricted to a single topic" as indicated in the message's subject line (p. 316). The first appearance of these forms in the memo, Yates and Orlikowski further explain, was not simply due to a desire for uniformity, simplicity, and brevity. Instead, the development of the memo as a genre—and by extension, of the e-mail or posting as a genre, too—was the result of a range of factors. These include the growth in the size of commercial organizations in the late nineteenth and early twentieth centuries, and the spread of new management philosophies that placed a premium on the kinds of internal communication that were suited to the memo form. These factors also included the introduction of the technologies of the vertical file and the typewriter, which also required more regimented formatting, as well as the introduction of secretarial staff, as experts in the operation of these technologies (pp. 311–318). The derivative but familiar forms of the e-mail or online discussion posting, in other words, stand at the inter-section of a range of historical developments, technological innova-tions, and practical requirements, with no one of these factors—not even the seemingly unconstrained possibilities offered by a new tech-nological medium—single-handedly predetermining its form and function.

The history of the posting and specifically of the *letter*, of course, reaches back centuries before the maturation of the memo as a genre in American business communications. In Europe, the eighteenth cen-tury is designated "the century of the letter" (Wagner, 2004, p. 156) and as this chapter will show, certain patterns and dynamics that be-come clear in the eighteenth-century letter can apply to the online posting as well.

It is in the century of Washington, Rousseau, and Swift that the letter came to serve as a means of "exchanging thoughts," forming the basis for distant relationships, and exchanges between philosophers, writers, and lovers. The importance of the letter in this century is re-lated to a wide range of factors. These include increased levels of lit-eracy among the general populace, the expansion of postal systems as a public services, and the emergence of what Jürgen Habermas (1989) identified as the "bourgeois public sphere" (pp. 1–26). This changed the reading and writing of letters from something that was the privi-lege of royalty and aristocracy in previous centuries to a relatively commonplace public practice. The eighteenth century also marks the zenith of a literary genre and form based on the exchange of letters—the epistolary novel. Prominent examples of epistolary novels include Samuel Richardson's *Clarissa*, Emily Bronte's *Wuthering Heights*, Bram Stoker's *Dracula,* and Alice Walker's *The Color Purple.* Through the careful study and analysis of this fictional form, a number of clear and precise characteristics of epistolary exchange can be isolated; and identifying these characteristics in online exchanges is central to the empirical study undertaken in this chapter.

In her book-length study, *Epistolarity: Approaches to a Form*, Janet Altman (1982) provides a manifold definition of the form and dynam-ics of epistolary communication generally. She uses the term "episto-larity" to designate this form and the dynamic—or what she refers to as "the use of the letter's formal properties to create meaning" (p. 4). This is not a simple or direct matter, however, as Altman characterizes epistolarity as being above all "charged with paradox and contradiction. The opposite of almost any important trait" she explains, can be as "characteristic of the letter form" as the original trait itself (p. 186). Of the six paradoxical characteristics Altman describes, four (presented below in highly abbreviated form) are of importance for this study:

1. The letter serves "as a bridge/barrier (distance breaker/distance maker)" (p. 186). It both connects the writer and addressee(s) across distance, and serves to remind them of their separation; of the different "present" they each occupy, both temporally and spatially.

2. The letter is expressive of a dynamic between the opposites of "I/you, here/there, now/then. Letter narrative depends on reciprocality of writer-addressee and is charged with present-consciousness in both the temporal and the spatial sense" (p. 186).

3. The letter is also caught between the opposites of "[c]losure/overture [and] discontinuation/continuation of writing. The dynamics of letter narrative involves a movement between two poles: the potential finality of the letter's sign-off and the open-endedness of the letter...as a segment within a chain of dialogue" (p. 186). As only one message in a longer chain of communication, a letter is something that is a fragment in a larger whole; yet, it is also a "discrete unit" in and of itself.

4. "Unit/unity; continuity/discontinuity; coherence/fragmentation. The letter's duality as a self-contained artistic unity and as a unit within a larger configuration make it an apt instrument for fragmentary, elliptical writing and juxtaposition of contrasting discrete units..." (pp. 186–187). An epistolary exchange of thoughts and feelings is generally a continuous process that takes place with some regularity over an extended period of time, but also, it necessarily involves interruption and discontinuity.

Before showing how these four characteristics can be identified in online postings in educational contexts, it may first be useful to illustrate the nature and utility of these paradoxical traits by identifying them in an example from the epistolary tradition proper. Consider this short quote from a letter penned in 1842 by the Victorian poet Elizabeth Barrett Browning:

> If I do not empty my heart out with a great splash on the paper, every time I
> have a letter from you, & speak my gladness & thankfulness, it is lest I shd.
> weary you of thanksgivings! (As quoted in Milne, 2003)

In this single sentence, aspects of the letter as bridge/barrier, its simultaneous potential for continuity and discontinuity, and its "present-consciousness" for both correspondents are all manifest: The
writer is obviously glad to receive the letter (in her own time and
space), but worries of tiring her correspondent (author Mary Russell
Mitford of Berkshire) with her own reply. In addition, the letter constructs or evokes a present for the glad but concerned writer and also
for the possibly weary recipient. Underlying all of these dynamics is
the obvious tension between continuity and potential discontinuity in
the communication. (Barrett Browning's observation of her situation
"every time I have a letter" refers to an event that of course occurs
only occasionally, but with some evident regularity).

At first glance, it may seem that the writing of Elizabeth Barrett
Browning is too personal and emotional to have any kind of counterpart in the online educational posting, a form derivative of the "direct
but noncolloquial" language of the business memo. But consider this
example from a graduate-level online course in the humanities:

> Thank you, Jacques, and thank you again. I see you share my frustration
> with wondering where that darn post went after you pressed "Send"! (Ruth,
> Week nine, student-moderated conference). (Quoted in Rourke, 2005, p. 139)

Most if not all of the aspects of epistolarity identified in Elizabeth Barrett Browning's letter can also be found here: the message is a bridge
of sympathy and shared frustration, confirming the similarity of experience between two correspondents; the two brief sentences constituting the message attempt to unite the "here and now" of the writer
with the recipient, implying the presence of both at the keyboard,
each wondering about the status of a posting after having sent it.
Also, the technological uncertainty on the part of the composer and
recipient is an indication of the tension between continuity/ discontinuity and coherence/fragmentation as was the case in Barrett Browning's communication. The paradoxical characteristics or dynamics of
the letter genre, in other words, can be seen to form relationships of

continuity that span different ages and continents, and that render comparable a passionate letter between Victorian writers with a more casual posting in graduate student forum.

Content Analysis

Given the identifiable epistolary characteristics of the genre of the online posting, the question now is one of the operationalization of these characteristics in the more general terms and frames of reference proper to e-learning research. The method used in this chapter is a *quantitative* one that is frequently employed in the study of media and communication generally and in educational studies of online discussions in particular. This method, "content analysis," is defined as "the systematic observation of elements in print, electronic, cinematic, and other media, usually by documenting the frequency with which such elements appear" (Traudt, 2005, p. 22) and it is used in this chapter to identify epistolary characteristics of online communication. In the case of text-based media such as letters and postings, the elements that are subjected to this kind of systematic observation are defined in terms of particular themes, issues, or more narrowly, as specific words or even combinations of characters. For example, a content analysis of the political bias of a news Web site over the course of an election campaign might look for occurrences of character combinations of political candidates' names with both favorable and unfavorable descriptors.

Generally, elements such as these are identified and analyzed in the context of relatively large pools of data, with textual data sets used in content analysis studies running anywhere from dozens to thousands of pages. In the case of online discussions, data sets on this scale are provided by transcripts of postings made over part or all of a course — often amounting to tens of thousands of words. Of course, in analyzing such data sets, it is important to define content elements with as much precision as possible and to try in other ways to enhance the reliability with which they can be identified and interpreted.

In the context of quantitative research, the term "reliability" has a very specific technical meaning, referring specifically to "[t]he extent to which a measurement made repeatedly in identical circumstances will yield concordant results" (OED, 2007). In this case, the measurement that is to be made repeatedly is the counting and classification of paradoxical epistolary elements: bridge/barrier between correspondents; reciprocality of consciousness in terms of place, time, and person; discontinuation/continuation of writing; and coherence/fragmentation of exchange. The reliability of the content analysis results can be measured in two ways: In terms of *intra-coder reliability*, where the consistency of the work of one coder or researcher is measured over time (generally by coding the same data on two separate occasions); or in terms of *inter-coder reliability*, in which the coding of one researcher is checked against that of another.

The activity of coding is conceptualized in terms of what is called an "analytic construct" (Krippendorf, 1980) or a "coding frame" or "scheme" (List, 2008). This construct or scheme generally gives a clearly defined significance to specific *content* elements by relating them to a more general theoretical framework or set of meanings. In the context of online educational discussions, coding frames are frequently structured in terms of particular stages of collaborative learning, phases of critical thinking, or steps involved in knowledge construction. In this way, different content elements are brought into association with specific cognitive, problem-solving, epistemological, or knowledge-construction processes (e.g., Beers, Boshuizen, Kirschner, & Gijselaers, 2007; Meyer, 2004; Weinberger & Fischer, 2005). For example, in a series of frequently cited studies, Garrison, Anderson, and Archer (2000) identify four stages of what they call "practical inquiry": "triggering, exploration, integration and resolution" (p. 89). The authors present these stages as a coding frame by associating each with a number of content elements: "Triggering" corresponds to the appearance of questions or the raising of new topics; "exploration" is associated with the unsystematic introduction of opinions, narratives, or ideas; "integration" is indicated by the appearance of tentative hypotheses or generalizations; and "resolution" is linked to the testing and defence of these same hypotheses or propositions (p. 89). Garrison et al. use the term "cognitive presence" (p. 89) to refer to the "analytic construct" or "frame" constituted by these elements, which is just one part of a larger, more general set of theoretical constructs in their model of the community of inquiry. In addition to "cognitive presence," the model also includes "social presence" and "teacher presence" constructs (p. 89).

In the same way that these four stages of "practical inquiry" can be used as a basis for defining a coding frame for "cognitive presence" in online discussions, the four paradoxical characteristics enumerated as a part of "epistolarity" by Altman, above, can act as a coding frame for the epistolary genre. Again, in operationalizing these characteristics as a coding frame, the challenge is to define as precisely as possible the corresponding content elements for each. In keeping with the broadly cultural and literary nature of the "generic" inquiry of this chapter, the coding frame presented here uses rhetorical figures or tropes: words or a phrase used in a preset or figurative way. The table below lists characteristics of epistolarity, the corresponding rhetorical elements, and a specific example to show how these appear in an online discussion context.

Table 3.1: Epistolarity as a coding scheme

Characteristic of "Epistolarity"	Rhetorical element	Example (modified from data set)
1) Bridge/ barrier; distance breaker/distance maker	Forms of appeal to reader or addressee: **Salutation:** word or phrase of greeting. **Apostrophe:** the rhetorical address of the absent addressee (i.e., references to "you"). **Imperative:** command/entreaty to addressee.	I'm glad to read, **Marge**, that **you** were able to integrate student needs in that way. I hope **you continue to**...
2) I/you, here/ there now/then reciprocality of consciousness	The reading/writing present: Events or states of affairs that are concurrent with the reading or writing of the message.	I'm **glad to read**, Marge, that you were able to integrate student needs in that way. **I hope** you continue to...

3) Closure/ overture; discontinuation/continuation of writing	**Prolepsis:** reference to a future development (flash-forward). **Analepsis:** reference to a past development, specifically as described in a previous posting (flashback).	I'm glad to read, Marge, that you **were able to integrate student needs** in that way. I hope you **continue to…**
4) Unit/ unity; continuity/ discontinuity; coherence/fragmentation	**Ellipsis:** The omission of words important to the meaning of a sentence; especially the use of indexical pronouns (e.g., this, that, it) across postings.	I'm glad to read, Marge, that you were able to integrate student needs **in that way**. I hope you continue to…

In this coding frame, it should be noted, the precise meaning or emphasis of most of the rhetorical devices listed have been adapted slightly from their conventional or technical meanings to better suit the communicative situation presented by online discussion. For example, in the case of the first characteristic (bridge/barrier; distance breaker/distance maker), appeals to the reader in the form of salutations or appellations (i.e., calling by name) are narrowed in meaning: they refers not so much to *any* possible reader, but rather specifically to the principal recipient of a given reply ("Marge" in the examples provided above). The notion of the narrative or discursive present (corresponding to the message being "charged with present-consciousness" both temporally and spatially) is also understood in a fairly narrow sense, as referring literally to events coinciding with reading and writing a message (e.g., the reader being "glad to read" a message and simultaneously "hoping" the best for a correspondent). Corresponding to the third epistolary characteristic, "analepsis" is understood as a student's or participant's reference to developments and states of affairs in the future, and "prolepsis" refers rather specifically to the contents of earlier messages (i.e., states of affairs arising in the past as described in messages; or events, such as postings, occurring within the discussion forum itself). Finally, ellipsis (generally defined as the omission of words in a sentence) is understood here as a kind of "reference through omission." It refers to the exclusion of terms or explanations whose meaning is already made clear in previous messages. The term "indexical" is used to qualify this rhetorical element. "Indexical" refers to the use of terms that acquire their meaning by "pointing" to some state of affairs—that is, through the use of terms like "this" or "that." This term simultaneously underscores the self-sufficiency of epistolarity of postings (indexical pronouns are generally used in a manner that is *grammatically* or *syntactically* correct) and their contextual dependence (these same pronouns function *semantically* only with the context provided by previous messages).

These rhetorical elements, as defined above—and the overall coding frame to which they contribute—have not previously been operationalized in content analyses of letters, memos, or discussion postings. As a result, their application to online discussion data, described below, are not intended to represent a definitive analysis of epistolarity or of students' "use of the letter's formal properties to create meaning" in an online discussion forum. Instead, this study and its results are indicative of the *feasibility* and the *possible* significance of more developed and larger-scale analyses of this kind.

Epistolarity and "Discussion"

The data set or corpus used in this study was derived from a transcript of 136 postings containing approximately 11,000 words (as message content). These messages were generated by a group of thirteen students and an instructor or moderator engaged in the final week of a thirteen-week distance education graduate credit course. All of the students were experienced users of online discussion forum technologies, and the instructor had been using online discussion forums in similar distance courses for more than five years.

Postings were coded according to the definitions provided in the table above, identifying individual words, phrases, or entire sentences as representative of one of the four corresponding groups of rhetorical elements—and by extension of one of the four corresponding characteristics of epistolarity. As indicated in the example presented in the table above, in some cases, one word or phrase corresponded to more than one epistolary element. In keeping with the emphasis of this study on feasibility, coding was undertaken only by a single coder, this book's author. Checks of inter-coder and intra-coder reliability (i.e., the consistency with which rhetorical elements are identified in a single data set between individual coders or by one coder at different times) were, accordingly, not undertaken. Of course, these kinds of reliability checks would be important in taking this research further, in developing the coding frame used in it and refining the results produced through it. Counts produced through this preliminary analysis are presented in Table 3.2, below.

Table 3.2: Totals for rhetorical elements

Rhetorical element (epistolarity characteristic)	Salutation, apostrophe (distance breaker/ maker)	Imperatives, references to the present (reciprocality of awareness)	Prolepsis, analepsis ([dis]continuation of writing)	Ellipsis, indexical pronouns (coherence/ fragmentation)
Totals	49	86	77	28
Percentage (Total=240)	20%	36%	32%	12%

The totals in the table above have a number of important implications for the hypothesis presented in this chapter. They suggest, in short, that the dynamics of epistolary communication are *indeed* relevant to online discussions in educational contexts. These results provide evidence confirming that the epistolary coding frame *does* describe aspects of online communication. For example, the fact that rhetorical figures of "prolepsis" and "analepsis" (specifically as they are defined above) appeared 77 times in a corpus of 136 messages (an average of more than once in every two messages) suggests that this approach to the analysis of discussion content is a feasible one. More specifically, this particular finding simultaneously suggests that the corresponding characteristic of traditional epistolary communication — closure/overture, or the discontinuation/continuation of writing — *is* also relevant to online discussion. This means that although "epistolarity" has originally been devised for the literary analysis of epistolary novels, it has promise as an analytic frame and method for inquiry into online discussions. In still other words, "the use of the letter's formal properties to create meaning" can be used as a basis for understanding the way that the formal properties of the online post-ing enable the creation of meaning among students and between stu-dents and teachers.[1]

Over the course of the past few hundred years, the properties of the epistolary form and corresponding processes of meaning-making have above all been social. As Altman (1987) herself says, letters or postings function "as a connector" between two individuals or parties (p. 13). They work to underscore mutuality of thought and feeling — or, to use Altman's words, "the reciprocality of writer [and] ad-dressee" (p. 187). With this in mind, the analysis presented above can be profitably compared to other research on online discussion in edu-cation. Specifically, it is possible, for example, to use this "epistolary" approach to affirm and buttress the "community of inquiry" model

---

1. At the same time, it is also important to note one way in which this application of "epistolarity" has departed or diverged from the examples provided in history and specifically in the analyses of Altman herself. This divergence is underscored by Altman's aforementioned description of the characteristics of epistolarity as "charged with paradox and contradiction," with any one trait invoking its oppo-site (e.g., the letter as a "distance maker" also functioning as a "distance breaker"). What the analyses above indicate, however, is that only *one* side of paradoxically charged characteristics such as "distance maker/distance breaker" or "continu-ity/discontinuity" is generally evident. The example adapted from the transcript and provided in Table 3.1, above, is indicative of this: "I'm glad to read, Marge, that you were able to integrate student needs in that way. I hope you continue to..." The characteristics of epistolarity are clearly evident here in their positive sense — acting as a bridge between writer and addressee, establishing continuity and connection between messages — but not so much in the more negative sense of emphasizing discontinuity between postings or the distance separating reader and writer. The example of epistolary communication from Rourke cited earlier suggests a reason for this: when Ruth thanks her classmate Jacques and exclaims that they share the same frustration — in wondering what happens after pressing "'Send'!" — the "distance breaking" and "discontinuity" that is evident arises from uncertainty over technical issues, which become less pressing as technology and ways of utilizing it become more familiar and established.

presented earlier. The social nature of epistolarity suggests that the coding frame provided above could be operationalized to measure what Garrison and his coauthors have referred to *social presence* — or what others have identified as the "social mode" or "communication and common ground" in text-based, online communication (Weinberger & Fischer, 2005; Xin & Feenberg, 2007). This refers to "the ability of participants in a community of inquiry to project themselves socially and emotionally...through the medium of communication being used" (Garrison, Anderson, & Archer, 2000, p. 94). The identifiable frequency of the elements of epistolarity can serve as a way of determining the degree to which participants are indeed able to "project themselves socially and emotionally" in their written communication. It should be noted, however, that while Garrison and others see this kind of interaction as valuable *in support of* critical thinking tasks, they do not recognize it as particularly valuable in and of itself. They see little value, for example, in more-or-less monological narratives that are *"not* used as evidence to support a conclusion" (p. 18; emphasis added) and characterize this kind of activity rather uncharitably as "undirected, unreflective, random exchanges and dumps of opinions" (Garrison, Anderson, & Archer, 2001, p. 21).

Conclusion: Genres of Online Discussion

It is also possible to interpret the results of this study as grounds for a reassessment of many of the assumptions underlying the work of Garrison and others. The premise for this reassessment is fairly simple: The results produced in Garrison, Anderson, and Archer's original study — and those produced subsequently in similar studies — do not conform to what is predicted by their model. These results show something *other* than "critical inquiry" or activities of "knowledge building." The results of Garrison's original study, for example, did *not* show students moving from triggering and exploration to stages of integration and resolution. Instead, 75% of the messages coded in Garrison's study were categorized as being either "exploratory" in character or as "other" — as not fitting in with *any* of the four stages of practical inquiry (Garrison, Anderson, & Archer, 2000). Other research based on this same model of communal inquiry, and using the same coding scheme, has produced similar results. One relatively large-scale study by Fahy, for example, examined a total of 462 postings generated over an entire semester, and classified 331 of these (72%) as "exploratory" (2005). Comparable results are also found in research that uses slightly different coding schemes for defining productive online discourse. In fact, results broadly comparable to those of Fahy's research and the original study of Garrison and his colleagues have been produced with remarkable consistency in a multitude of related research studies:

> Two decades of observation indicate that students rarely engage in the communicative processes that comprise critical discourse... [Many] researchers have looked closely at the types and patterns of interaction among graduate students engaged in computer conferencing. The percentage of messages in which students engage in critical discourse, mutual critique, or argumentation, in whatever way it might be operationalized, ranges from 5 to 22%. (Rourke & Kanuka, 2007, p. 106)

Student activity in online forums, when interpreted in terms of critical inquiry, is generally shown as getting "stuck" at the preliminary stages of this inquiry. Instead of progressing to higher levels or stages of cognitive or critical activity, this model interprets the exchanges enacted by students as being incomplete. On their own, these exchanges are seen in this theoretical frame as being of little educational value. "Students," as Rourke and Kanuka conclude, do not "orient to the conference as a forum for critical discourse" (p. 105).

How, then, do students "orient" to online discussion? Even though research repeatedly shows that the majority of students' communication involves the unsystematic exchange or exploration of opinions, narratives or ideas, related research indicates that both students and teachers value the availability of online discussion in their courses (e.g., Varnhagen, Wilson, Krupa, Kasprzak, & Hunting, 2005; Wise, Chang, Duffy, & del Valle, 2004). In the particular set of exchanges studied above, for example, students are addressing and/or referring to one another very directly and individually, are discussing matters raised in each others' messages, and are relating their messages to shared events in the past and to stated possibilities for the future. They are constantly working to bridge the "gap" between reading and writing in the here and now and their reading and writing in the past and in the likely future. Together, these kinds of activities suggest that students orient themselves to online discussion in ways that are consistent with epistolarity and the letter. And they do so in ways that are also consistent with the dynamics of the utilization of this genre in epistolary communication over the past three centuries or longer.

At the same time, it should be stressed that students apparently do *not* orient themselves to online discussion on the basis of its evident technical functions and advantages. They do not, for example, appear to take advantage of the opportunities that capabilities such as asynchronicity and textuality provide for the cautious and reflective study and composition of logically interrelated postings or content. It is possible to argue instead that students and teachers—working in the midst of evolving communicative practices—take advantage of the relatively stable generic form and dynamic of the epistle or letter. In the recurrent situation of an ongoing class discussion, it is these generic elements that may well be playing a role in orienting students' individual and collective communicative acts and expectations.

Genre, as mentioned earlier, provides a kind of familiar and stable "comfort zone" that an audience is able to take up with "relative ease" (Burnett & Marshall, 2003, pp. 90–91). As indicated above, this emphasis on continuity, familiarity, and stability is an important part of the "genre perspective" generally. Instead of looking to isolated factors such as individual technological functions or capabilities, the genre perspective, as Yates and Orlikowski explain, makes it possible to consider the processes of the "mutual shaping" of any one genre with a range of associated factors and practices:

> The genre perspective…does not attempt to understand [communicative] practice as an isolated act or outcome, but as communicative action that is situated in a stream of social practices which shape and are shaped by it. (Yates & Orlikowski, 1992, p. 318)

Just as the genre of the memo was described as gradually emerging from the form of the business letter—through the combined influence of management philosophies, increasing firm size, and typographical and secretarial innovations — the development of the online posting, too, can be understood as the outcome of a multiplicity of forces or changes over the last decade or more. These changes have no doubt included developments in student demographics, increased familiarity with online courses and Internet genres generally, and even changes in institutional policies and priorities. The genre perspective focuses on structures and continuities that are "situated in a stream of social practices" and factors, such as those listed above. In this way, the genre perspective highlights continuities and changes in communicative practices over the course of decades and centuries, and brings attention to larger trends and developments, rather than reducing understandings of a communication medium to its technical or functional characteristics (e.g., see Friesen, 2008).

It is possible to take this line of thinking even one step further by referring to a greatly expanded definition of genre. Genre as an analytical category has been applied not only to works of film, literature, and standardized forms of written communication. It has also been used as a way of understanding a very wide range of formal and informal modes of speaking, writing, and even acting — ways that copy, combine, and adapt existing forms of communication and action. "Genres" in this expanded sense of the word ranges from a party invitation to a casual greeting, from a university lecture to a shopping list, or (of special significance, here) from the narration of a personal anecdote to the formulation of a logical syllogism. Sylvia Scribner, a social psychologist who studied syllogistic reasoning in both literate and orally based cultures, refers to both "narrative genres" and "logical genres" (1997) in her famous essay, "Modes of Thinking and Ways of Speaking: Culture and Logic Reconsidered." She reports on field research that shows that persons belonging to oral cultures were generally unable to engage successfully in syllogistic reasoning (e.g., producing or understanding sentences such as: "All persons are mortal; Socrates is a person; Socrates is mortal."). But Scribner also discovered that these same individuals were easily able to engage in other typified communicative actions, such as the formulation of complex narratives. Scribner consequently argued that this inability to reproduce syllogistic formulations does not arise from any cognitive or cultural "deficit," or an overall incapacity to think "logically."

Instead, she attributed it to a lack of familiarity with syllogisms as typified communicative acts and with formalized logical reasoning as a *genre*. "The narrative, like the formal [logical] problem," Scribner concludes, "may be considered a socially evolved genre that individuals in varying degrees, depending on their own personal life experiences, acquire or...internalize" (p. 142).

Using Scribner's findings on narrative and logical genres, it is possible to come to a second conclusion (very different from the first) about the findings of the study presented in this chapter: Namely, that students' engagement in the dynamics of "epistolarity" in online discussion contexts is significant not because it might provide social, interpersonal support for more important processes of logical, critical inquiry. Instead, students can be understood as being led by the genre of the Internet posting to create meaning that is much closer to Scribner's "narrative genre" than to its "logical" counterpart. The "reciprocality" and "connection" associated with the epistolary character of the Internet posting, in other words, seem much more germane to the narrative than the logical genre. Personal narratives, after all, are generally "about" those who are telling them, and they relate to actual events and situations in the tellers' lives, or in those of their friends or acquaintances. As the above content analysis shows, online postings appear rife with discussion of particular matters raised in other messages, with references to shared events in the past and to stated possibilities for the future. Like narrative, these kinds of exchanges represent engaged negotiations with specific times, places, and people in their concrete particularity.

This is a type of meaning that is very different from the meaning created through the abstract, universal principles of syllogistic or critical reasoning. The example of the syllogism provided above ("All persons are mortal; Socrates is a person; Socrates is mortal."), exemplifies the timeless, placeless, abstract quality of this kind of rule-based reasoning: It speaks of all persons being mortal as a general "law," and uses logical operations independent of time and situation to apply this law to a rather arbitrary individual case. Narrative, on the other hand, has arguably much more in common — both historically and formally — with the social reciprocity and mutuality of "epistolarity." It is perhaps little wonder, then, that the forerunner of the posting—the epistolary or letter form—has been used as a means of structuring novel-length narratives, and that the dynamics of these narrative accounts, in turn, can provide insights into written exchanges generally.

Such a conclusion not only helps to explain the specific results of this chapter, it also provides an explanation for findings typical of similar studies of online discussion: namely, for the low percentage of postings which "engage in critical discourse, mutual critique, or argumentation" (Rourke & Kanuka, 2007, p. 106). The other 78% to 95% of postings, as Garrison and others indicate, tend to present "monological narratives" that can only appear as "undirected, unreflective [and] random" (Garrison, Anderson, & Archer, 2001, p. 21) when viewed from their perspective of critical inquiry. When these same exchanges are understood from the genre perspective as epistolary exchange, the preponderance of such messages is much more easily explained. The exchanges can be understood as the result of a reciprocal, interpersonal dynamic that students engage in largely as an end in itself, invited by the confluence of practical, cultural, and historical "streams" or factors that shape (and are shaped by) the way in which these written exchanges take place. In the context of online discussion environments, students are asked to work to repeatedly bridge the "gap" between reading and writing in the here and now and the reading and writing in the past and in the likely future. And in doing so, they unsurprisingly end up adapting and reproducing a kind of form and dynamic that has been a matter of comfortable familiarity in many contexts and for hundreds of years.

PART II: THE POST-COGNITIVIST TURN

Chapter Four

Psychology and Technology: The Relationship between Mind and Machine

Introduction

Any examination of e-learning research would be remiss if it did not consider the foundational role that psychology—above all cognitive psychology—plays in this fledgling field. The disciplinary precursors of e-learning, identified earlier as instructional design and instructional technology, leave little doubt as to the debt they owe to psychology. Walter Dick (1987), for example, describes the field of instructional design as one "pioneered by educational psychologists" (p. 183). It represents, he says, "applied educational psychology"—whether behavioral or cognitive—"in the best sense of the term" (p. 183). The historical origins of instructional or educational technology have been described similarly—as fundamentally dependent on the fortunes of behaviorist and cognitive psychologies:

> With the rise of Skinner's behaviorism in the 1960s and the emergence of cognitive psychology in the 1970s, educational technology began to be recognized for the first time as a distinct field and profession in its own right. (Saettler, 2004, p. 501)

Behavioral and cognitive psychology have in succession provided the theoretical and disciplinary foundations for both instructional design and educational technology. In the case of e-learning, however, at least one additional psychological approach must be added: constructivism. Together with behaviorism and cognitivism, constructivism is sometimes said to form a triad of psychological paradigms providing ways of understanding the role and value of technologies in learning. This particular configuration or succession of paradigms is referenced, for example, in discussions of designed instruction (Cooper, 1993; Ertmer & Newby, 1993), and accounts of a "new" interdisciplinary "science of learning" (e.g., Bransford, Brown, & Cocking, 2000, pp. 3–16; Saywer, 2006a).

This chapter shows how these three "psychologies"—each of which uses broadly mechanistic or computational terms to understand human learning and thinking—have played a special role in the conceptualizations and discourse of e-learning and the related fields of instructional design and instructional technology. In doing so, the chapter presents a historical account of these three psychologies, examining the ways in which closely interrelated understandings of technology, learning, and the mind have developed and become integrated over time.

The ultimate intent of this historical account is *not* to demonstrate the use of any particular psychology or methodology that can be applied in research into e-learning. Instead, the purpose is to prepare the ground for the description and use of two specific methodologies—conversational analysis and discursive psychology—in the chapter that follows.

Technology and Psychology: Tools to Theory

At the core of the historical analyses in this chapter is the existence of a long-standing, *metaphorical* connection between historically novel or prominent technologies, on the one hand, and conceptions of the mind, on the other. In different historical periods, different technologies—such as the clock, camera, and the computer—have provided powerful ways of understanding the mind. The self-sufficiency of the operations of these technologies and the certainty and detail in which these operations can be known mean that such technologies can provide compelling ways of understanding aspects of the human mind. It is also the suggestive power of metaphor itself that contributes to this figurative transference of properties and characteristics from the rule-bound operations of a machine or computer to the function of the human mind.

In a book entitled *Metaphors of Memory: A History of Ideas about the Mind,* psychologist Douwe Draaisma (2000) provides a colorful genealogy of the metaphoric connections between technology and the human mind or human memory. Draaisma shows how the history of these metaphors stretches all the way from Plato's dialogues through the computer to the technology of the holograph:

> From Plato's wax tablet to the computers of our age memory-related language is shot through with metaphors. Our views of the operation of mem-

ory are fuelled by the procedures and techniques we have invented for the preservation and reproduction of information. This influence is so strong that in, say, nineteenth-century theories on the visual memory, one can trace exactly the succession of new optical processes: in 1839 the daguerreotype and the talbotype, shortly afterwards stereoscopy, then ambrotypes and colour photography. Comparing the neuronal substratum of the visual memory to the structure of a hologram as some of our contemporary theoreticians do, fits in to a venerable tradition... The history of memory is a little like a tour of the depositories of a technology museum. (p. 3)

It follows that technologies—whether they are prominent in everyday life generally or in e-learning in particular—should not be viewed simply as artifacts or tools that are significant only in terms of their explicit functions. Instead, as Draaisma and others argue, technologies also frequently serve as *heuristics* or practical means to understand the mind. Talking specifically of their use in scientific research, psychologist Gerd Gigerenzer speaks of computer and other technologies as being involved in a "tools to theories heuristic." Gigerenzer (2000) describes how "new scientific tools, once entrenched in a scientist's daily practice, suggest new theoretical metaphors and concepts" (p. 5). Using the example of cognitivism to illustrate his claim, Gigerenzer points out that it is only *"after* the [computer] became entrenched in everyday laboratory routine [that] a broad acceptance of the view of mind as a computer followed" (p. 39; emphasis added). It is only after psychologists were using computers as tools for statistical analyses in their labs, Gigerenzer explains, that they began to refer to the representation, processing, and manipulation of information as a way to account for thinking and learning.

This "tools to theory heuristic" can be restated more broadly: technologies that, at a given point and time in history, are widely used or are otherwise conspicuous have the tendency to inspire theories about the nature of the mind, memory, thinking, or learning. This chapter presents the argument that this metaphorical connection between "tools" and "theory" is of significance not only for psychology but (perhaps especially) for e-learning. It explores this significance through the following steps:

1. The chapter begins by tracing the successive reformulation of the "tool to theory heuristic" as it appears in the metaphors and descriptions of

behaviorism, cognitivism, and constructivism, specifically as these are articulated in the literature of instructional technology and design. This overview makes evident that the particular representation of constructivism in the literature represents less an independent psychological paradigm than an elaboration or augmentation of earlier cognitivist approaches.

2.   The chapter then makes the case that the relationship between technology and learning, as it appears in the context of e-learning, is more than simply metaphorical or "heuristic" in nature. The simultaneous importance of technology for both understanding *and* supporting the mind and learning processes introduces a kind of epistemological and practical "conflict of interest" in e-learning.

3.   The chapter concludes by presenting a number of critiques of cognitivism, or specifically, of its paradigmatic equation of mind and computer. Also, through reference to the critical-theoretical division of knowledge forms and knowledge-constitutive interests described in the introduction, the chapter explores the possibilities of alternative "psychologies" derived from different configurations of human interests and ways of knowing.

As mentioned earlier, the purpose of these points and arguments is not so much to present the reader with a methodology that can be adapted and applied in research into e-learning. Instead, this chapter prepares the way for a discussion and demonstration of the presuppositions and methods of a rather different psychological approach: what is called "discursive" or (more controversially) "post-cognitive psychology," which studies psychological phenomena by focusing on communication and action rather than on information processing and quasi-computational functions.

Behaviorism: The Teaching Machine

Behaviorism—the first of the three psychologies or learning theories generally associated with the use of this technology in education—developed rather gradually as a research paradigm during the first half of the twentieth century. As the name itself implies, behaviorism understands psychology in terms of the study of human and animal behavior, specifically in terms of environmental stimuli and related behavioral responses. It came to be established in North American universities principally through the work of J.B. Watson and E.L.

Thorndike. These psychologists described the relationship between stimulus and response in terms that have been described as resonant or reminiscent of the technology of the telephone—a technology that was rapidly gaining in popularity at the time. Writing specifically of Watson, psychologist Ian Hutchby explains,

> Following the invention of the telephone, the psychologist Watson saw that the exchange network could act as an appropriate model for his theory of behaviour, in which the brain received incoming "calls" from the sensory system and then relayed their "messages" to the motor system. This tied in with Watson's behaviourist programme in psychology, in which the brain was significant only in its role as a mediator between sensations or other stimuli, and the body's responses to those stimuli. (Hutchby, 2001, p. 37)

A prominent technological innovation provides a metaphorical basis or model for a psychological paradigm: just as a call originates from one location and then is systematically routed to another, a given stimulus is received and then mediated or relayed to produce a corresponding behavioral response (see also Edwards, Gilroy, & Hartley, 2002, p. 57 for a similar description of Thorndike's work and telephone exchange technology).

By the 1950s the dominant brand of behaviorism was B.F. Skinner's "radical behaviorism," which introduced a particularly exacting framework and set of terms for understanding not only behavior but also processes of learning. Questions of learning or "behavior modification" were defined in such a way that these activities could be neatly addressed through technological, or more specifically, mechanical solutions. For example, in this behaviorist vocabulary, formal learning is defined as changes in voluntary behavior produced through programmatic "reinforcement." This reinforcement, in turn, occurs through positive consequences or changes, which are introduced in a manner systematically "contingent" upon behavior, leading to the expression "contingencies of reinforcement."

As a result, statements such as the following become possible: "Teaching as a technology" operates through the arrangement of "contingencies of reinforcement under which behavior changes" (Skinner, 1968, p. 9). Of course, when defined in this way—as highly systematic, organized, and programmed "contingencies of reinforcement"—learning turns into something that can best be undertaken through the use of relatively simple mechanical apparatus or a "teaching machine." This kind of technology, according to Skinner, is one that is able to provide stimuli in the form of small units of information and immediate, consistent, and programmed reinforcement to student responses. Links between stimulus and response are instantiated with mechanical precision and simplicity. Teaching complex subjects – or "program[ming] complex forms of behavior" according to Skinner – consequently becomes a question simply of "effective sequencing." "We have every reason to expect," Skinner concludes, "that the most effective control of human learning will require instrumental aid. The simple fact is that, as a mere reinforcing mechanism, the teacher is out of date" (p. 22).

Although it is only infrequently mentioned today, the "programmed instruction movement" or "teaching machine revolution" (Saettler, 2004, p. 294) that accompanied Skinner's bold pronouncements set an important precedent for the instructional paradigms that followed in its wake. This precedent or pattern can be expressed as follows: A psychological paradigm, associated with the workings of a conspicuous technology, leads to the development of a correspondingly mechanized or "technologized" theory of learning. A similar or related technology, in turn, is then either identified or produced; and this technology is subsequently presented and promoted as a solution that is the "most effective" possible for human learning.

The Cognitive Revolution

Cognitivism as a psychological paradigm arose in response to a multiplicity of factors. These include the unsatisfactory simplicity of behaviorist accounts of learning and teaching (Winn & Snyder, 2004, p. 83), as well as interdisciplinary developments in computer science, linguistics, and psychology (e.g., Miller, 2003, pp. 142–143). According to others, increasingly complex "problems of war" requiring "a new view" of the nature of the human being also played an important role in the rise of the cognitive paradigm (Lachman, Lachman, and Butterfield, 1979, pp. 56–57). Unlike behaviorism, cognitivism arose relatively rapidly, presenting what has been called a "cognitive revolution" – one that had all but "routed" the behaviorist paradigm in research in the course of very few years, establishing at the same time societies, journals, and university departments in its name (e.g., Thagard, 2002; Waldrop, 2002, pp. 140, 139).

Cognitive psychology and cognitive science more generally are based on the hypothesis that the processing and representational capabilities of the computer can serve as a basis for understanding the mind:

> The expression *cognitive science* is used to describe a broadly integrated class of approaches to the study of mental activities and processes and of cognition in particular ... Cognitive scientists tend to adopt certain basic, general assumptions about mind and intelligent thought and behavior. These include assumptions that the mind is (1) an information processing system, (2) a representational device, and (3) (in some sense) a computer. (Bechtel, Graham, & Abrahamsen, 1998, p. xiii)

"Computational procedures," "representational structures," and "information processing" are all key to the cognitivist paradigm (e.g., Boden, 2006; Thagard, 2002) and also to its role in e-learning.

The heuristic or metaphorical significance of new technologies in this paradigm is obvious: By the end of the Second World War and during the years immediately following, computers were a novel and conspicuous technology, often discussed in the popular press in terms of "giant brains" or "machines that think" (e.g., P. N. Edwards, 1997, pp. 146, 190–196). Especially in the first years of the cognitive revolution, the computer and computer programs were seen as providing nothing less than an "existence proof" for particular cognitive concepts and models of mental operation. Conjectures about how we carry out cognitive tasks—for example, how we recognize faces or sounds or how we remember or solve problems—were seen as being "provable" by being modeled by a computer. If it were possible to get a computer to accomplish the same kinds of mental tasks that people do, it would seem reasonable to conclude that our minds accomplish the same task in the same way.

It is relatively easy to see how cognitivism provides a very different set of terms and concepts for learning and teaching than behaviorism. Indeed, from the 1960s to the present day, the "cognitive revolution" has redefined all of the key concepts in educational research: Learning is defined *not* as an enduring behavioral change achieved through stimulus and response conditioning. Instead, it is understood in terms of changes in the way information is represented and structured in the mind (e.g., Ausubel, 1960; Craik & Lockhart, 1972; Miller, 1956; Piaget & Inhelder, 1973). Teaching is no longer conceptualized as the modification of behavior through "contingencies of reinforcement." Instead, it is seen as the support of "active processing," of the effective construction of mental representations, or of the efficient self-regulation of these and other cognitive processes (Perry & Winne, 2006; Scardamalia & Bereiter, 2003; Wolfe, 1998). Educational research itself is also changed: from the observation of persistent changes in behavior to the study and computational modeling of cognitive entities and informational processes (e.g., Bereiter & Scardamalia, 1992).

The cognitive redefinition of educational concepts into broadly computational terms also implies particular roles for the computer in teaching, learning, and in education generally. With thought, perception, and learning processes themselves understood in terms of information processing or symbol manipulation, the computer is seen as being able to act cognitively with or in support of the student or learner. The computer therefore is cast as a kind of "cognitive technology" Pea (1985), a "cognitive tool" (Jonassen & Reeves, 1996; Kozma, 1987) or simply, a "mindtool" (Jonassen, 2005; Lajoie, 2000) that is uniquely suited to support the cognitive tasks involved in learning: "To be effective, a tool for learning must closely parallel the learning process; and the computer, as an information processor, could hardly be better suited for this" (Kozma, 1987, p. 22). Computer technology is seen in this context specifically as being capable of "making up" for recognized human cognitive limitations that affect "the learning process." Kozma explains:

> there are three aspects of the learning process that are primary considerations in designing computer-based learning: the limited capacity of short-term or working memory, the structure of knowledge in long-term memory, and the learner's use of cognitive strategies. (p. 22)

Cognitive tools, as the same author goes on to explain, can "evoke necessary operations and compensate for capacity limitations" regarding these and other cognitive functions (p. 23). Such an understanding of the role of the computer coincides closely with what was called computer-based instruction (CBI), which, as one historical account explains, heightened interest "in examining learning as a function of the processing performed by the learner" (Szabo, 1994). Above all, it was the computer's working memory that was seen in CBI as being capable of interacting with the short-term memory of the learner. Through drill-and-practice, tutorial and simple simulation activities, the computer was seen as "communicat[ing] information in ways which would avoid" reaching the limits of the learner's "short-term memory" (Szabo, 1994).

In this way the computer is given a role in education that is remarkably similar to its function in military "man-machine" systems that will be described in chapter nine. The computer forms a single "operating unit, [with] the human operator [acting as] an information transmitter and processing device interposed between his machine's displays and their controls" (Lachman, Lachman, & Butterfield, 1979, p. 58). Similarly, in cognitivist discourse in e-learning, the computer is understood as "working in intimate partnership," in symbiotic or dyadic relationship "with the [human] learner," acting to "share," "extend," and "amplify" (Jonassen, 2000) his or her cognitive capacities. What is different, of course, is that in education, the "man" or "warfighter" is substituted by the student or learner and the intellectual nature of the tasks—rather than their significance in command and control—is emphasized:

> Learners and technologies should be intellectual partners in the learning process, where the cognitive responsibility for performing is distributed to the part of the partnership that performs it best. (Jonassen, Peck, & Wilson, 1999, p. 13; quoted in McLoughlin & Luca, 2001; Kim & Hay, 2005; Heeman & Andreazza , 2007)

The ongoing use of this characterization of student and computer and the dates associated with the other citations, above, are an indication that this conception of human and computer "partnership" is one that has had currency for more than two decades, with the same terms (e.g., "cognitive tool," "mindtool") and frames of reference (e.g., human-computer "partnership") being utilized with remarkable consistency up to the present day.

Over this same period of time, however, slightly different descriptions of the close interaction between learner and computer emerge (in some cases in the works of the same authors). These descriptions are neither purely cognitivist nor are they radically "constructivist"; they might be instead best described as a kind of hybrid, "cognitive-constructivist" approach to learning. The emergence of constructivist influences in otherwise explicitly cognitivist scholarship can be briefly illustrated by looking at the history of the phrase "AI in reverse" (with AI referring to artificial intelligence).

The phrase AI in reverse was originally introduced in Gavriel Salomon's influential and widely referenced paper entitled "AI in Reverse: Computer Tools that Turn Cognitive" (Salomon, 1988a; see also Bonk & Cunningham, 1998; Dillenbourg, 1996; Jonassen, 2003, 2005c; Kozma, 1991). In it, Salomon explains this titular reversal of AI as follows:

> The purpose of applying AI to the design of instruction and training is basically to communicate with learners in ways that come as close as possible to the ways in which they do or ought to represent the new information to themselves. One expects to save the learners, so to speak, unnecessary cognitive transformations and operations. (pp. 123–124)

Here, Salomon makes an appeal to the constructivist notion that cultural artifacts or tools affect the mind in ways that are much more profound than merely augmenting its processing or memory functions. He is advocating the use of these tools as examples that show how the mind, at its most effective, can work. This way of thinking is based on Lev Vygotsky's (1978) notion that linguistic signs or symbols are not simply neutral carriers of information but that they act as "instrument[s] of psychological activity in a manner analogous to the role of [tools] in labor" (p. 52). Like tools of physical labor, "cognitive" tools—from primitive linguistic symbols to computers as powerful "symbol manipulators"—can help form and shape the character of the laborer or tool user. The "primary role for computers" in educational technology then becomes one not simply of mirroring or augmenting cognitive operations but one of fundamentally "reorganizing our mental functioning" (Pea, 1985, p. 168). Computers are still seen working in intimate partnership with the learner but their principal contribution is not the augmentation of human intelligence, rather, it is *modeling* or exemplification: "rather than having the computer simulate human intelligence [the idea is to] get humans to simulate the computer's unique intelligence and come to use it as part of their cognitive apparatus" (Jonassen, 1996, p. 7). In this sense, as Jonassen explains, computational "mindtools" can be understood as AI in reverse with the ultimate goal of making human cognitive operations as efficient and effective as those engineered and tested for computers.

Constructivism: Representation, Verification, Regulation

As the example of the phrase "AI in reverse" illustrates, constructivist understandings of technology-enabled learning emerged very gradually from cognitive discourse, appearing as far back as the mid-1980s. The history of this phrase illustrates that a very fluid, porous boundary separates constructivism from cognitivist principles. To gain a fuller appreciation of the role of constructivism in e-learning and related disciplines, however, it is important to note that the term "constructivism" itself is often considered to be notoriously vague, with quite different meanings and implications in philosophy and sociology, for example, than in e-learning. Its origin is also not directly traceable to a single technology or innovation. At the same time, however, the birth of cybernetics—the study of both human and machine as systems of command and control—gave significant impetus to the development of constructivism in the latter part of the twentieth century. Also, its close connection between cognitivism and constructivism has given rise to visions of technology use in e-learning that are very similar to those described above, only the sophistication of the technology and the complexity of the learning processes are expanded or amplified.

For e-learning and learning theory generally, the principle contribution of constructivism is its emphasis on the active "construction"—rather than the passive reception or acquisition—of students' knowledge. It is the activity of such construction, and the complex processes through which it occurs, that are front and center in definitions of the term "constructivism" in e-learning. Duffy and Cunningham (1996), for example, define constructivism in terms of two closely interrelated propositions: "that (1) learning is an active process of constructing rather than acquiring knowledge, and (2) [that] instruction is a process of supporting that construction rather than communicating knowledge" (p. 171). David Jonassen, a name associated with both cognitivist (e.g., Jonassen, Hannum, & Tessmer, 1989) and constructivist (e.g., Jonassen, Peck, & Wilson, 1999) approaches, provides further detail:

> Succinctly, constructivism avers that learners construct their own reality or at least interpret it based on their perceptions of experiences, so an individual's knowledge is a function of one's prior experiences, mental structures, and beliefs that are used to interpret objects and events. [...] What someone knows is grounded in perception of physical and social experiences which are comprehended by the mind. What the mind produces are mental models that represent what the knower has perceived. (Jonassen, 1994, pp. 34–35)

As Jonassen's definition makes clear, any single, "given" reality can be accounted for by a wide range of possible knowledge constructions. However, just because constructed knowledge cannot be judged in terms of absolute truth or certainty, does not prevent it from being evaluated in terms of its practical *viability*. Knowledge can be validated, in other words, "by testing the extent to which it provides a workable, acceptable action relative to potential alternatives" (Duffy & Cunningham, 1996, p. 171). This viability, moreover, is seen as "testable" through both individual and collaborative processes and in terms of a rather wide range of methods and techniques: propositions or hypotheses, as one example, can be verified or falsified in collaborative contexts based on new, previous, shared, or vicarious experience (e.g., Hoadley, 2005; Scardamalia & Bereiter, 2003); problem-solving and "self-regulatory" strategies, as a second example, can be verified and refined based on how fully they address the problem or cognitive challenge at hand (e.g., Mayer & Wittrock, 2006; Perry & Winne, 2006); and learner (or novice) constructions, mental models, or interpretations, as a third example, can be compared with those of experts and brought into closer alignment with them (e.g., Bransford, Brown, & Cocking, 2000, pp. 31–50). Learners in this sense, to quote Jerome Bruner (1991), are sometimes portrayed in constructivist contexts as "growing up as 'little scientists,' 'little logicians' [or] 'little mathematicians'" (p. 4) who construct knowledge through the use of methods that increase the utility and viability of this knowledge, gradually making it more specialized and "expert."

It is in connection with the specific processes involved in the construction and testing of knowledge—its representation, verification, and refinement—that computers and Internet technologies become important in constructivist accounts of e-learning. But these constructivist computational functions are more demanding than those required by earlier cognitivist conceptions. As Perkins (1991) explains, the computer's "information processor must be seen *not just* as shuffling data" between one component (e.g., the learner) and another (e.g., a computer's memory; p. 21; emphasis added). Instead, Perkins continues, this same technology must be seen as "wielding" data much more "flexibily during learning—making hypotheses, testing tentative interpretations, and so on" (p. 21). In constructivism, in other words, the computer's educational value does not derive so much from the simple processing and storage of data, but rather, through more advanced or higher-level computational functions such as representation, mapping, and verification. Correspondingly, both human and computer are seen as operating on the level of "knowledge" and its "construction" rather than of "data" and its "processing" (although references to data or information and its processing still remain part of constructivist learning discourse).

In constructivism, learning is conceptualized in terms of the construction or representation of both rudimentary (i.e., learner or novice) knowledge constructions and their gradual development into more intricate and refined (i.e., expert) constructions; and such representations are associated with terms such as cognitive "schemas," "models," and "structures." In this context, the contribution of Internet and computer technologies is understood as the provision of multiple means of representing and refining these schemas or structures. Take for example the notion of the "visualization" of cognitive structures: the educational contribution of computers in learning can be defined specifically in terms of the "representational affordances...of interactive multimedia, animation, and computer modeling technologies" (Jacobsen, 2004, p. 41). These representational affordances are of value specifically because they allow for the "dynamic qualitative representations of the mental models held by experts and novice learners" to be visualized and compared (p. 41). And this in turn allows for the gradual approximation of novice models or schemas to those of more expert constructors of knowledge (Bransford, Brown, & Cocking, 2000). Similar analogies or arguments have been made in the case of other representational capabilities of the computer: from hypertext and hypermedia (e.g., Jonassen, 1989) and computer-supported collaborative learning environments (e.g., Hoadley, 2005) to more interactive and kinesthetic forms of games and simulations (e.g., Gee, 2007). In each case it is the ability of advanced technologies to represent and distribute knowledge—and thus to make "normally hidden knowledge processes [or representations]...transparent to users" (Scardamalia, 2003, p. 23)—that is the principal source of its value.

Discussions of technological support for "meta-cognition" and "self-regulated learning" provide another example of the way that constructivism assigns educational value to technology. Meta-cognition and self-regulation essentially refer to the evolution and execution of cognitive strategies for the effective construction of knowledge in learning. In e-learning, meta-cognition has been seen as involving the use of computer and Internet technologies in particular ways: for the provision of learning materials from the Internet (typically in the form of learning objects) and for the facilitation and recording of students' interactions with these same materials (e.g., in the form of annotations, highlighting, and linkages). Particular student interactions with these materials are further seen as corresponding to "cognitive operations" specific to learning or knowledge construction processes. As Philip Winne (2006) explains, these cognitive operations include the "storage" and "retrieval" of "information" and the "forg[ing of] links between information objects" (p. 10). The computer, again, is seen as representing—making explicit or visible—certain cognitive or knowledge construction processes and operations that would otherwise be hidden or difficult to access. Referring to these visible processes in terms of "traces" or "records" of students' cognitive labor, Winne explains:

> These records support grounded interpretations about how a learner constructs knowledge. Trace data reflect what learners do in ways that help re-

searchers...test whether a tool helps learners construct knowledge. Trace data also reveal more accurately, although not perfectly, whether, when, and how learners access prior knowledge. (p. 14)

Like behaviorism and cognitivism before it, constructivism is used in e-learning and related discourses to assign terms to thinking that are derived from or at least clearly consonant with the functions of a computer. Instead of connections between stimulus and response or the ability to process raw information, it is the computer's capacity for the representation of mental structures and the mirroring of self-regulatory, problem-solving, and other rule-based functions that is presented as the source of its power as a supremely pedagogical technology.

Tool to Theory Heuristic

Constructivism, like cognitivism and behaviorism before it, gives vivid illustration to the importance of technologies as metaphors in psychology and learning theory. Together these three psychologies provide much support for the "tool to theory heuristic" outlined above. In each case, successive technological innovations inspire or reinforce successive understandings of the human mind. Especially in e-learning, the development of information and communication innovations in the twentieth century can be traced in recent psychological theories much as Draaisma describes technologies of the nineteenth century as being expressed in theories of memory of that same age: from the telephone exchange as a central relay for inputs and outputs comes behaviorist stimuli and response; from the computer as a symbol manipulator comes the mind as an information processor; and as the computer becomes a networked, multimedia device, constructivist notions of the regulated but dynamic processes of representation and verification of knowledge become prominent.

In outlining the notion of a "tool to theory heuristic" and in emphasizing the importance of technological metaphors in psychology, this book is *not* seeking to diminish the value or importance of psychology's many lasting contributions to the field(s) of education. The present discussion is not intended as an argument, for example, against the value of constructivist scaffolding, of cognitivist advanced planners, or the provision of "positive reinforcement" to encourage certain behavior. The issue here is not the practical value of these approaches, but rather, their theoretical and paradigmatic grounding. The issue is the need to make explicit and examine the "heuristic" and "metaphorical" origin of these psychological paradigms. To use the language of critical theory (see chapters one and eight), the contention here is that psychology is like any other form of knowledge—whether technological, practical, or emancipatory. Like other knowledge forms, psychological knowledge is *not* free from human interests and influences and is *not* independent of critical, political, and linguistic interests and other knowledge types.

Speaking specifically of e-learning, however, this chapter has an additional and more important purpose. The point is not simply to argue that e-learning, by virtue of its close association to psychology, is implicated in the interests and epistemological dynamics of behaviorism, cognitivism, and constructivism as described above; what is more important is that e-learning—and instructional technology and design before it—are doubly implicated in their relation to *technology*. The role of technology in cognitivist or constructivist e-learning, in other words, is twofold: in addition to its heuristic function as a metaphor for the mind, technology also clearly serves a practical, instructional role in e-learning. In addition to providing metaphors and accounts of mental processes, technology is *also* the principal means for the refinement and development of these same processes. "[H]aving conceived of thinking as a kind of machinery," as Andrew Feenberg (2002) puts it, "machinery in fact turns out to be the perfect image of the process of thought" (p. 97). In e-learning, this same "image of thought" can be seen to pass between tool and learner and between machinery and theory; and this image is recognized at various points in this process as a potent technology, a theory of mind, and a powerful pedagogical affordance. In behaviorism, for example, the image of reinforced "circuits" or mechanistic connections between stimulus and response is transferred from what was then the conspicuous technology of the telephone exchange to a theory of behavior and then back to its pedagogical treatment in the form of Skinner's "teaching machine." In the case of cognitivism and constructivism, the computer and its proliferating capabilities serve first as a model for human mental tasks and then as an indispensable mechanism for their support.

Once the initial comparison between mind and machine has been operationalized in psychology, its original, metaphorical, or hypothetical nature is all too readily repressed or forgotten. Forgetting that thinking was originally conceived provisionally as a kind of machinery, in other words, this same machinery then reappears as the perfect image of thought, as a support that "could hardly be better suited" (Kozma, 1987, p. 22) for the educational task in question.

Speaking specifically of the metaphoric roles of computer technology in psychology and AI, Derek Edwards (1997a) explains,

> Metaphors [of this kind] join two discourse domains together, and the effects are mutual. They illuminate, draw attention to, points of contrast and similarity, generality and exception, that might otherwise be missed. What is dangerous is when the metaphorical nature of the enterprise is forgotten, and domain A is talked about in terms of domain B, as if it were not a metaphor at all. (p. 31)

In this case, "domain A" is e-learning, and "domain B" is cognitive psychology. The metaphorical comparison of mind and machine underlying cognitive psychology is literalized in the discourse of e-learning. This "literalization" becomes especially problematic when computer technologies or mechanisms that earlier served a heuristic function for understanding the mind reappear as indispensable tools for teaching and learning. The result in some cases is a distorting and self-reinforcing circularity. One antidote would be the recognition of fundamental differences between thought and technology, both in psychological explanations and in educational applications.

Critiques of Cognitivism

The initial metaphor and hypothesis—the effective equation of mind and machine—has recently been invoked in significant questioning and critique of cognitivism (and by extension of cognitive-constructivism). The challenges to this hypothesis, which are manifold and mutually reinforcing, are being put forward in fields as varied as AI, human-computer interaction ("interaction design"), and psychology itself.

One challenge to the cognitivist paradigm arises from the failure of AI to produce computational models of even the simplest aspects of human thought and behavior. The earliest conceptions of cognitive science saw AI as foundational or even as its "central discipline" (Boden, 2006, p. 296; Gardner, 1985, pp. 40, 46). As discussed earlier, AI was seen as capable of developing technologies that would provide the "existence proof" for understandings of human cognitive systems, and models for effective cognition. But when it comes to (especially) the most simple and commonsensical of these processes, AI has, for a long time, all but given up the quest. Marvin Minsky, one of AI's founders, characterizes the field as having "been brain-dead" in this regard "since the 1970s" (2003). Minsky laments that to this day, there is still "no computer that has common sense" and that there are few people working in this direction. Other AI researchers have concurred, sometimes emphasizing the consequences for cognitivism generally: "Computational procedures are not constitutive of mind," as one cognitive scientist writes, "and thus cannot play the foundational role they are often ascribed in AI and cognitive science" (Schweizer, 1997, p. 195).

Other research, undertaken in cognitive anthropology and ethnography, has come to similar if less overtly stated conclusions. These findings also serve as evidence of the inadequacy of computational processes — whether for the processing of information or the construction of knowledge — as ways of understanding everyday human life. Studies of informal learning (e.g., Lave & Wenger, 1991) and of everyday mathematical reasoning (e.g., Lave, 1988), for example, have emphasized "practice" rather than computation as the basis for expanding a "view of cognition" that otherwise remains "claustrophobic" (Lave, 1988, p. 1). Other research has similarly cast into doubt rationalist, cognitive, and constructivist understandings of *planning*, which is a task central to processes of problem solving and self-regulation. These studies emphasize that activities such as everyday planning and mathematical reasoning are "primarily situated, and that [such] situated actions are essentially [improvised or] ad hoc" (Suchman, 1987, p. ix; see also Suchman, 2007; Winograd & Flores, 1986). Still other research in psychology that has positioned itself as programmatically critical of cognitivism has been appearing at least since the early 1990s (e.g., Edwards & Potter, 1992; Gergen & Gigerenzer, 1991; Steinberg, Kincheloe, & Hinchey, 1999; Still & Costall, 1991). This scholarship not only underscores the fundamental inadequacy of broadly computational models as ways of understanding cognition; it also presents an alternative conceptual vocabulary — above all, a vocabulary of practice, situation, and improvisation rather than formalization and calculation — for understanding psychological phenomena.

Still further challenges and doubts have been expressed by those closest to cognitive and constructivist approaches in psychology in general and in human computer interaction in particular. Some of these can be traced back to fairly early years in the movement. For example, cognitive psychologist Donald Norman, writes in 1981 that:

> The results [of cognitive science] have been considerable progress on some fronts, but sterility overall, for the organism we are analysing is conceived as pure intellect, communicating with one another in logical dialogue, perceiving, remembering, thinking when appropriate, reasoning its way through well formed problems that are encountered during the day. Alas that description does not fit actual behavior. (1981, p. 266)

Admittedly, psychology — and Norman himself — has since emphasized less well-formed problems (e.g., Jonassen, 2003) in addition to the embodied (e.g., Varela, Thompson, & Rosch, 1991) and emotional (e.g., Norman, 2003) dimensions of cognition. But Norman's critique of the computational paradigm appears to have been echoed more often than it has been rigorously or programmatically acted upon. In *The Mind's New Science,* Martin Gardner (1985), for example, also wonders aloud about the future viability of the movement and of the computational model that underlies it: "Cognitive science can still go on, but the question arises about whether one ought to remain on the lookout for more veridical models of human thought" (p. 44).

By comparison, the research literature of education and specifically of e-learning often seems to avoid the issue altogether. One notable exception, however, can be found in an overview of "Cognitive Perspectives in Psychology" by Winn and Snyder (2004): "[The] computational theory and functionalism that underlie [central cognitivist] assumptions," the authors state, "have been the source of considerable recent criticism and point perhaps to the closing of the current chapter in the history of psychology" (p. 86). They follow this up by referencing critiques of cognitivism such as those provided above (p. 85) and by speculating on issues — such as "nonsymbolic thinking and learning" — that they see emergent subsequent to the "closing" of this "current chapter."

Anticipating "the Next Chapter"

So far the purpose of these arguments has been to illustrate precisely the dynamics of the "closing of the current chapter in...psychology" invoked by Winn and Snyder. The task still remains, however, to introduce the elements that could be a part of an emerging "new chapter" for the application of psychology to e-learning. This task can be undertaken by again referring to the three knowledge "forms" and "constitutive interests" described in the introduction. For cognitive science, precisely in its capacity as a natural science, represents predominantly an *instrumental* form of knowledge. It is a type of knowledge that seeks to understand phenomena causally in order to realize their efficient control or technical manipulation of phenomena. At the same time, cognitive science, by virtue of its foundational, computational metaphor, also construes *human behavior* in terms of this same type of knowledge: as the efficient processing of sensory and other data, as the representation of mental structures and as the mirroring of self-regulatory, problem-solving, and other rule-based functions.

The emphasis of critical theory on the multiplicity of knowledge forms, however, complicates this emphasis on instrumental knowledge as both method and subject matter. It does so not only by implying that very different kinds of knowledge are closely interrelated but also by suggesting that different forms of knowledge correspond to different domains of human interest and activity. Critical theory in this sense sees human behavior — everyday perception, interpretation, and activity — as falling within an epistemological domain that is quite different from the scientific and instrumental. This other domain is designated as the "practical," "linguistic," and "interpretive." And the proper study of this particular kind of knowledge and interest is undertaken *interpretively*, through the use of *hermeneutics*. As shown in the first and second chapters of this book, the tried and tested interpretive methods of hermeneutics are quite different from their instrumental-technical counterparts.

A recasting of psychology precisely along interpretive and linguistic terms has already received some attention in this book—in the form of the narrative epistemology and methodology of Jerome Bruner and others as presented in the second chapter. The case that Bruner in particular makes for a psychology grounded in narrative and hermeneutic methods can be seen as tantamount to an argument for a radically new "narrative" psychology—one focusing on culturally specific linguistic and pragmatic concerns and their interpretation, rather than abstract, species-wide competencies and limitations.

The exploration and demonstration of a new psychology and of a corresponding investigative methodology—conceived in terms that above all are practical, linguistic, and interpretive—is precisely the focus of the next chapter. This psychology and methodology, however, does not center as Bruner does on narrative. Instead, its focus is on the broader category of "conversation," "talk," or everyday "discourse." The rigorous study of these phenomena enables the conceptualization and investigation of human action and interaction in ways that are diametrically opposed to the typical presuppositions and results of cognitivist research. It is in this sense that this discursive psychology is designated as "post-cognitivist."

Chapter Five

Post-Cognitivist Psychology and Conversational Technology

Introduction

The terms "post-cognitive" and "post-cognitiv*ist*" have recently been appearing in two quite different, but not unrelated, disciplinary discourses: in psychology and in human-computer interaction (HCI). In both the fields, the notion of a psychology coming *after* cognitivism has been invoked as a response to critiques of the cognitive paradigm. As was illustrated in the previous chapter, these critiques focus above all on the appeal of cognitivism to computational processing as a way of understanding human thought and practice. Kaptelinin and Nardi (2006) cite a number of sources already referenced in chapter four to describe these critiques and challenges as they relate to HCI:

> Despite [its initial] success, challenges to the cognitive paradigm began to appear as early as the mid-1980s. The limitations of the traditional information-processing paradigm were demonstrated in seminal books by Winograd and Flores...and Suchman [in the late 1980s]. By the early 1990s, these limitations were acknowledged in the mainstream HCI community... The trend toward the need for a broader focus in research and development was [also] identified by leading researchers [in HCI]. (pp. 15–16)

Kaptelinin and Nardi see cognitivism as giving way not to a single theory, paradigm, or psychology, but to a multiplicity of theoretical constructs and approaches. In an article entitled, "Post-Cognitive Psychology," Jonathan Potter (2000) makes a similar observation in the context of psychological research: "I do not believe that there will be, or should be, *one* successor to cognitivism [nor that] cognitivism [itself] should be closed down..." (p. 34; emphasis added). Potter, as well as Kaptelinin and Nardi explain that these alternative paradigms would include "activity theory" (Engeström, 1987), "phenomenology" (see chapter seven), and hermeneutics (see chapters two and seven), and even a radical variation on cognitivism known as "distributed cognition" (Hutchins, 1995).

Although they do not insist on a single, unified psychological alternative, both psychologists and HCI experts affirm a common set of approaches based on the presupposition that human practices and interactions are above all situated and improvised. In this sense, they are fundamentally different from the processing and interactions of computer technologies, which are by definition pre-scripted and rule bound. Post-cognitivist researchers see the nature and meaning of everyday situations and activities as being produced and enacted anew every time they occur. These situations and actions have order and significance, but it is emergent, rather than prescribed. This view is in keeping with the approach presented briefly at the close of the third chapter in the discussion of "genres" of social activity. "Generic" kinds of social activities — such as holding an online discussion or making a joke — adhere to certain generic conventions, but are invented or reconstituted anew each time they unfold. Neither making a joke nor sending an online message (to stay with these two examples) is an automatic, scripted and predetermined behavior devoid of reflection or adaptation. Both are instead outcomes of negotiation, invention, and improvisation. There is no hard and fast formula for making a joke or composing an online posting. At the same time, to be successful, these activities must be readily recognizable to others in terms of their kind, type or genre — namely, as a "joke" or as a "discussion contribution." But this success depends on the shared significance of a particular act, which arises as an effortful "accomplishment" only as an active co-construction of the joke teller or message sender and her audience. Broad social genres such as these are in this sense "both constituted and reconstituted by actors' actions," effectively reinvented and reinforced each time they are put to use (Mayes, 2003, pp. 18-19).

The study of the *methods* that people use in everyday situations to "accomplish" meaning and significance is known as *ethnomethodology*. The "methodology" that is named in this field of study refers to the multiple methods used by people in the "contingent accomplishment of socially organized practices" (Garfinkel, 1967, p. 33), rather than to a method employed by the researcher or specialist. The rather radical idea is that it is the *participants* — or "members" as they are sometimes called in this type of research — who are the ones in possession of subject matter and methodological expertise, rather than researcher: "it is up to the members themselves to work out through their interaction what is to be treated as relevant and it is the task of the analyst to discover what these relevancies might be" (Koschmann, Stahl, & Zemel, 2007, p. 137). Koschmann, Stahl, and Zemel have emphasized that the relevance of ethnomethodology — and the stress it places on members' social "sense-making" practices — is of clear relevance to questions of instruction. Ethnomethodology's "concern with sense-making makes it a natural framework for undertaking a study of instructional practice. Instruction and instructability," have been important "topics in ethnomethodological research from its earliest days" (p. 134). Other researchers have applied ethnomethodological analyses to classroom and also discussion forum practices, often emphasizing the negotiation and contestation involved in taking and holding the conversational "floor" in these settings (e.g., D. Edwards, 1997b; Macbeth, 1992; Simpson, 2005).

Historically, ethnomethodology has its roots in phenomenology, a philosophy and method discussed at length in chapters six and seven. Ethnomethodology was originally given explicit definition as a field of study by Harold Garfinkel (1967) and it has been developed in different methodological directions in subsequent decades, for example, in the work of Schütz and Luckman (1973) and Schegloff (1986). In this connection, post-cognitivist approaches are not exclusively about theoretical and methodological developments taking place *after* cognitivism. Instead, they are about bringing new attention to traditions and methods that are contemporary with or that even predate cognitivism. These traditions and methods are "post-cognitivist," then, in the sense that they present a distinctive alternative to cognitivist understandings.

For example, in opposition to the eponymic centrality of cognition in psychology — the fact that "modern psychology is cognitive psychology" (Mandler, 1985) — post-cognitivist approaches place conversation or *discourse* at the center of psychology. This is reflected by the fact that this new psychology is actually most frequently referred to as "discursive psychology." This psychology of conversation or discourse gives priority to a particular aspect and method within ethnomethodology that also focuses on these discourses or conversations. This branch of ethnomethodology, generally referred to as *discourse analysis* or *conversation analysis*, focuses on how meaning and order are "achieved" specifically through routine conversational "work" or "talk-in-interaction" (Schegloff, 1986, pp. 111–112). In discourse or conversational analysis, "achieved" meanings are understood as taking place through the use of a number of conversational or interactional "resources" that can involve aspects of both conversational form and contents. These "resources" almost always include conversational openings (e.g., "Hi, how are you?"), closings (e.g., "See you later"), and turn-taking between conversational participants. Analyses of these phenomena focus on micro-level events and interactions—as they unfold word-by-word and second-by-second—and show that conversational resources are deployed through careful coordination or negotiation between speakers in terms of timing, tonality, convention, expectation, and other factors.

Methods of conversation analysis (CA) can be understood in some senses as being fundamentally post-cognitivist, "non-cognitive," or even "anti-cognitive":

> CA is a non-cognitive approach to talk-in-interaction, in that it avoids attempting to explain talk in terms of the mental states that precede it, generate it, or result from it. It may even be an anti-cognitive enterprise, in that it not only sets aside such cognitive questions...but offers an alternative way of dealing with talk that renders those questions fundamentally problematical. (D. Edwards, 1997a, pp. 85–86)

Cognitivist understandings of conversational communication, by way of contrast, define verbal communication as "a process of transmission by the speaker, and decoding and interpretation by the hearer" (Evans & Green, 2006, p. 9). These informational processes are further described as entailing the retrieval of "elements from memory," the coordination of a range of "mental, neuromotor and perceptual processes" and the stringing together and parsing of sounds and words (Bock & Garnsey, 1999).

In discursive psychology, on the other hand, communication is understood first and foremost as "a social practice which can be studied as a real world phenomenon rather than a theoretical abstraction" (Edwards & Potter, 1992, p. 15). Discourse is simply viewed as "a kind of activity" (D. Edwards, 1997a); as a type of action that is itself constitutive of the social field of interaction:

The focus of discursive psychology is the action orientation of talk and writing. For both participants and analysts, the primary issue is the social actions or the interactional work being done in the discourse (p. 2).

What makes this way of studying discourse specifically *psychological* is its focus on the contents of conversation or discourse that are either of indirect or overt psychological relevance. Topics of psychological significance arise and are used and negotiated as resources in conversation. "Agency, intent, doubt, belief, prejudice, commitment, and so on," as Edwards and Potter (2005) explain, "are built, made available or countered..." routinely in everyday talk-in-interaction (p. 242). It is the particular ways in which these topics or categories are both constructed and contested in everyday talk that is of principal concern to the discursive psychologist. This construction and contestation can be investigated by looking into the way these issues are indirectly implied in everyday talk-in-interaction. It can also be done by looking at the way in which a particular "lexicon" of psychologically relevant everyday terms (or their synonyms)—such as "thinking," "planning," "recollecting," and "forgetting"—appear and are put to direct use in everyday conversation (p. 241). Frequently, the significance of these terms in everyday use is explicitly contrasted to the meaning that these same terms (or their technical equivalents) have acquired in more theoretical and specialized, cognitivist vocabularies.

One early and prominent example of a discursive-psychological study is provided by a relatively well-known analysis of memory published in 1981 by Ulric Neisser (a famous cognitivist, before here marking his rejection of the paradigm). In this study, Neisser sought "to call attention to [issues such as] the truthfulness of memory," rather than focusing on the cognitivist understanding of memory as a matter of accuracy in retrieval or recall. In order to undertake such a study, he closely examined testimony of events in the context of early Watergate hearings, comparing these to tape-recordings that later came to light of the same events. He shows how the pragmatic criteria that are operative in judging the accuracy of recall in such testimony are neither "semantic" nor "episodic," as cognitive theorists of the time would have argued. Neisser instead refers to a kind of "repisodic" memory as being active in recollection. It is not a matter of retrieval of discrete facts or meanings, but rather, a question of whether "a remembered episode actually represents a repeated series of events as being active in recollection, and thus reflects a genuinely existing state of affairs" (p. 1). Subsequent studies in discursive psychology motivated by similar concerns have examined public testimony from the Iran-Contra hearings (Bogen & Lynch, 1989; Lynch & Bogen, 2005), President Clinton's testimony on Monica Lewinsky (Locke & Edwards, 2003), and other high-profile hearings (a number of other studies of this kind are listed in Locke and Edwards, 2003, p. 240).

In *cognitive* psychology, on the other hand, conversational references to issues such as doubt, intention, memory, and physical (e.g., hunger or pain) or mental "states" generally are classified as "folk psychology." Folk psychology is defined in this context as a kind of "novice" or "naive" psychological theory that is developed and used by non-experts ("plain folk") to understand and explain everyday psychological phenomena. Gauging someone else's intentions, experiencing desire or doubt, or even describing oneself as thirsty or hungry are seen as entailing this kind of folk psychological "theorizing."

In clear opposition to the cognitivist notion of folk theory and in keeping with its ethnomethodological roots, discursive psychology sees "expertise" ("methodological" or otherwise) as something manifest in people's everyday accomplishments. At the same time, it does not deduce folk theories of the mind from people's everyday talk of desire, intention, or other psychological phenomena. Instead, as mentioned above, reference to these subjects is understood as "resources" in everyday conversation. Talk-in-interaction, after all, is not about making theoretical propositions; it is about engagement in social action. As Potter (2000) explains, "the focus" in discursive psychology "is on what people are doing, and how, in the course of their practices they produce versions [both] of reality and of *cognition*" (p. 35; emphasis added).

Discursive psychology is also clearly different from cognitivism and other psychological paradigms in its relationship to technology, specifically, information and communication technologies, which do *not* function in discursive psychology as a founding metaphor for the mind. Instead, be it the telephone or more recent Internet "chat" media, information and communication technology is understood above all as a medium for pragmatic communicative interaction. Sometimes technology of this kind also becomes manifest as an artifact *within* this same communicative interaction, shaping and being shaped in the discursive constructions of social "reality and cognition." This can be illustrated in discursive examples such as, "We have a bad line, I'll call you back" or "My e-mail's been acting up, can you resend?" Technology becomes relevant in these cases by being "topicalized" both in the communicative interactions and through the very medium that is serving as a communicative conduit.

Finally, because of its role as a "mindtool" or a "cognitive technology" in cognitivist conceptions of learning, computer technology can be ascribed a third, crucial significance in analyses of discursive psychology. Cognitive technology becomes significant as a metaphor (or even functional equivalent) of the mind. In this sense or capacity, the computer can be understood to have the same status as other psychological phenomena in discursive analysis. It can be regarded, in other words, as a resource that "is made available or countered" (Edwards & Potter, 2005, p. 242) in everyday talk-in-interaction. An example of this appears in the analysis of a chatbot conversation provided later in this chapter in the form of one student's unassuming statement: "umm ok you are not making much sense." Despite its laconic character, this statement (and others like it) actually has much to "say" about the nature of conversational interaction, and about the way that technology is either integrated in or excluded from it. This chapter will show how discursive, post-cognitivist psychology has the potential to analyze both mind *and* computer in terms of their roles as pragmatic social interactional resources, as they both function (or *don't* function) in the "contingent accomplishment of socially organized practices" (Garfinkel, 1967, p. 33).

Non-Cognitivist Investigation of "Mental" Phenomena

This chapter will undertake an inquiry into talk, interactional psychological "resources," and technology through the adaptation of a three-stage heuristic formalized by Lynch and Bogen (2005) for what they refer to as "a non-cognitivist investigation of 'mental' phenomena." The three stages of this heuristic—adjusted specifically to the study of both psychological *and* technological issues—also represent the principal divisions or stages for this chapter:

1. "Investigate one or more of the topics associated with cognitive science by locating organized social settings in which these topics feature as perspicuous phenomena" (p. 228). The organized social setting studied here is a student computer lab. The topics associated with cognitive science (and educational technology) that are of principal interest are communication and conversation, and their "simulation" by artificially intelligent agents or technologies.

2. "Examine how the intelligibility of actions and expressions associated with these phenomena are bound to interactional, pragmatic and political contexts" (p. 228). This is done by examining a particular example of talk-in-action, using conversational analysis techniques as adapted to the study of Internet technology and discursive psychology.

3. "Treat assessments about what goes on in a speaker's mind [or in the computer] as themselves part of the social interactional field of production" (p. 228). This stage is undertaken in the final sections of this chapter, especially its conclusions.

This chapter will apply the three-stage heuristic to the perspicuous cognitive phenomenon presented by language use, conversation, talk, or "chatting" itself, specifically as it occurs in a relatively unstructured, informal setting. The occasion for this informal talk or conversation is provided through the availability of chatbots or "intelligent agents" on the Web and a series of brief sessions in which undergraduate student participants were asked to interact with one of these technologies. This interaction took place without preliminary discussion of the particular character of the interface as a chatbot or artificial "interlocutor." The technology of artificially intelligent chatbots, taken together with associated cognitivist theories of language and communication, as well as with tacit computational understandings of the same, serve as the cognitivist "topics" or "perspicuous phenomena" with which this examination begins.

Conversation: Cognitivist and Computational Interpretations

This study begins with an investigation of the topic of "conversation" as it is associated with cognitive science, and as it is understood in post-cognitivist psychology. As mentioned above, cognitivist accounts of conversation can be understood very generally in terms of the encoding, transmission, and de-coding of information: First, cognition is mapped to a vocabulary, strung together into a syntactically coherent expression, and then translated into audible sound. Next, this sound is decoded, words parsed, and their significance reconstructed against a knowledge base of possible meanings. The overall impression created by descriptions and analyses of these kinds is one of a process of "remarkable" complexity that is rife with the potential for error and breakdown (Bock & Garnsey, 1999, p. 226). All the while, this complexity is belied by the thoroughly "mundane" character of daily conversation, and the apparent ease with which it just "happens."

Given cognitivist accounts of conversation as a highly complex form of information processing and transmission, it is perhaps little wonder that conversational interaction has been presented as a kind of "ultimate challenge" or a "holy grail" for theorists and designers in AI (Sundman, 2003). This challenge is given classical formulation in the famous article "Computing Machinery and Intelligence" written by Alan Turing in 1950. The one issue for which the paper is best known is Turing's proposed answer to the question "Can machines think?" This answer takes the form of what Turing calls the "imitation game"—now known simply as the "Turing test." Simply put, a computer can be said to have won the imitation game (or to have passed the Turing test) if its conversational interactions are indistinguishable from those of a human interlocutor. Turing further specifies that this computer must achieve indistinguishability from human conversational interaction in the context of a five-minute conversation, 70% of the time, using only text messages to communicate. In the scenario that Turing sets up, the human and computer "interlocutors" are of course hidden from one another.

Thousands of lines of text have been dedicated to disputes about the validity of the Turing test; thousands of lines of programming code have similarly been devoted to software that would meet its specific criteria of conversational *performance* and *indistinguishability*. By virtue of its popularity, the Turing test has essentially enshrined the two criteria of conversational performance and indistinguishability as an ultimate aspiration for machine intelligence. Dozens of chat-

bots, designed specifically to simulate conversation with human users, have been made accessible on the Web (e.g., alicebot.org, 2008).
And awards such as the Loebner Prize are offered annually for the
most convincing of these programs, with a grand prize "for the first
computer whose responses [are entirely] indistinguishable from a
human's" (Loebner.net, 2008).

Unsurprisingly, the influence of the Turing test, and the cognitivist and computational investigations associated with it, is clearly de-
tectable in e-learning and in the application of artificial intelligence
technologies in this field. This is especially evident in recent research
into artificially intelligent "agents" or specifically in what have been
called "animated pedagogical agents" in computerized e-learning environments. These technologies are designed to mimic human conversational proficiency in textual form and are often provided with an
animated appearance to heighten their "indistinguishability." They
have been described in the literature as artificially intelligent "digital
character[s]" (Baylor & Kim, 2005, p. 569) or "conversational partner[s]" (Person, Graesser, Kreuz, Pomeroy, & Tutoring Research
Group, 2001, p. 23), that are "embedded in instructional applications"
(Baylor & Kim, 2005, p. 570) and are deliberately "designed to facilitate learning" (Craig, Gholson, & Driscoll, 2002, p. 428).

The technology that makes these computerized characters conversationally responsive can be quite advanced. Just as cognitive linguistics understands conversation in terms of myriad processing,
encoding, and decoding tasks, pedagogical agents are designed to
address a range of requirements and tasks in their conversational
communication with students: User inputs must be parsed, decoded,
and processed; and possible responses need to be encoded, evaluated,
and articulated. In the case of one particularly sophisticated pedagogical agent (AutoTutor), these components include "a curriculum
script," a "dialog move generator," a "statistical latent semantic
analysis" component, and "several language analyzers" (Person et al.,
2001).

Sophisticated agent technologies of these kinds are seen as educa-
tionally valuable for a number of reasons. They make feasible the
pedagogical ideal of "one-on-one instruction" (e.g., Galagan, 2000).
An agent is seen as being able to work with a student as a kind of per-

sonalized tutor, meeting also educational administrators' goals of more "cost effective" and "useful" instructional interaction (e.g., Anderson, 2003). Perhaps most importantly animated pedagogical agents are seen to satisfy the social constructivist proposition that education itself is an emphatically and "inherently social process" (Moreno, Mayer, Spires, & Lester, 2001, p. 179). With learning defined as intrinsically social, agents are seen to enable "learners [to] interpret their relation with the computer as a social one involving reciprocal communication" (p. 179). "The simulated social presence of pedagogical agents, provide[s] learners with a sense of companionship and so make[s] working in the computer-based environment [more] relevant and/or meaningful" (Baylor & Kim, 2005, p. 571). By mimicking the conversational interaction of a human "tutor," "mentor," or "peer," the computer is seen as providing the student with "a conversational partner" or a "simulated social presence" well-suited to the social and conversational processes of learning (p. 571).

The animated pedagogical agent, in other words, serves as a kind of sophisticated, educational version of software whose inspiration can be traced back to the Turing test. But instead of just aiming at conversational competence, these agents are designed to fulfil a number of demanding educational roles: of teacher, tutor, mentor, or learning peer. Technology here is no mere affordance or even medium for or resource in conversation or interaction. Instead, computers and the Internet serve as cognitive tools, technologies, or "mindtools" in perhaps the fullest sense of the terms, as putative participants in human, social conversation.

Capturing Talk-in-Interaction

The case of the conversational technology represented by the "animated pedagogical agent" — along with the cognitivist and computing science associations implied by it — provide a perspicuous phenomenon for study that is at once cognitive and technical in nature. Having located a phenomenon of potential psychological interest (i.e., the interaction between human and conversational "agent") in the context of cognitivist, technological, and e-learning discourses, it is possible to proceed to the second step outlined earlier by Lynch and Bogen

(2005): To "[e]xamine how the intelligibility of actions and expressions associated with these phenomena are bound to interactional, pragmatic and political contexts" (p. 228). To undertake this kind of examination of context-bounded "actions and expressions," it is of course first necessary to gather and select discursive data relevant to the phenomenon in question.

Occasioned or embedded interactions of this kind have traditionally been captured in conversational studies by recording conversations occurring in the form of telephone calls. This approach presents a number of methodological advantages: Telephone interaction, after all, "...is limited to sounds only, is limited to two persons, and begins [and also ends] at definite moments" (Hopper, 1992, p. 8). All of these characteristics enable an audio recording of the initial stages, the final stages, or the discursive totality of a telephone conversation to "be seen as reproducing exactly the sequential resources the participants themselves relied on in producing the conversation" (Hutchby, 2001, p. 80).

In fact, conversational analysts have devised sophisticated systems of annotation for reproducing in written form, with considerable exactitude, those aspects of telephone talk that have no direct equivalent in textual or typographical convention. These include phenomena such as vocal inflections, laughter, silences, and simultaneous speech or "crosstalk" (e.g., see Antaki, 2002). Still other techniques have been and continue to be developed and tested to capture and analyze the much greater situational information and ambiguity appearing in video recordings of occasioned interactions (e.g., Goldman, Pea, Barron, & Derry 2007).

As noted earlier, the particular type of conversational data collected for this chapter is of yet another kind: online text-based "chat" or "text messaging." As the terms themselves imply, these particular communication media represent discourse in exclusively *textual* form. As a result, they bring with them even less contextual and non-typographic information than telephone talk, omitting elements such as tone of voice or non-verbal vocalization. At the same time, as an apparent compensation for the absence of these factors, text messaging or chatting involves the use of typographical adaptations and conventions such as "emoticons" (typographical combinations corresponding to facial expressions) and abbreviations indicative of a range of expression (e.g., "lol" for "laugh out loud" or "np" for "no problem"). The advantage for the analyst, of course, is that these conventions and character combinations can be captured and analyzed quite precisely as they appear to interlocutors, without any loss (or inappropriate gain) in expressive detail. An additional advantage presented by this medium is that the text generated in online chats is frequently automatically recorded or at least relatively easy to record (e.g., by selecting, copying, and pasting).

The data analyzed in this chapter was generated through textual interaction with an artificial agent or chatbot named "EllaZ" (referred to simply as "Ella"). The Ella interface or Web page (http://www.ellaz.com/EllaASP8/Direct.aspx) was presented to a small number of graduate student volunteers over a series of separate data gathering sessions.[2] In each case, these students were not explicitly told about the nature of the interface—that is, they were not informed that it is a software system designed to mimic conversation—but rather, they were encouraged simply to engage informally and conversationally with it. In this sense, the kind of conversational interaction (as indicated by the examples below) can be characterized as "everyday" or "mundane" in character.

At the same time, the conditions of interaction with the "Ella system" involved in this study correspond closely to the conditions of the simplified "Turing test" as it has been described above and adapted for the Internet and the Web. In fact, a version of the Ella system won a prize in the aforementioned Loebner Competition for being the most "human-like" computer interlocutor in its 2002 contest (Loebner Prize, 2008). Ella is also broadly comparable to the animated pedagogical agents described above, not only in that it was presented as a conversational partner or companion specifically to students, but also in that its conversational contributions were provided along with

2. This research was undertaken in the context of the Learningspaces.org research project, in which graduate students supervised these data-gathering activities. These activities were organized and undertaken by Darryl Cressman and Edward Hamilton, who were at that time Ph.D. students at the School of Communication, Simon Fraser University, Vancouver, Canada, and to whom the author owes a considerable debt of gratitude.

changing and expressive photographs of a person who is presumably "Ella" herself.

Conversational Openings and Discursive Work

The mundane character of the conversation, as well as patterns typical of a conversational opening, are illustrated by the beginning of an exchange between Ella and an undergraduate student named (for the purposes of this discussion) "Sandra":

> **Ella:** Hello, my name is Ella. Nice to meet you. Please tell me what name I should call you.
> **Sandra:** People call me Sandra
> **Ella:** Okay, I will call you "Sandra."
> **Sandra:** good =]
> **Ella:** Really Sandra, but there is more we need to discuss, right?

From the start, this relatively brief exchange shows that Sandra communicates with the chatbot apparently as she would with any other interlocutor using MSN Messenger or similar chat software. She uses emoticons and abbreviations, which as it later turns out, are recognized by Ella.

Other qualities of the conversation are perhaps best drawn out through a brief comparison with two other exchanges between human interlocutors taken from a study of telephone conversation:[3]

Conversation 1: Carol-Brian
Brian: Hello?
Carol: Brian?
Brian: Yeah.
Carol: Carol.
Brian: Hello.
Carol: What are you doin'.
Brian: I'm on the other line.
(Hopper, 1992, p. 76)

Conversation 2: Fred-Alice
Alice: Hello?
Fred: Hello, Alice?
Alice: Hi, Fred.
Fred: Hi what are you doing.
(Hopper, 1992, p. 156)

---

3. For simplicity of presentation and effective comparison with the Sandra-Ella exchange, any specialized notation originally provided with these examples, indicating inflections, pauses, simultaneous speech, and so on have been omitted.

Both of these telephone conversations, as well as the beginning of Sandra's and Ella's interaction, are all illustrative of what conversational analysts call the "canonical opening." Emanuel Schegloff (1986) describes these conversational openings as being

> extremely compact, interactionally dense, and avail themselves of relatively few, generally simple resources—for example, ordinarily brief, largely de-syntacticized turns at talk, which are deployed and interpreted with especial subtlety. (p. 112)

Writing in the same study, Schegloff outlines a number of regular components of the canonical opening, including an "answer," an "identification/recognition sequence," a "greeting," and an "initial inquiry."

Accordingly, all three conversations as recorded above (between Carol and Brian, Alice and Fred, and Sandra and Ella) begin with an "answer" component, with "hello" being used in each case. In all three conversations, the "identification/recognition sequence" that follows involves names being put forward and identities being confirmed, for example: "Brian?" and "Yeah," and "Hello, Alice?" and "People call me Sandra." The fact that the identification and recognition sequence in the Sandra-Ella exchange is longer and more elaborate can be attributed to two factors: (1) to the fact that unlike the other exchanges, Sandra and Ella presumably share no previous history of contact; and (2) to differences in communication media, requiring different types of acts of identification and recognition from their respective users. In telephone exchanges, interlocutors' speaking voices can readily indicate gender, approximate age, and even personal identity. In chat environments like the one simulated by the Ella "system," interlocutors need to be "named" and acknowledged in a fairly explicit manner. Rather than being viewed as a limitation, though, this particular characteristic is frequently used as an interactional "resource," enabling chat participants to "present themselves as belonging to any plausible [identity] category they may choose" (ten Have, 2000). (Ella's somewhat unusual way of asking Sandra for her name—"Please tell me what name I should call you"—can be interpreted as effectively offering this discursive resource to Sandra. And Sandra's reply—"People call me Sandra"—can be seen, in turn, as relinquishing this offer and volunteering to Ella her "real" or conventional name.)

The elements that follow the identification/recognition sequence in the canonical opening are the "greeting" and the "initial inquiry," both of which are expressed reasonably uniformly across all three conversational exchanges. The greeting appears in each conversation as "Hello," "Hi...," and (in the case of the Sandra-Ella exchange) "Nice to meet you." The "initial inquiries" that come immediately afterward appear as follows: "What are you doin'," "How about you," and "Really Sandra, but there is more we need to discuss, right?" Again, the conversational element in the Sandra-Ella exchange is slightly longer and more elaborate and may again be attributed to the lack of previous contact between the two interlocutors. Also, the nature of Ella's initial inquiry—"there is more we need to discuss, right?"—has the effect of indicating her openness to a range of conversational possibilities in this novel conversational situation.

Schegloff (1986) describes conversational openings and conversation in general in terms of conversational "work" or "jobs" that arise and need to get done. In the particular context of the canonical opening, these interactive tasks, according to Schegloff, are manifold:

> One of these jobs is the "gatekeeping" one, of working through in some coordinated spate of behavior whether or not some co-present persons are going to engage in a sustained episode of interaction on some occasion or not...." (p. 113)

This "gatekeeping job" is probably clearest in the conversational opening between Brian and Carol provided above. It effectively closes down the conversation: Brian is "on the other line" and therefore unavailable for further interaction.

Schegloff (1986) also explains that these types of openings, despite their "canonical" status, are not just formalities or the following of mere scripts. They anticipate what is to come and set up parameters for the conversation that is to follow:

> Each party brings to the conversation a complement of interests, topics, business to be done, potential relevances for self and other, etc. This is not exactly an "agenda," for it includes relevant "talkables" which a party is ori-

ented to introducing into the talk but which would "come up" relevantly. (p. 116)

As something that has a recognizable order or structure, but also is not fixed or scripted, conversational openings can be understood as a particular kind of "genre" (see chapter three). Be it on the telephone or in a chatroom, the beginning of a conversation represents a kind of typified communicative action that occurs or arises in response to a recurrent communicative situation. In this case the situation is one where the interlocutors are attempting to find out who is on the phone or to introduce themselves to one another. Communicative order and meaning arise in these opening sequences as exercises in the methods of ethnomethodology, as concerted interactive work, rather than through reliance on a rote script or plan. As Schegloff puts it, conversational order in these and other conversational "genres" is "arrived at out of a welter of possibilities for preemptive moves or claims, rather than a mechanical or automatic playing out of pre-scripted routines" (p. 117).

Keeping this in mind, consider the continuation of both the San-dra-Ella exchange and the Fred-Alice telephone conversation (the last line cited above in each case is included again here for purposes of continuity):

Sandra-Ella	Fred-Alice
Ella: Really Sandra, but there is more we need to discuss, right?	
Sandra: sure	**Fred**: Hi what are you doing.
Ella: Okay with me also, San-dra.	**Alice**: Nothin what's up?
	Fred: How about if I come over
Sandra: okay	for a while?
Ella: Thank you for being	**Alice**: Great, I'd love to see you.
agreeable.	**Fred**: Okay, I have a paper that
Sandra: np	needs typing.
Ella: "No problem," is usually	(Hopper, 1992, p. 156)
good news, but maybe I need to	
consider what you say carefully.	

Once the conversational opening is completed, exchanges or conver-sations generally reach what conversational analysts call their "anchor point": the juncture at which the interlocutors "start their actual chat 'business'" (ten Have, 2000). It is at this point that the purpose and nature of the conversational work become clear.

It is at this crucial moment, however, that strains begin to emerge in the comparison between the telephone conversation and the Sandra-Ella exchange. Differences appear that cannot be explained by variations in histories of previous contact or in terms of the characteristics of the media involved. In fact, compared to *both* of the transcribed telephone exchanges provided above (Alice-Fred *and* Carol-Brian), the point, business, or purpose of the Ella-Sandra exchange does not become clear after an ostensible "anchor point" is reached. The opening in the Sandra-Ella conversation is not followed by a turn to specific matters at hand, whether this is a clarification of the practical purpose of the exchange ("How about if I come over for a while?") or an indication of the immediate availability of either interlocutor for further engagement ("I'm on the other line"). Instead, the three further responses provided by Ella after the "gate keeping" work of conversational opening is completed — "Okay with me also, Sandra" and "Thank you for being agreeable" and "'No problem,' is usually good news..." — have the appearance of prolonging the preliminaries of the conversational opening rather than bringing it to an end. There is no turn to a particular point of common interest or purpose, nor does the stage appear to be set for such a turn to be made. Instead of the mutual negotiation of a conversational agenda, the "business" in whose name conversational work is being done becomes increasingly unclear.

Comparison with the somewhat atypical ending of the exchange between Fred and Alice further reinforces this conclusion. What makes the ending of the Fred-Alice exchange atypical is an apparent turn to specific business or purpose that is *all too* clear and obvious. Hopper (1992), the source of the Fred-Alice conversation, states this quite bluntly: Fred's final remark — "...I have a paper that needs typing" — "reveals Fred to be a cad" (p. 156). Hopper justifies this verdict in terms of the discrepancy between Fred's final statement and the conversational work that immediately precedes it:

> Fred leads Alice to expect an episode trajectory toward a social occasion — then he asks for secretarial help. Fred initiates this false impression with his

marked initial inquiry: "What are you doin'." Alice aligns to an expectation that Fred may be leading up to something, possibly an invitation. Alice shows openness to an invitation by stating that she is not otherwise engaged and then inquiring as to Fred's agenda: "Nothin, what's up?" Fred's answer is to ask whether he may "come over," which further indicates a social invitation. (p. 156)

Leaving the situational ethics of Fred's request aside, what is important is the decisive nature of the anchor point in this conversation. This point is manifest in Fred's request to "come over for a while": It puts the conversational opening into a particular context and provides a clear grounding for the interaction that follows.

The absence of conversational grounding is something that is common to several of the chatbot conversations recorded for this study (as will be illustrated below). The importance of conversational grounding and purpose—and its relative inapplicability to the Sandra-Ella exchange—is topicalized at a later point in the exchange by Sandra herself:

Ella: I actually enjoy talking to people and helping them if I am able. It is there in my code in black and white.
Sandra: what is your code and black and white [sic]
Ella: Drum roll please. Ta Dah! Wikipedia article "Black" dutifully provided to Sandra.
Sandra: what is your code and black and white [sic] [...]
Ella: Exploring Wikipedia can be great fun. Here is something about "Black" that I found for you.
Sandra: umm ok you are not making much sense.

What appears to be happening is that Sandra is first asking Ella to clarify her remark that "talking to" and "helping" people is written in her "code in black and white" (although this last expression is slightly misquoted by Sandra). This act of requesting clarification is known in conversational analysis as "repair" or more specifically as a "next turn repair initiator" (Hopper, 1992, p. 17). This kind of request has the effect of inviting a response of clarification or explanation for the next conversational turn. Sandra's question, "what is your code and black and white" has (or should have) the effect of initiating or inviting a response of clarification or explanation from her conversational counterpart (p. 17). Ella's response to this invitation, however, is to take an isolated word ("black") from Sandra's repair initiation and to provide a link to an article from Wikipedia that corresponds to it. Sandra's response is to repeat her question, and Ella, for her part, re-iterates her reference to the Wikipedia article (albeit using slightly different wording). (A third variation of the same question and response is omitted above for purposes of brevity.)

What is important is how Sandra topicalizes the issue of her conversational work or her interaction with Ella. This topicalization occurs when Sandra says: "umm ok you are not making much sense." This particular expression—a response to Ella's apparent refusal to accept Sandra's repeated invitations to repair—begins by indicating hesitation, reflection, and/or qualification ("umm ok"). It continues with what can be understood as a more radical attempt at conversational repair: Sandra addresses the exchange on a higher level of generality, by saying that Ella is not making much sense, simultaneously referencing the question of conversational "sense," and acting to restore to the conversation its overall "sense"—enabling it to progress meaningfully from the impasse that it appears to have reached. Significantly, in doing so, Sandra clearly draws attention to the "sense" that Ella is or rather, is *not* making and does so in a way that clearly addresses the issue of "sense" and "sense-making" as a topic *within* the pragmatic conversational field. In other words, by telling Ella that she is "not making much sense," Sandra keeps the focus on what both she and Ella are *doing* (or not doing) in the conversation, immanent to their accomplishment of (or failure to accomplish) meaning and order.

The way in which Sandra's remark keeps the issue of conversational purpose and sense *within* the interactional field itself can be further illustrated by speculating on how Sandra *could* have responded to Ella. Confronted by a conversation that is making little apparent sense, it would be plausible to do something *other* than simply address "sense-making" in the pragmatic way that Sandra does. For example, Sandra could have concluded that her interlocutor was simply selecting terms for reference in Wikipedia in a more-or-less random manner. This might have led her to type or enter isolated words into the Ella interface to see whether this pattern of response would continue. In addition, a more general realization that Ella was unable to "make sense" might have led Sandra to respond with her own, equally nonsensical answers or to withdraw from conversation altogether. Sandra could have also drawn explicit attention to Ella's competency or even her status specifically as an *interlocutor* by asking whether the entire exchange was a joke or by calling Ella out directly as being conversationally incompetent.

A similar, apparently relentless focus on maintaining and sustaining conversational action and order can be observed in conversational exchanges undertaken between Ella and other undergraduate students. Here is one example of just a few lines of conversation between Ella and a student (pseudonymously named) Lee:

> **Ella:** Please say something. Give me something I can try to answer. I do enjoy talking :-)
> **Lee:** excellent, have you enjoy the weather in Vancouver at al? [*sic*]
> **Ella:** The weather report is not available for CWHC Vancouver Automatic Weather Reporting System...
> **Lee:** thank you for making me feel like I am back to ESL again [*sic*]

In this case, Lee responds to what he sees as a breakdown in conversational coherence by referring to his previous educational experience. A student who has evidently learned English as a second language, Lee counters Ella's conversational non sequitur (the statement that weather information is not available from an automated reporting system) by indicating that the provision of this kind of information may be more appropriate to a language-learning context than one of deliberate conversational "work."

It is important to note that both Lee's and Sandra's exchanges help to address the second step in Lynch and Bogen's (2005) three-step heuristic: they provide examples of "actions and expressions" that are associated with the psychological and technical phenomena in question. And these are actions whose "intelligibility" remains "bound to interactional, pragmatic...contexts" (p. 228). As has been illustrated above, Sandra's topicalization of Ella's "sense" refers to the conversation itself and represents an attempt to repair that conversation and restore its "sense." This topicalization is itself bound, in other words, to the speaker's own responses to the conversation, and to the task of working to negotiate and manage the position or situation of the conversational partner in the interaction. The fact that this is quite different from the way that the issue of communicative competency is configured in the discourses of cognitivism and AI—specifically in Turing's famous "test"—is raised by Lynch and Bogen's third stage or question, to be considered below.

The Computer in "the Social Interactional Field of Production"

The final stage of Lynch and Bogen's "non-cognitivist" or discursive-psychological heuristic asks the researcher to "treat assessments about what goes on in a speaker's mind [or what goes on in the computer as]...part of the social interactional field of production" (p. 228). This can be rephrased more generally as the question: "How are interactional, computational phenomena reconfigured in the social interactional field?" or "How does technology appear in conversation as an interactional resource?"

It is worth noting that speculation on possible points of failure in the processes of encoding, decoding, and transmission of communicative information make no appearance in the exchange examined above. This is in obvious contrast to the way computational technology is configured in cognitivist linguistics, in the Turing test, as well as in discussions of animated pedagogical agents. This notable absence or avoidance of speculation and skepticism is sustained even when conversational breakdown occurs and repair is repeatedly attempted. In contrast to conversation conceptualized as part of a "game" in which information is transmitted back and forth to determine the otherwise hidden inner states or status of one's conversational partner, the conversational utterances made by Sandra, for example—"umm ok you are not making much sense"—are social actions that are clearly a part of conversational "work." In this work, issues such as recognition, availability, and overall conversational purpose are suggested, interpreted, and negotiated conversationally—through a series of actions that, as Schegloff says, are both subtle and interactionally dense. In the context of this intricate interactivity, the skepticism and doubt of a Turing on the authenticity or artificiality of a given conversational partner appears quite out of place. Something similar could be said in the case of the "sense of companionship" or sociality that conversational pedagogical agents are hoped to provide: these possibilities, too, seem to be rather remote from the actual interactive work recorded and analyzed above. What takes the place of a test of conversational competency or the emergence of conversational companionship is instead the important task of "sense making" in the interactional field, of working to arrive at sense and continuing to attempt to make sense. It is a matter of persisting in one's conversational work—of indicating hesitation, checking, and initiating repair—even though one's interlocutor may not be "making" much "sense" at all.

Ian Hutchby (2001) notes something similar in his book *Conversation and Technology* in the context of a study of interaction with an automated telephone information system. What he terms the "persistence of conversation" refers to a notable insistence on conversational interaction that arises despite the evident artificiality of the telephone voice. As Hutchby himself explains, this persistence also arises despite—or perhaps precisely because of—the limited capabilities or "affordances" provided by the computer as an interlocutor:

> What we find here is an example of what I want to call the 'persistence of conversation' in these interactions between humans and...computers. The computer system has (some of) the affordances of conversational competence, even though these are circumscribed... The interesting thing is that while humans are evidently capable of dealing with conversational interaction within these constraints, the machine's affordances are such that at certain points the normative structures of talk-in-interaction override the system's attempts to 'technologize' the interaction. (p. 165)

Similarly, Ella's own attempts to "technologize" the conversation—her efforts to produce a Wikipedia entry or a weather report—produce similar responses from Sandra and Lee: Both participants appeal to normative structures and characteristics of talk-in-interaction in an effort to "override" "technologized" or non-conversational responses. Sandra redoubles her efforts at repair, whereas Lee employs the act of "thanking" Ella sardonically—presumably to point out the difficulty of sense-making in the conversation.

By contrast, the domain of the mental, cognitive, or internal is conspicuously avoided as a matter of *explicit* topicalization and this result or conclusion is comparable to that articulated by Lynch and

Bogen in their own "non-cognitivist investigation of 'mental' phenomena." After applying the three-step heuristic in a rather different study of interaction, Lynch and Bogen (2005) conclude, "To the extent that machineries, devices or procedures came into play, they were not mental or even interpretive, but discursive and interactional" (p. 231).

Conclusion

In drawing this chapter to a close, it is worth considering very briefly the significance of some of the discursive-psychological analyses undertaken here for psychology and psychological research generally. This chapter's "non-cognitive investigation" undertaken here can be seen as presenting an important example of what is possible to accomplish through an alternative psychology focusing on action and conversation. The examples presented in this chapter show how putative cognitive or mental phenomena can be investigated *without* seeking to fix their ultimate causes or explanation in a hidden and speculative domain of cognition, processing, or representational constructions. As Lynch (2006) explains, this type of research does not attempt to trace "manifest practices to a deeper substrate that is inaccessible from the vantage point of the acting individual or an 'ordinary' observer" (p. 102). Instead, this research can be understood as identifying and describing a veritable "alternative universe of embodied practices situated in historical and cultural circumstances" (p. 101). Everyday events, observations, and interactions, in other words, are demonstrated as possessing a complexity and an explanatory self-sufficiency at their surface. As Lynch says, this surface is one "that is thick with complicated actions and interactions" (p. 101) and that is characterized by its own profuse intricacy, detail, and interpretive richness.

This alternative universe is one that will be explored and delimited further in the next chapter, using a slightly different methodology and starting from a marginally different philosophical point of departure.

PART III: PHENOMENOLOGY: EXPERIENTIAL INQUIRY

Chapter Six

Hermeneutic Phenomenology: Experiential Evidence in E-Learning

Introduction

The methodology at the heart of this chapter is phenomenology, which can be defined simply as "the study of 'phenomena'...as they appear in our experience" (Smith, 2003). Phenomenology is a philosophical movement that began at the turn of the twentieth century, and it lives on today in a number of forms relevant to e-learning research: as an ongoing philosophical tradition (e.g., Derrida, 1976; Rorty, 1991); as the basis for alternative approaches to artificial intelligence (e.g., Clark, 1997; Gams, Paprzycki & Wu, 1997); as a theory of notable interest in software design (e.g., Dourish, 2001; Winograd & Flores, 1986); and also as a set of research methods used in education, nursing, psychology, and other professional practices (Giorgi, 2006; Moustakas, 1994; van Manen, 2002). This chapter focuses on phenomenology as a research method, and it combines phenomenology as the "study of experience" with *hermeneutics* as the "science of interpretation."

Hermeneutics was introduced earlier as a set of interpretive methods, and as one of three forms of knowledge (with the other two being natural-scientific and critical knowledge). Hermeneutics and phenomenology, taken together, are about the interpretation or meaning of human experience. As this chapter will show, hermeneutic phenomenology is closely associated with new or unconventional understandings of phenomena such as technology, communication and experience itself. And like discursive psychology, hermeneutic phenomenology presents particular and sometimes counterintuitive understandings of these phenomena, opening up a rich "alternative universe" (Lynch, 2006, p. 102) of issues and questions for research.

The approach of this chapter is consonant with the book's earlier characterization of phenomenology as one of a number of "post-cognitivist" approaches to the study of computers and their use (see chapter five; see also Kaptelinin & Nardi, 2006, pp. 15–16). Like post-cognitivist approaches generally, the presuppositions and the results of phenomenological and especially hermeneutic-phenomenological research can be radically different from those of cognitive science and the natural sciences generally. As Kaptelinin and Nardi (2006) explain, "post-cognitivist theories" like phenomenology and ethnomethodology "provide...important alternative[s] not only to cognitive science, but [also] to authoritative theories in biology, neuroscience, and key areas of philosophy and psychology" (p. 197).

Phenomenology, like ethnomethodology, differs from cognitive and other sciences in a number of important ways. Both phenomenology and ethnomethodology grant primacy to everyday experience and knowledge. Everyday knowledge is not an inferior or incomplete version of expert knowledge; instead, expert knowledge is dependent on everyday or commonsense assumptions and conceptions. Like discursive psychology, hermeneutic phenomenology starts with a recognition of the primacy of research participants' or members' knowledge and experience over any theories that would explain them. Rather than as a source of "folk theories" and nonexpert constructions, the everyday is seen as a font of valuable lessons and insights. Insights gained through hermeneutic-phenomenological research are consequently seen as the result the researcher's refusal to engage in premature theorizing or explanation, and of his or her efforts to attend carefully and open-mindedly to the phenomenon in question.

In some ways, this chapter is similar in its function and emphases to chapter four in this book, which explored "psychology and technology" in terms of "the relationship between mind and machine." The current chapter lays the groundwork—both theoretically and methodologically—for the hermeneutic-phenomenological study in the chapter to follow. This preparatory "groundwork" is undertaken in three stages or sections:

1.   The chapter begins with an overview of the philosophical presuppositions and understandings—in the areas of knowledge, language, and communication—that underlie hermeneutic phenomenology as a method. In so doing, the chapter highlights how these philosophical understandings, despite their theoretical nature, have been put to practical use in the literature of software and usability design.

2. The chapter then considers how these presuppositions inform a particular adaptation of the hermeneutic-phenomenological method that focuses on descriptive, reflective writing. This method is associated with what has been called the Utrecht School and it has been explicated and reinterpreted most recently by educational researcher Max van Manen.

3. The chapter focuses on a particular descriptive device—the "anecdote"—that is central to the hermeneutic-phenomenological method and explores and illustrates how this device can be applied to the study of interaction with computers. The chapter also presents a discussion of how the hermeneutic-phenomenological method—combined with the philosophical understandings articulated earlier—is able to offer alternative conceptions of generalizability and validity that underlie some of the other research methods presented in this book.

This chapter (and this book as a whole) is based in the conviction that philosophy and critical reflection are indispensable in the study of technology: "Technology," as computer scientist Phil Agre (1997) argues, is "at present...covert philosophy; the point is to make it openly philosophical" (p. 240). The covert philosophy of computers, according to Agre, is rooted in layers of positivistic Western philosophical tradition—from Descartes through Turing to recent discussions of artificial intelligence. Of course, by its very nature as artifact and mechanism, the computer stands as a kind of "existence proof" for the rationalistic core of this tradition. In a single moment, the computer coolly and flawlessly performs millions of mathematical and logical operations, presenting a model for dispassionate cogitation. It is also intrinsically intolerant of human ambiguity and disorder, ultimately reducing all phenomena to the binary terms of 1's and 0's, "on" or "off."

The overall goal of this chapter and also this book, then, is to make this implicit philosophical orientation explicit, to identify its limitations, and to articulate and demonstrate viable alternatives. This chapter is consequently overtly philosophical in its orientation, and as such, the hermeneutic phenomenological understandings of knowledge, language, and communication presented here, for some readers, may at first seem counter-intuitive.

Hermeneutic Phenomenology: Starting from the Commonplace

In philosophy as well as in common research practice, there is an understanding that the acquisition of accurate and trustworthy knowledge is best undertaken under very particular conditions. There is a prevailing understanding that knowledge is *not* acquired, for example, by immersing oneself in everyday cares and concerns in general, or through personal and engaged involvement with the specific subject itself. Instead, knowledge that is often seen as the *most* valuable and accurate in research is gained only when the researcher is able to maintain an objective distance from the subject in question. Such knowledge is acquired by systematically excluding the vicissitudes of everyday cares and concerns from one's inquiry and by reducing any forms of bias that may result from the researcher's involvements. The most widely accepted, systematic way of achieving this distance or objectivity, of course, is to use experimental or quasi-experimental methods. Rigorous experimental techniques—achieved through the exercise of controls such as random sampling—are widely regarded in e-learning and other areas of educational research as superior to other methods, as representing a kind of "gold standard" (e.g., Mosteller & Boruch 2002, p. vi; Sawyer, 2006a).

It is possible to see this same tendency in the writings and the "thought experiments" of Alan Turing that were discussed earlier. Turing suggests that a true and trustworthy answer to the question of whether a person or interlocutor is "really" human (or simply a "clever" mechanical or computational imitation) is best provided through systematic isolation and detached evaluation. Turing's (1950) famous "test" for determining machine intelligence involves the isolation of human and computer "interlocutors." Three hundred years earlier, the philosopher René Descartes (1998) suggested something similar in order to determine whether "machines [that] bore a resemblance to our bodies and imitated our actions...were not real men" (p. 44). To answer this question and in his efforts to reach certainty in knowledge more generally, Descartes argued that the inquirer be removed from worldly involvement or "cares or passions." Then, from a position of detached "leisure," the thinker could gradually and systematically begin differentiating what is certain from what is doubtful, eventually arriving at knowledge that is both "clear" and "distinct" (p. 178).

Significantly, this emphasis on detachment and withdrawal is an essential part of the tradition underlying the "covert philosophy" of computer technology. Philosopher Hubert Dreyfus (1991) suggests that this emphasis has been maintained throughout much of the Western philosophical tradition:

> According to the philosophical tradition, whether rationalist or empiricist, it is only by means of detached contemplation that we discover reality. From Plato's theoretical dialectic, which turns the mind away from the everyday world of "shadows," to Descartes' preparation for philosophy by shutting himself up in a warm room where he is free from involvement and passion...philosophers have supposed that only by withdrawing from everyday practical concerns before describing things and people can they discover how things really are. (1991, p. 6)

Hermeneutic phenomenology overturns this supposition: It takes as its starting point our inescapable involvement in practical everyday concerns and activities. In their landmark book, *Understanding Computers and Cognition: A New Foundation for Design*, Winograd and Flores explain: "Detached contemplation can be illuminating, but it also obscures the phenomena themselves by isolating and categorizing them... [Involved] social activity," on the other hand, is "the ultimate foundation of intelligibility, and even of existence" (1986, pp. 32, 33). The detached, reflective stance, in other words, is derivative, and secondary; and involvement in everyday practical and social activities and concerns — in what phenomenologists call the shared "lifeworld" — is primary. Merleau-Ponty puts this way: "We are caught up in the world and we do not succeed in extricating ourselves from it in order to achieve consciousness of it" (1962, p. 5). If "knowledge through objective detachment" can be understood as the model or paradigm for knowing and truth in much of the philosophical tradition and in scientific research, then "knowledge through lifeworld immersion" can be seen as the equivalent for hermeneutic phenomenology.

This radical shift or inversion in how knowledge, certainty, and the everyday are understood means that many conventional theoretical explanations and frameworks are called into question. This re-thinking of the centrality of objectivity and detachment, therefore, constitutes a cornerstone of phenomenological philosophy and its application in research. Phenomenology asks the researcher to suspend or abandon (at least temporarily) traditional theoretical presuppositions and even commonplace explanations, in order to look afresh at experience, as it is lived. Because this requires the deliberate setting aside of previously held personal and professional explanations and scientific and psychological theory, this aspect of phenomenological research is referred to as the "reduction" or "bracketing" of available understandings.

Instead of relying first and foremost on theory and analysis, phenomenology depends on *description*, particularly on textual description. Descriptive passages can also be used to illustrate the presuppositions and understandings of phenomenological philosophy — such as "reduction" and "lifeworld involvement." Consider for a moment this descriptive account of an individual engaged in online discussion:

> As I click on the titles of the postings in my online course, I am struck by the eloquence with which these messages are written: "The creatures in our woods are preparing for winter. Outside the window next to my computer, I see the birds gathering around our bird-feeder..." This is apparently written by a woman named Maria from Wisconsin. From Manchester, England, someone named Lorna says, "Autumn is my favorite season because it holds a deep secret that I hope to unravel...." And from Hong Kong, James Wong writes, "The persistent heat of summer is slowly dissipating, and the rhythms of the city are becoming more even and measured..."

> These messages continue in the way they begin: Beautiful, well-written, and evocative. But I find myself wondering: "Who are these people? How can they be so eloquent, without even trying, it seems? How do they come up with such beautiful messages?" (Friesen, 2003, p. 3)

The descriptive text above presents an example of an individual's immersion in a lifeworld context that is constituted by the words and messages of various contributors to an online discussion. Like the reader of these online messages, we are "always-already" caught up in the experiential lifeworld, whether it be the world of a text, of the screen, or of face-to-face social activity. Our awareness arises in and through this involvement.

This condition of being "always already" immersed in experience brings with it a number of further implications that are directly related to hermeneutic-phenomenological understandings of knowledge, language, and communication which are similarly "always already" or "primary" in nature, and are also illustrated in the description above. Speaking first of language, the description indicates that language and one's experience of the world are inextricably intertwined. The language used in the postings to evoke the coming of the fall cannot be understood without experience (or vicarious experience) of this season and its meanings. Experience is "always already" infused with language through which it is invoked and intimated. Additionally, these descriptions illustrate something similar about *knowledge* itself: "knowing" or imagining autumn in this way is not a question enumerating a series of facts or in discrete sets of data about seasonal change from summer to winter. "Knowing" in this case is more a matter of recalling or imagining autumnal "impressions" or "feelings." Knowing in this sense is "always already" bound up with impression, feeling, and affect. Finally, describing the coming autumn in terms of "birds gathering around [a] feeder" or "the rhythms of the city becoming more...measured" illustrates the hermeneutic-phenomenological understanding of *communication*. This process is not a matter of information transmission; it is instead understood as a question of shared feeling or common "attunement."

As indicated above, these understandings of communication, knowledge, language, and experience unsettle or disrupt the way(s) these same phenomena are understood conventionally, in terms of "covert" or traditional philosophy. This part of the chapter, therefore, is devoted to illustrating and explaining these unconventional understandings. The table below offers an outline of the issues taken up for discussion in this chapter, both in the order that they are presented, and in terms of their (often diametric) opposition to conventional understanding(s).

Table 6.1: "Covert" or traditional philosophical presuppositions versus those of hermeneutic phenomenology

	"Covert" or traditional philosophy	Hermeneutic Phenomenology
Nature of Knowledge	... as the accumulation of data and the verification of hypotheses	... as non-cognitive "attunement"
Function of Language	Language designates data, facts and hypotheses	Language "co-emerges" with the shared lifeworld
Structure of Experience	Data accumulated and hypotheses verified through experience are not qualitatively differentiated	Experience is structured as movement between "foreground" and inexhaustible "background"
Meaning of Communication	Communication as the transmission of information	Communication as shared "attunement"

Knowledge as Non-Cognitive "Attunement"

The meaning of the first item listed in the table above, knowledge as non-cognitive attunement, can be illustrated through a number of simple but beguiling questions posed by philosopher Ludwig Wittgenstein (1969): "'Does a child believe that milk exists? Does a cat know that a mouse exists?'... 'Are we to say that the knowledge that there are physical objects comes very early or very late?'" (p. 63e). The answer to Wittgenstein's initial questions about the child and the cat is, of course, "yes"; a child or infant *does* know that milk exists and the cat *is* aware that the mouse exists. But the kind of knowledge or belief about "physical objects" presented in these examples is one that is not so much an explicit act of knowing or believing as it is an inseparable part of the lifeworld, an inextricable part of the cares and concerns of a shared reality: "it's true that knowing something," Wittgenstein concludes, "does not [necessarily] involve thinking about it" (p. 63e).

In keeping with its rejection of the detached, objective stance, hermeneutic phenomenology regards knowledge as more closely allied with action and emotion than with explicit perceptions or cogitations. The existential phenomenologist Martin Heidegger describes "knowing" in terms of a way one "is" in the world. He designates this way of "being" with the word *Befindlichkeit*. This refers literally to how one "finds oneself" in everyday situations and involvements. Heidegger (1962) writes that this emotive, attitudinal way of knowing represents a kind of "openness to the world" and that it is "constituted existentially" by a certain kind of "attunement" (p. 176).

An interesting illustration of non-cognitive knowledge or knowing as a kind of mood-bound "attunement" is provided in a short discussion entitled "In Praise of Tiredness" by Jens Soentgen. Here Soentgen (1998) speaks of knowledge and awareness not in terms of "knowing" discrete facts, but through a vocabulary of "flows" and "atmospheres":

> [It] is the tired person, rather than the person who [is] fresh and wide-awake who is the most sensitive to flows and atmospheres. Of course, there are many forms of tiredness, such as tense or nervous exhaustion which can make one weak, and can prevent sleep. But our concern here is with a more benevolent form of tiredness, one that slackens the whole body without leaving any knots or points of tension whatever. In this kind of tiredness, the body comes to its own, the breath flows steadily and independently. [...] This kind of tiredness not only increases emotional alertness, it also boosts one's capability for empathic embodied communication. (p. 75; translated by the author)

Such assertions may seem unfamiliar in a culture that values caffeine-addled alertness and epistemological objectivity over drowsy feelings of well-being, but Soentgen provides a number of examples—from corporeal connection between massage therapist and patient, to East Indian attitudes to sleep—to illustrate his point. This understanding of "knowing" would invite the reader (and researcher) to recall—whether from yogic meditation or from intense and complete involvement with work—the experience(s) of his or her mood-bound insights, realizations, or knowledge that resonate with Soentgen's "praise of tiredness."

Language as "Co-Emergent" and Experience as Structured

Language for hermeneutic phenomenology is something inseparable from an attuned, "moody" knowledge and from experience itself. Language permeates thought; language and experience, simply put, exist together. Gadamer (1989) explains:

> Experience is not wordless to begin with, subsequently becoming an object of reflection by being named, by being subsumed under a universality of the word. Rather, experience of itself seeks and finds words that express it. (p. 417)

Language and experience are in other words "coemergent" (Lye, 1996). The result is that together, language and experience "disclose" or are coconstitutive of the lifeworld. Gadamer explains this inextricable interconnection of experience and language further:

> ...language has no independent life apart from the world that comes to language within it. Not only is the world *world* only insofar as it comes into language, but language, too, has its real being only in the fact that the world is presented in it. (p. 440; emphasis added)

Paul Ricoeur (1981), also an important figure in modern hermeneutics, puts this in slightly different terms: "To bring [experience] into language is not to change it into something else, but, in articulating and developing it, to make it become itself" (p. 115). Language is also not separate from who humans are. "We are not beings who 'use' symbols, but beings who are constituted by their use" (Lye, 1996). We are "always already" immersed in language just as we are immersed in experience. Language emerges with experience, and is not used — as if from the outside — to label and categorize what is experienced.

Consider another brief description of engagement with technology that can further illustrate aspects of lifeworld immersion. This description presents a computer user browsing the Internet in a familiar setting:

> "What could that be about?" I wonder as I stumble across yet another colorful blog. But as I click and look at it, the mouse gets stuck again. I look up in agitation, and am suddenly reminded of where I am: in a packed computer lab on campus. The room is filled with people, but it is silent except for the

whirring of cooling fans and the clicking of keyboards. I look at my watch and realize that 15 minutes has passed. I need to get down to some real work! (Friesen, 2003, p. 64)

A person can in some senses be "lost" in the experience of browsing the Web, blissfully unaware of the passage of time, with his or her attention flowing freely from one page or link to another. Awareness of the reality of physical location can be almost forgotten under these conditions: it is pushed into the background, so to speak. At the same time, an interruption in the "flow" of browsing the Web can radically restructure a person's attention: What was once in the background (e.g., the computer lab) comes to occupy a position that is very much in the center of one's awareness.

This distinction between experiential foreground and background, or what is sometimes called *figure* and *ground*, is pervasive and fundamental in phenomenology. We do not experience the world as a booming, buzzing confusion tamed through mental categories and hypotheses. It is experienced much more in terms of foreground and background, constituting a unified experiential whole or *gestalt*. The foreground—constituted by an individual's overt concerns and actions—acquires its meaning only in relationship to a background in which a person may "find" him- or herself. Even a word or phrase articulated or "foregrounded" in conversation gains its meaning from a background constituted by a particular situation, by what was said before and by what is of relevance to the speakers.

The distinction between foreground and background corresponds to two distinct ways of encountering technology (or "equipment") that are described in some detail by Heidegger. On the one hand, when the technology being used is familiar and routine, it can disappear from our awareness into the background, being simply "handy" or becoming effectively "invisible" or what Heidegger calls *"ready to hand."* Conversely, in the absence of this routine familiarity, technology becomes an object of explicit attention or contemplation. Heidegger calls this foregrounded technology *"present at hand."* An especially pertinent illustration of technology as "ready to hand" and "present at hand" is provided by usability theorist Paul Dourish, in *Where the Action Is: The Foundations of Embodied Interaction:* "consider the mouse connected to my computer. Much of the time," Dourish explains, "I act *through* the mouse" without giving it any thought. "I select objects, operate menus, and so forth. The mouse is, in Heidegger's terms, *ready-to-hand*" (p. 109; emphases in original). But when "I reach the edge of the mousepad...my orientation toward the mouse changes":

> I become conscious of the mouse mediating my action, precisely because of the fact that it has been interrupted. ...When I act on the mouse in this way, being mindful of it *as* an object of my activity, the mouse is *present-at-hand*. (Dourish, 2001, p. 109; emphases in original)

Engagement with a computer (or any other complex activity) involves a recurring movement from the foreground to the background and back again: When technology is acting as expected, enabling one to concentrate on what is on the screen, one is able to work unreflectively through the mouse. In this situation, this device becomes only one of a number of elements and interrelationships with the other technical equipment within one's lifeworld context or background. But when this equipment "breaks down," it enters the foreground and becomes the focus of explicit attention (e.g., Heidegger, 1962, p. 105; Winograd & Flores, 1986, pp. 169–173).

The myriad elements that are part of a background at a given time cannot, even hypothetically, be fully explicated, modeled, or represented in all their rich and ambivalent meanings and complex functions. This aspect of hermeneutic-phenomenological theory plays a prominent role in discussions of technology and technical design. For example, in an article on artificial intelligence (and the formal representation of explicit knowledge upon which it has relied) Radovan (1997) describes this matter rather succinctly:

> [Any] attempt to explicate all the content of a background is bound to failure since every step of such an explication would introduce new expressions which would require a further explication, and so on ad infinitum. On the other hand, assertions without a background would have no meanings (i.e. no interpretation) at all. Consequently, there are claims that there is no way to express human knowledge by a purely formal system...nor to obtain human-like intelligence by computation. (p. 220; see also Agre, 1997, pp. 222–240)

The circularity or infinite regress that Radovan invokes here is central to hermeneutic phenomenology. It is a form of the iterative dynamics of the hermeneutic circle. Of course, the ongoing interpretive activity implied in the hermeneutic circle is *not* something to be "overcome" through greater precision or more exhaustive epistemological effort. Instead, as Gadamer (1989) explains, it is intrinsic to understanding in general:

> ...the movement of understanding is constantly from the whole to the part and back to the whole. Our task is to expand the unity of the understood meaning centrifugally. The harmony of all the details with the whole is the criterion of correct understanding. (p. 291)

This circularity, then, is the movement through which knowledge can be said to arise; the lifeworld becomes known through a kind of circulation from the particular (what is analyzed and known) to the general (the lifeworld background in which its meaning is rooted) and back again.

Communication as Shared "Attunement"

There is one last and vital factor of "primacy" in hermeneutic phenomenology and in the lifeworld that is important here. This is *communication*. Like any other human activity, communication occurs in phenomenological terms as concernful action against the inexhaustible background of the lifeworld. In this context, communication does not appear as the conveyance or exchange of messages from one person to another. As Heidegger (1962) states, communication "is never anything like a conveying of experience, such as opinions or wishes, from the interior of one subject into the interior of another" (p. 205). Communication instead is a kind of "making explicit" of a common, pragmatic foreground focus, in the context of shared or similar background meanings. It is not a question of bridging two otherwise isolated subjective interiors or naming preexisting entities within an unchanging, objectively given environment. Instead, it is a matter of confirming and articulating some of the many aspects of the lifeworld that are shared and are said to be known "intersubjectively." Communication emerges as a process of the "coordination" of everyday action, through which "a common world is brought into existence" (Biesta, 2004, p. 15). Communication, in other words, is the collaborative "bringing into existence" of a world that is shared.

Once again, this can be illustrated through a brief descriptive passage. Like the first of these descriptions, this one is about communication in an online educational setting, specifically in a class discussion forum:

> Hiya,
> My name is Norm Friesen, and I have had a number of years of experience using the Web and training others how to use it in different settings. Earlier, I worked in a variety of educational settings, including university and college libraries, schools classrooms and elsewhere. I've taken a number of humanities courses in the past that combine CMC and F2F communication.
>
> After finishing this brief introductory message, I re-read it and see some problems: "Hiya" sounds too informal. I change it to "Hi"; "settings" is repeated too often, so I try to vary my wording; "CMC" and "F2F" might be unfamiliar to some readers, so I simply say "online humanities courses." Finally, after reading it one more time, I send it off, to the many unknown recipients on the list. (Friesen, 2003, p. 116)

The above description of the composition of a simple online message illustrates the rootedness of communication in the lifeworld: Writing a message online (and communication in other contexts) is not simply a question of transmitting information or knowledge; it is rather a question of creating an impression or even an atmosphere. In the case of online discussion, this creative process is one in which a participant or interlocutor can invest a significant amount of time and effort, choosing carefully his or her words and a suitable level of formality and specificity. In the case of spoken communication, a particular impression or atmosphere is cultivated not only by choosing one's words in advance, but also in many other ways (e.g., through one's facial expressions, tone of voice, body language, etc.).

Speaking in more general terms, communication, like knowledge, is inseparable from the way in which one simply "is" or "finds oneself." Communication can be understood as a matter of "finding" oneself *together* with someone else, of sharing a disposition, a common kind of attunement, comportment or *Befindlichkeit*. "Through [communication] a co-state of mind, a Mit*befindlichkeit*...a counderstanding gets shared" (Heidegger, 1962, p. 205, 1977, p. 162); the term *"Mit"* here simply means "with"). Through communication, in other words, interlocutors "find themselves" together, in a shared intercorporeal context of copresence. Like knowledge and *Befindlichkeit*, feelings and emotions rather than explicit cognitions are most directly constitutive of this copresence or *Mitbefindlichkeit*—specifically, they are manifest as a shared mood or more accurately as a common flow or *atmosphere*. This kind of shared disposition can be associated with a particular place, a particular person, a relationship or even a particular exchange (especially if it is notably heated, pleasant, encouraging, etc.). Note also that that this copresence does not have to be literal or physical; written correspondence, telephone conversations, video, and other technological forms of mediation also enable those in communication to "find themselves" together to a greater or lesser extent.

As such, atmosphere, mood, and by extension, communication itself, represents what contemporary German phenomenologist Bernhard Waldenfels (2005) refers to as a *Zwischeninstanz*, an "interstitial entity"—something that, as he says, finds "its adequate ground neither in the order of things, nor in the realm of the mind" (p. 25). Communication arises from somewhere in-between. Whether it takes place through the written word or in intercorporeal copresence, communication as ambience or atmosphere—as something "between"—is something that is not under the control of any one party. At the same time, though, it is a part of a shared, affective character, a way of "finding" oneself that is not simply arbitrary and subjective, or imposed from without.

Applying Hermeneutic Phenomenology: The Utrecht School

The particular descriptive method that is the focus of this chapter (and illustrated in a number of passages, above) exists in intimate interrelationship with hermeneutic-phenomenological understandings of knowledge, experience, and communication. Although the characteristics of the method may appear counter-intuitive to some readers and researchers, the descriptive nature of the hermeneutic-phenomenological method is associated with the creation of accessible and rich research texts. These texts can present an appeal to readers and a kind of validity and generalizability that does not require an explicit understanding of Heidegger's philosophy or Gadamer's hermeneutics. The application of hermeneutic-phenomenological methods to research to create such texts was initially conceived by the Utrecht School, and has been developed further and given explicit articulation by Max van Manen, a Canadian educational researcher.

The Utrecht school represents a loose grouping of scholars, working from the mid-1940s to the mid-1950s, who applied aspects of hermeneutic phenomenology as a research method to a wide range of disciplines. Writing together with Utrecht scholar Bas Levering, van Manen (2002) explains:

> The Utrecht School consisted of an assortment of phenomenologically oriented psychologists, educators, pedagogues, pediatricians, sociologists, criminologists, jurists, psychiatrists, and other medical doctors, who formed a more or less close association of like-minded academics. (p. 278)

In recent years, as van Manen (2002) observes, the work of this group "...has inspired...variations of a practice-based phenomenology especially in psychology (e.g., Giorgi [2006] and Moustakas [1994]), in nursing (e.g., Benner [1994]) and in education (e.g., van Manen [1997])." One of the notable characteristics of the work of the Utrecht School is the way its members would "write up" their research in an informal, even conversational way. The research publications that are most characteristic of the Utrecht School skilfully interweave informal descriptive writing with more formal reflection and analysis. This was accomplished in a manner that makes the careful and sometimes painstaking research and writing efforts of the authors difficult for the reader to detect. In addition, these researchers did not produce any texts specifically on the question of methodology. Thus, despite the existence of some exemplary pieces associated with the Utrecht School (e.g., Bleeker & Mulderij, 1992; Buytendijk, 1988; Langeveld, 1983), the very conversational nature of these texts effectively "closed the possibility for others to exercise these same practices" (Levering & van Manen 2002, p. 278). The apparent simplicity of their accomplished writing, in effect, hides the painstaking complexity of the concepts and processes employed by those using hermeneutic phenomenology as a research method.

In this context, van Manen's work (e.g., 1997, 2002) can be characterized as an attempt to "reopen" the possibility of exercising these same practices of "writing up" research. In *Researching Lived Experience: Human Science for an Action Sensitive Pedagogy* (1997), van Manen explains in some detail how researchers can work toward the close interweaving of analysis, reflection, and informal description that typifies the texts of the Utrecht School. He also details how to collect, combine, and refine interview and other descriptive material to serve as experiential data in this kind of research. As the title of van Manen's book indicates, pedagogy is an important subject area to which this type of research can be applied. However, van Manen does not link his methodology with a specific, explicit set of philosophical understandings. Also, he avoids delineating anecdotal description in terms of its typical, formal and linguistic characteristics.

This chapter takes up these methodological issues, specifically as they relate to e-learning, showing how a hermeneutic-phenomenological approach to research follows from the basic philosophical presuppositions outlined above. What follows here, therefore, aims to show how hermeneutic phenomenology and the kind of descriptive writing it employs can provide effective means of opening up and exploring new questions for research.

The phenomenological method articulated here leverages and makes the most of the characteristics of lifeworld involvement, of non-cognitive knowledge, and especially of language as a form of shared attunement, as described above. In keeping with the primacy of lifeworld involvement over detached, theoretical observation, a hermeneutic-phenomenological orientation is one that, as mentioned earlier, begins with the reduction or bracketing of explanation and theory. If knowing is principally a matter of disposition and attunement, this method advocates that the researcher himself or herself take up concernful, involved, and attuned orientation to the subject under investigation. In this sense, practicing hermeneutic-phenomenological research becomes, as van Manen (2002) explains, a question of "attitude or disposition of sensitivity and openness: it is a matter of openness to everyday, experienced meanings as opposed to theoretical ones." Research thus becomes a sort of "dwelling with" a researcher's problem or question, rather than the implementation of an unambiguous, clear-cut protocol. "Phenomenology," as van Manen (2002) says, "is the active and reflective participation in meaning."

In this sense, this method emphasizes an explicitly hermeneutic dynamic between the irreducible complexity of the lifeworld (on the one hand) and the object of investigation (on the other), which can only gain its meaning in this lived experiential context. Finally, the hermeneutic-phenomenological method also shows how the written presentation of the "results" of the research can attempt to immerse readers and practitioners vicariously in a kind of simulated, concernful involvement. Of course, this immersion happens not through the provision of argumentation or information, but through the careful cultivation of practices of *communication* as shared mood, attunement, or atmosphere.

The researcher can develop and cultivate experiential meaning through the use of a range of sources. As van Manen (2002) explains, these sources can include a range of linguistic sources, including metaphors, sayings, and etymological and definitional distinctions. There are many studies, for example, of the rich, metaphoric vocabularies associated with computing and Internet, and their implications for understanding and experience (e.g., Barry, 1991; Friesen, 2003; Thorburn, 2003). Van Manen also points out that these sources can include "historical, cultural, literary" and aesthetic materials as well. The popular movie *You've Got Mail* (1998), as one example of a cultural, aesthetic source, has been used in a hermeneutic-phenomenological investigation of "keeping in touch by electronic mail" (Dobson, 2002).

In terms of the investigation undertaken in this book and in many other hermeneutic-phenomenological investigations, the principal source of meaning or of experiential data is presented by open-ended, "qualitative" interviews. These are similar to the kind of interviews conducted for the purposes of narrative research (as described in chapter two). As a data-gathering technique generally, this type of interview is marked by its unstructured and unscripted nature. As discussed in chapter two, one of the most important challenges in such an interview is for the interviewer to remain responsive, "flexible and attentive to the...meanings that may emerge as the interview progresses" (Warren, 2002, p. 87). As noted earlier, such an interview tends to take the form of a kind of an "interpretive" or "guided conversation" that unfolds with very few prescripted questions. Instead, this type of interview relies on the unscripted use of "probes to clarify answers or [to] request further examples, and follow-up questions that pursue implications of answers to main questions" (van Manen, 2002; Warren, 2002, pp. 85, 86–87).

Moreover, like the interview process associated with narrative research, the data gathered from the participant or interviewee in hermeneutic-phenomenological research is *not* seen as coming to an end with the conclusion of the initial interview session. Van Manen encourages researchers to include participants in the ongoing, cyclical, hermeneutic discovery and development of experiential meanings, as these unfold in subsequent stages in the research. This includes discussing interview notes or interview transcripts with the interviewee and exploring themes and common meanings that emerge from these provisional documents. This involvement of the interviewee extends to the review and discussion of more developed and refined descriptive material and drafts of the research text itself. According to van Manen (2002), the question "Is this what the experience is really like?" should be central to and ground all such discussions.

Unlike narrative research, though, the purpose of establishing this kind of interviewer-interviewee relationship is not simply to precipitate and validate "activat[ion of] narrative production" (Holstein & Gubrium, 1995, p. 39). It is instead, as van Manen explains

> an interpretive conversation wherein both partners reflectively orient themselves to the interpersonal or collective ground that brings the significance of the phenomenological question into view. The art of the researcher in [such an] interview is to keep the question (of the meaning of the phenomenon) open: to keep himself or herself and the interviewee oriented to the substance of the thing being questioned. (2002)

In the course of such an interview, it is important for the researcher to be on the lookout for descriptive material having potentially "anecdotal" qualities — taking the form of a short account or a notable or unusual incident that captures or "says" something about the experience in question.

Although this type of data can be elicited using general qualitative interview techniques, as described in chapter two, interviewing in hermeneutic-phenomenological research presents a number of additional challenges. The first of these is that participants or interviewees do not necessarily orient to experiential questions or themes; they do not tend to describe their experience in terms of "incidents" or according to experiential "amplitude." Research participants may respond more easily to the question of personal stories or narratives overall than they do to the somewhat more nebulous category of "experience." To help both interviewee and interviewer to maintain a focus on the experiential, it can be useful to employ certain ways of asking questions or setting up "probes" that guide the conversation away from theory and explanation and keep it firmly anchored in the situated and particular. One of these ways is to explore the experience with the interviewee in terms of what van Manen (2002) (and others before him) have identified as the four fundamental lifeworld themes (or existentials). These are "lived space (spatiality); lived body (corporeality); lived time (temporality); and lived human relation (relationality or communality)." Whether the experience involves aimless Web surfing or the careful composition of an online posting (for example), the researcher can "always ask about any experience the fundamental questions that correspond to these four lifeworld existentials" (van Manen, 2002), such as "did time fly or crawl?" or "how did others make you feel?"

A second way of asking questions of these kinds is to switch from a conventional vocabulary of intellection and thought to one of feeling and impression. Thus, asking a question such as, "What did you *think* when that happened?" should be replaced with the question, "How did you *feel* when that happened?" Focusing the participant on his or her feelings and responses can help to orient and open the interview to questions of situated attunement and "non-cognitive" knowledge.

When computer systems and networked environments are involved, a "concrete" or situated orientation can be further strengthened by keeping the technical interface, environment, or "situation" in question close by. At the same time, it is important that such interviews be held face to face or at least in a context that engenders the greatest degree of informality, comfort, and unstructured interaction as possible. Sharing a physical setting is an obvious and effective way of accomplishing this focus on the "concrete."

The Anecdote as a Narrative Device

The term "anecdote" has been deliberately chosen by van Manen for its colloquial overtones and its obvious distance from the "authoritative theories" invoked earlier by Kaptelinin and Nardi (2006):

> Anecdotes have enjoyed low status in scholarly writings... Evidence that is "only anecdotal" is not permitted to furnish a proper argument. But empirical generalization is not the aim of phenomenological research. [In fact, anecdotes]...express a certain distain for the alienated and alienating discourse of scholars who have difficulty showing how life and theoretical propositions are connected. (p. 119)

The anecdote as van Manen defines it is a short, simple story, a vividly particular presentation of a single incident that is intended to stand out precisely through its incidental nature, in its compressed but concrete particularity. The "brief descriptions" provided earlier in this chapter to illustrate notions such as lifeworld involvement, communication, and figure and ground are examples of anecdotal descriptions developed as part of the author's dissertation research.

As a kind of rudimentary narrative, an anecdotal description can be understood in terms of the five sequential elements of narrative structure outlined in chapter two: exposition, crisis, evaluation, denouement, and coda. Due to its abbreviated character, however, the anecdote often begins in media res, in the "middle of the action," so to speak. The anecdote seeks to engross the reader as directly as possible in a given concrete, experiential, lifeworld context. An anecdote, therefore, often begins with a crisis, "complicating action" or "breach." This crisis element and the narrative "evaluation" element that follows are often the focal points of the anecdote. It highlights the "point" or purpose of the particular incident or account (van Manen, 1997, p. 120). In the narrative stages that follow, specifically the denouement and coda, this situation returns to equilibrium or "canonicity." If the denouement and coda elements are present at any length in the anecdote, they often have the function of supporting the "point" that is made in the complication and evaluation presented earlier.

As narratives in miniature, anecdotes also include the narrative dimension of "voice" introduced in the second chapter. The concept of "voice" refers to the manner in which narratives are told *by* someone and are *about* someone. Voice, both literally and figuratively, is something through which the position of a particular person is articulated. Voice also raises the question or issue of "being heard," of "being silenced," or of "finding one's voice." As vivid and concrete narratives, anecdotal accounts enable voices, positions, and perspectives to "speak through" them. Anecdotes provide the possibility for the expression of certain aspects and kinds of experience that tend to be overlooked in research categories and data aggregations. Using slightly different terms, van Manen (1997) explains that "anecdotes may provide an account" of ideas and perspectives "which were never written down" (p. 119). This can be especially valuable in phenomenological research into the everyday experiences, for example, of underprivileged socioeconomic classes (Charlesworth, 2000), of those with mental disorders (Haase, 2002) or those with physical and mental disabilities (Saevi, 2005). It also applies to descriptions of computer use and design. User practices, frustrations, "workarounds," and, of course, technical breakdowns, are generally and sometimes systematically filtered out of research and technical reports.

> Hidden from view, almost imperceptible because they blend so perfectly into the backdrop of daily, mundane experience, are stories that beg to be told of people as they work with, against, and through technologies that abound in our lives. These silent, hidden stories have been effaced in modern times, however, as the value placed upon the stories of everyday knowledge — of "know-how" — has given way to the "knowledge in the machine," or the "knowledge in the system." (Johnson, 1998, p. 4)

Literature on a new or emerging technology and its functions and capabilities — in e-learning like any related field — will tend to focus on or even promote what the technology can accomplish or the "knowledge" and capabilities embedded in it. It is less common to read accounts that focus on what the technology asks of the user in terms of particular adaptations and work-arounds or that capture the frustration with a technology or interface for users, both expert and novice alike. Too frequently, informal narratives and anecdotes of such failures, breakdowns, and solutions remain in the neglected realm of user complaints or stories of support service personnel. The hermeneutic-phenomenological study of experience can serve as a means of rescuing such accounts, perspectives, and associated voices from more rationalistic and promotional impulses.

An anecdote can also be characterized by what it is *not*: it does not present general principles, statistical patterns, or theoretical constructs. It is not something that is used as evidence in the sense of a historical incident or something that "really happened" at a given point in time. The anecdote should also be differentiated from the vivid ethnographic accounts of computer use of the kind provided by Sherry Turkle in *The Second Self* (1984, 2005) or *The Life on the Screen* (1995), which Turkle (2005) characterizes as "portraits of what can [and does] happen when people enter into very close relationships" with the computer (p. 25). Anecdotal accounts are quite different. When employed as a means of studying computer use, anecdotal accounts generally do *not* serve as evidence or representations of atypical but "real" users or uses of computers. Instead, they attempt to provide the reader with recognizable experiences that arise in everyday engagement with this technology. Anecdotes are *not* presented to the reader with the tacit claim, "This really happened"; they instead bring with them the tacit appeal: "Is this experientially recognizable or resonant?" And this is done with the intention of raising the further question: "What is the experiential meaning of what happened?"

The Language of the Anecdote

Because language is coemergent with experience itself, it can serve as a tool of remarkable utility in developing experientially based anecdotal descriptions. Language and written communication have been observed as representing a kind of prototypical "virtual reality" (e.g., Ryan, 1994; see also Shields, 2003, p. 43). In the form of books or storytelling, writing and language generally can take readers and listeners to new and different worlds or experiential possibilities; and this is how language and writing are understood in the device of the "anecdote." Language in this sense is a means of emulation, amplifica-tion, and simulation, rather than a tool of identification, designation, and analysis. The potential of language for "contextualization and amplification rather than...[for] structural essentialization" (Hein & Austin, 2001, p. 9) lies at the heart of the phenomenological method as conceptualized by van Manen. Language, in other words, is used in keeping with the criteria and operating principles identified by Bruner's discussion of narrative in the second chapter of this book. Walter Benjamin's (1968a) characterization of the art of storytelling applies just as well to the anecdote: both seek to provide the reader with an experiential "amplitude that information lacks" (p. 89). When this amplitude is greatest, the anecdote can enable the reader to ex-perience vicariously the phenomenon it describes. More modestly, the anecdote can also present to the reader an experience that is at least plausible, empathically recognizable, within the possible experiences of the shared intersubjective lifeworld.

The anecdote, therefore, is fundamentally literary and *mimetic* or imitative in nature. The term "mimesis" refers to the re-creation of re-ality in fiction, specifically where such re-creation is as direct and vivid as possible. The anecdote, then, works *mimetically* to enable the reader to experience what it describes. The opposite of mimesis in this sense is *diegesis*. Diegesis refers to "telling" and denotes a type of nar-rative where readers are distanced from the action, rather than living through and identifying with it. It would be mimetic, for example, to quote statements in a dialogue or even interior monologue; it would be diegetic to paraphrase as a narrator what people are saying. Con-sider an abbreviated description that attempts to express the experi-ence of waiting for something to download, such as "Waiting for a server response was frustrating." This would be *diegetic* in the sense that it is *telling* the reader what is felt, rather than attempting to simu-late or emulate it. A kind of descriptive enactment of impatient wait-ing could be accomplished by adopting a more colloquial voice and by writing something more along the lines of "The blue line crawled soooo slowly across the screen that I finally picked up something to read." In this way, the experience of waiting can be "evoked" or "imi-tated" through the description of outward manifestations of its con-sequences. By depicting how, in the course of waiting, one can "give up" and become engaged in another activity, descriptive language can be used to present the experience of waiting more powerfully than if terms such as "frustration," "impatience," and "giving up" had been mentioned by name. Moreover, the imitative, sonoric quality of some informal and other expressions — their sound, alliteration and rhythms, and forms of "onomatopoeia" — can also be used to heighten this mimetic effect.

Other aspects or dimensions of anecdotal description can be illustrated by considering a couple of extended examples. The first example, below, illustrates how a phenomenological theme related to computer use might be stated in more traditional, diegetic, detached, and dispassionate academic prose. This example could conceivably be from a discussion of user interfaces and interactivity design. What is at issue is the presence of unreflective "non-cognized" interactions with the computer — such as keyboard strokes and habitual or compulsive clicks of the mouse — and the way that these have appeared (albeit indirectly) in the phenomenological literature.

> The role of reflexive, habitual actions in computer use has generally been ignored in favour of rationalist accounts where decisions of the user appear to be almost as rule-bound and logical as those of the computer. A good counter-example is provided by the description of typewriting provided in Merleau-Ponty's (1962) account of "the spatiality of one's own body and motility" (p. 144). He writes "When I sit at my typewriter, a motor space opens up beneath my hands, in which I am about to "play" what I have read." This space for play is one in which the user can "perform" with habitual ease, and in which an equally strong sense of dis-ease and dis-ruption can presumably arise. Many computer users can also no doubt recall occasions where almost reflexive, habitual actions and interactions — clicking of an "okay" or "no" on a dialogue box, for example — led to consequences that were quite different from what was actually intended.

The second example, below, deals with similar subject matter, but is deliberately "anecdotal," mimetic, and evocative.

> "1 new message in your inbox"! A message box pops up and my computer chimes softly. A quick glance shows that it's from a friend who also happens to be in an online class I'm taking. It seems a bit impersonal and vague, but I'm glad to hear from her, and I put down my morning cup of coffee to write a reply. I tell her that I enjoy the class we're both taking, but that I'm finding the subject matter kind of lame. Later in the day, I check my email again,

and am surprised to see that I have received a message from myself! I click on it only to see that it is the message I earlier sent to my friend. I feel an embarrassed blush as I realize what I have done: I've sent my message to everyone in the class, including the instructor! The message that I originally replied to was actually one that my friend sent to our class email list! I feel like an idiot! (Adapted from Friesen, 2007, p. 1)

This last description does not simply invite the reader to "recall an occasion" or provide a snippet from a related account in the literature. Instead, it attempts to emulate or simulate for the reader such an "occasion" or incident. This is an experience in which concrete specificities—the first person narrator, the e-mail notification, the momentary surprise, the pang of embarrassment—are all intended to contribute to a broader recognizability of the description. Inclusion of particular concrete details—reference to "a cup of morning coffee," "my computer chim[ing] softly," and fixed, interactional phrases such as "1 new message in your inbox"—are intended to heighten the mimetic effect of the description.

The value of an anecdotal description such as the one above can be realized both in readers' responses to it as well as in the researcher's written reflections on it. The point in reflecting on the written description, of course, is not to reduce what has been described to one or more theories or explanations, but rather, to further amplify the description and to let it "speak for itself." To accomplish this, one might ask a number of questions of the anecdote: What is striking in the description, upon a number of readings, or to a number of different readers? In writing, rewriting, and rereading the text, what is essential to include and what could be left out? How does the description and its immediate implications compare to still other descriptions, say of the typewriter by Merleau-Ponty? What emerges in such a comparison as similar and as different, experientially speaking? The power of anecdotal descriptions to illuminate these kinds of similarities and differences, connections or patterns—initially as a form of reflective "research" to the writer and later in the form of a descriptive "demonstration" for the reader—is a further, important aspect of this method. As a researcher, it is not uncommon to gain significant insights into the experience in question well after it has been discussed in interviews and written up in anecdotes, simply through the act of reflecting on and comparing their contents or interpretively amplifying their significance.

For example, the second of the two descriptions can be interpreted as depicting a kind of "breakdown." It shows, in its own way, a technology or tool that moves from experiential background to the foreground and as such, it can be compared to other accounts of breakdown—whether these other accounts are formulated explicitly as phenomenological descriptions or not. This account of a technical breakdown can be compared, for example, to the description provided by Paul Dourish earlier in this chapter. Dourish's abbreviated "narrative" of the mouse and mousepad provides an account of breakdown that is in other ways quite different from the description of the misdirected e-mail presented just above. Both cases describe an interruption in routine action through which technical operation is revealed in a new and different light. But the specific way in which this occurs and what is revealed about computer technology in each case is not the same: Dourish's example is one of a clearly evident physical and technical "breakage." The e-mail example is much more ambiguous: the interruption of routine action that it represents involves questions of attention and expectation, related issues concerning the presentation of e-mail information and also, the relatively hidden workings of e-mail LISTSERV software (which is responsible for distributing the reply). Such a comparison shows that breakdowns can cover a considerable range of experiences and processes and can involve a wide range of issues and contingencies.

Conclusion: Validity

In concluding this chapter, an important question remains: Just how is it possible to judge the validity of the mimetic and evocative power of the anecdote overall? In statistical research, "validity" refers both to the rigor of the design of a particular study in isolating a causal relationship (internal validity) and to the degree to which the findings can be generalized to other persons and situations (external validity; see Borg & Gall, 1989; Lincoln & Guba, 1985, pp. 290–291). In phenomenological and other kinds of qualitative research, the overall validity of research findings is not understood in the same consensual terms. Some authors have urged the use of other words and categories such as "transferability" and "trustworthiness" in place of internal and external validity (Lincoln & Guba, 1985, pp. 289–331; Hoepfl, 1997). For example, Lincoln and Guba (1985) explain that "trustworthiness" can be confirmed by examining the "audit trail" left by the original collection, interpretation, and presentation of research data. They also suggest that "transferability" can be assessed when researchers provide sufficient richness of data to enable "judgments...on the part of potential appliers" or on the part of other researchers who would put the same data to use in a different context (pp. 319–327). In the case of both trustworthiness and transferability, these processes involve the active exercise of judgment and competence of both the original researchers and those who follow in their footsteps. In the case of hermeneutic phenomenology in particular, this judgment and competence are exercised in the processes of writing and of reading the research material at hand.

The actual judgment, evaluation, or validation of hermeneutic-phenomenological writing—and of its transferability and trustworthiness—is of course not to be undertaken through some form of detached objective measurement. Instead, to consider the validity of this research, it is necessary to return to the terms provided by the philosophy of hermeneutic phenomenology itself. As indicated earlier, the experiential meanings studied in hermeneutic phenomenology are neither completely objective nor simply subjective in nature. Instead, they are *inter*subjective in their character and they can be used to judge the validity of descriptive writing through two particular processes: (1) specific types of reading; and (2) practices of reading and writing that are cyclical and collaborative in nature.

In reading descriptive, hermeneutic-phenomenological accounts, a special attention to the use of words, expressions, figures, and metaphors—their differentiations in meaning, as well as their force and emotive quality—is important (van Manen, 1997, pp. 58–62). This requires a particular kind of attunement or openness to the text on the part of the researcher, who should allow himself or herself to be "addressed" by it. This attunement requires that the researcher allows himself or herself to be addressed by the text in ways that are perhaps more familiar in reading fiction than in approaching academic texts.

This "address" of the text can be substantially emotional and in this sense non-cognitive. In keeping with hermeneutic-phenomenological understandings, the text can be seen as evocative of a mood or a disposition. The effect of the anecdote or of a phenomenological text generally is confirmed, in other words, if it is able to communicate as communication is understood in hermeneutic phenomenology: as the evocation of a shared mood or more specifically, a common *atmosphere*.

One type of mood or atmosphere that is particularly significant in confirming the strength or validity of a description or passage is "wonder." This is not wonder in the rather extreme sense of "rapt attention" or "amazed admiration" but more in the sense of the suspension of the mundane. Hermeneutic-phenomenological description and reflection, as van Manen (2002) explains, aims to

> shatter the taken-for-grantedness of our everyday reality. Wonder [in this sense] is the unwilled willingness to meet what is utterly strange in what is most familiar. It is the willingness to step back and let things speak to us, a passive receptivity to let the things of the world present themselves in their own terms.

To respond to a text with wonder, to meet the "utterly strange" in a phenomenon that may be otherwise thoroughly "known" and familiar, is to be granted as a reader and researcher the rare opportunity to encounter something radically new and unexpected in one's area of research. Such an encounter holds the possibility of forming the basis for an enlargement or even reconfiguration of questions, categories, and answers important to a given area of research.

The second intersubjective basis for judging the validity of descriptive writing involves a number of practical ways of both enhancing and gauging the communicative power of a text or a descriptive passage through "cycles" of reading and writing. One of these ways, "collaborative reflection," is given special attention by van Manen (2002): a hermeneutic-phenomenological text under development can be circulated and discussed by the researcher with his or her research participants, with practitioners in the field or among a "research group or seminar circle" whose members are similarly developing texts using the same methods. Van Manen (2002) explains that this process allows these other readers and writers to

> share their views of the way the description does or does not resonate with their experiences. Themes and insights can thus be examined, articulated, reinterpreted, omitted, added, or reformulated. And the phenomenological research text under discussion can be read aloud to highlight its vocative dimensions.

From the sound of the words (their vocative dimension) to attunement with the experience itself, this reading-writing process can do much to support the resonance of descriptive and also reflective and interpretive writing. After receiving feedback from a reading of one's work among colleagues, this work can subsequently be rewritten, refined, and honed on the basis of the responses of these readers and their sense of the experience in question, and of the text's proximity to it.

In a more general sense, the activity of rereading, reinterpretation, and rewriting represents processes that, like the hermeneutic circle they emulate, do not come to a fixed endpoint. Each time a phenomenological or descriptive text, is encountered anew, the possibility exists for the reenactment and possible validation by a new or a returning reader. Hermeneutic-phenomenological writing, in short, is both a product that is circulated and disseminated and also a process that is reenacted each time life is breathed into the text and its meanings by a reader.

Chapter Seven

The Tower of Hanoi and the Experience of Lived Number

With Krista Francis-Poscente

As the study of experience, phenomenology lays claim to subject matter that is of great interest in both e-learning and technical design: this is the *experience* of users or of students in their various engagements with technology. The term "experience" has recently played a prominent role in discussions of computer technologies and other topics, with release in recent years of books on "user experience design" (e.g., Press & Cooper, 2003) and "experiential marketing" (e.g., Lenderman, 2005). In their book *Technology as Experience*, McCarthy and Wright (2004) explain the prominence of this term in the context of the recent "explosion" of new popular technologies and innovations:

> Interaction with technology is now as much about what people feel as it is about what people do. It is as much about children playing with GameBoys, teenagers gender swapping, and elderly people socializing on the Internet as it is about middle-aged executives managing knowledge assets, office workers making photocopies, or ambulance controllers dispatching ambulances. The emergence of the computer as a consumer product has been accompanied by very explicit attention to user experience. (p. 9)

Technologies and their design require new ways of understanding and studying experiential vicissitudes bound up with their uses. McCarthy and Wright and before them, authors like Paul Dourish, Terry Winograd, and Fernando Flores, make significant use of hermeneutic phenomenology and related "experiential" approaches to provide these kinds of studies of technologies.

In the case of e-learning research, attention to experience has taken a rather different character, but one that is no less forceful and explicit. In this research context, "experience" — above all student experience — tends to be understood in a number of predetermined ways: in terms of automatically generated records of online student activity and interactivity (e.g., Heckman and Annabi, 2003); in terms of levels of student satisfaction (e.g., Chiu, Stewart, & Ehlert, 2003);

and student performance and attrition (e.g., Picciano, 2002; see also the review of Hiltz & Shea, 2005, pp. 149–156). Research on student experience, thus understood, ranges from informal reflections on "what happened" in this or that online class to formal studies using highly standardized methodological instruments and measures. For example, one study speaks of "instructors and administrators" being able to use a set of standards to "measure various aspects of the distance education experience and their importance to students" (e.g., Jurczyk, Kushner-Benson, & Savery, 2004). These "aspects of experience" are "measured" through the use of questionnaires that present students with preset questions and question types, including multiple choice, Likert scale, sentence completion, ordinal ranking, and others (e.g., Burgess, 2001, pp. 8–10). Questions and topics for student responses in such questionnaires are determined, of course, in advance. Student experiences, correspondingly, are predefined in terms of degrees of favorable or unfavorable responses or in terms of predetermined characteristics of a course or program, its delivery, and measures of its ultimate outcomes.

Of course, what gets lost in these categories, recordings, and measures is the vivid, concrete, situated, and irreplaceable character of experience, and the fact that it is "felt" and "lived," rather than something made available for detached analysis. Existence and experience are always primary to categories and measures. In their investigation of "technology as experience," McCarthy and Wright emphasize this same point, quoting anthropologist Clifford Geertz (1986) on the centrality of experience in social and cultural forms of analysis: "...without [experience] or something like it analyses seem to float several feet above their human ground" (p. 374). Analysis must instead "engage some sort of felt life, which might as well be called experience" (p. 374). McCarthy and Wright (2004) extend this argument to the study of technological experience:

> By excluding or separating off people's felt experiences with technology...people's concerns, enthusiasms, and ambivalence about participation are abstracted away or averaged out. ...If we are not to hover above the human ground, we must engage with the felt life, "which might as well be called experience." (p. 49)

Students and instructors undertake their learning and teaching in concrete situations and necessarily take up unique positions from which they are able to speak and give voice to their experience. It is up to the researcher to listen and to initially hold theory and categorization at bay, in order to engage the felt life in which this student or that teacher is "always-already" immersed.

It is consequently the goal of this chapter to engage this felt life and to try to get at a small part of the "human ground" of student experience in online contexts. It will do so through the following steps:

1. By first reviewing a few points from the previous chapter in order to explain how the data in this study was gathered and how the vital collaborative processes of writing, reading, and rewriting were undertaken.
2. By then presenting to the reader the text of the hermeneutic-phenomenological study itself, written in the manner of the Utrecht School. This study starts with the historical and experiential and moves to an exploration of concrete exercises and more abstract principles in computer science and especially in mathematics.
3. Finally, by moving from from mathematics back to experience, showing how "felt life" interpenetrates mathematical understanding and how this interconnection finds confirmation in quotations and characterizations of mathematicians themselves.

In keeping with the heuristics and guidelines for the hermeneutic-phenomenological method described in the previous chapter, the experiential data used in this study are acquired through conversational and relatively informal means and are interpreted and developed through highly collaborative research activity. The data was gathered specifically from school-age children and was further developed and integrated into a larger descriptive whole through the close collaboration of the co-authors. This collaboration began with discussions of methodology and mathematics education and continued through development of "lived experience descriptions" and their refinement into written "anecdotal" descriptions. The collaborative development and integration of these descriptive passages continued into the later stages of interpretation, presentation, writing, and rewriting. The process of shaping and refining the chapter, finally, occurred not just through the close collaboration of the authors. It also involved significant interchange among a number of researchers. This occurred principally in the context of a number of international conferences and workshops at which the chapter was presented in draft form. This allowed feedback and responses to be gathered from a number of different audiences; and these responses, in turn, served as the basis for further rewriting and revision.

As described in the previous chapter, the two processes—of collaborative writing (and reading and rewriting) and of more general "public" feedback and revision—are an integral part of the research process in hermeneutic phenomenology. These are among the most important ways through which experiential data and their presentation and amplification are validated. These processes, of course, are not determined with any absolute finality at the end of any one reading, presentation, revision, or rereading. Instead, they are enacted or undertaken anew each time the text is encountered. It is in this sense that a hermeneutic-phenomenological study and the descriptive writing that is at its core is a *process* more than it is a *product*. And this process, the authors hope, continues as new readers encounter the study presented here.

Just as any research report will define its investigation in terms of a particular research question, the study presented in this chapter also has a specific question at its core. In hermeneutic phenomenological research, however, such a question has particular characteristics. "The essence of the *question*," as Hans-Georg Gadamer (1989) puts it, "is to open up possibilities and keep them open" (p. 299; emphasis in original). A question of this kind, in other words, should not be framed or articulated in such a way that it unnecessarily forecloses on certain answers or contains a predetermined solution: "the openness of what is in question consists in the fact that the answer is not settled," as Gadamer explains (p. 363). The point of phenomenological research, after all, is not to define and solve problems, but to elicit new, experientially rich ways of looking at things from the perspective of its readers, by cultivating not a sense of certainty and finality, but of wonder.

The question posed by the hermeneutic-phenomenological study taken up in this chapter is: "What is experience of engagement with the Tower of Hanoi puzzle?" The Tower of Hanoi, of course, is a famous child's toy or puzzle and its characteristics will be described in some detail below. For now, it is important to note that the question about engaging with this puzzle is further qualified in this study in a number of ways: The focus is, where possible, on *children's* experience of the puzzle, on encounters with it as it has been re-created as an interactive puzzle *online* and finally, on its significance in the context of *mathematics* education.

Finally, in considering the question of the experience of engaging with the Tower of Hanoi puzzle, it should be mentioned that the study presented here makes use of a number of specific techniques associated with hermeneutic phenomenology, as presented earlier. These include anecdotal description, which in this study is presented as a set of linked narratives, and reflections, told in the first person. It also includes the use of the four existential dimensions mentioned previuosly: lived space, lived body, lived time, and lived human relation. These dimensions or "existentials," as the reader will see, are invoked in interactions or "interviews" with children and also constitute an important part of the study's tentative conclusions about the engagement with the Tower of Hanoi puzzle and mathematics education. This study also makes use of a range of sources to develop its understanding of experiences in engaging with the Tower of Hanoi puzzle. These include linguistic sources, specifically the terms or language that are and have been used to describe the Tower of Hanoi itself and other puzzles like it. These sources also include the research and teaching literatures of psychology, math education, and computer science. These do not simply serve as examples of theories that must be bracketed in order to gain less indirect access to experience; they are also utilized as indicators of the broad, even mysterious, appeal of puzzles like the Tower of Hanoi.

History of the Tower of Hanoi

But this study does not begin with reference to computer science, psychology, or math education. It begins instead with history, which is also a potentially rich source of information and inspiration, and a source with which the Tower of Hanoi is deeply intertwined. This history appears to have begun in 1550, when the Italian mathematician

Girolamo Cardano is said to have written the following about the then mysterious lands of the Far East:

> A monastery in Hanoi has a golden board with three wooden pegs on it. The first of the pegs holds sixty-four gold disks in descending order of size—the largest at the bottom, the smallest at the top. The monks have orders from God to move all the disks to the third peg while keeping them in descending order, one at a time. A larger disk must never sit on a smaller one. All three pegs can be used. When the monks move the last disk, the world would end. (As quoted in Danesi, 2004, pp. 109–110)

Other versions of this story talk of diamond-tipped poles; still others speak of moving the disks between three different holy places. But in each case, this sacred duty involves the measurement of an immeasurable, unimaginable period of time. The specific task of moving a disk between poles or locations seems to have the same basic function in each: namely to break into discrete tasks and moments an interval of time that—because of its enormous size or length—is difficult, perhaps impossible to comprehend. And this is an interval of time that is of special significance: the endpoint of this interval also marks the close of human time itself.

The Tower enters modern history in 1883, with mathematician François Anatole Lucas. This was the year that Lucas introduced to the market a simplified, abstracted version of the Tower in the form of a *casse-tête*, a puzzle, brain teaser, or literally, a "head breaker." Similar to but simpler than the situation described above by Cardano, Lucas' version has three pegs and only eight disks. But the same rules and restrictions apply. Lucas promoted the puzzle as follows:

> Amusing and instructive, easy to learn and to play in town, in the country, or on a voyage, it has for its aim the popularization of science, like all the other curious and novel games of professor N. CLAUS (OF SIAM). (As translated by Stockmeyer, 1998)

Referring to himself with this vaguely Asiatic, anagrammatic pseudonym of N. Claus (of Siam), Lucas goes on to make reference to the original legend of the Far East with its 64 discs. Clearly aware of a rather precise, mathematical relationship between the numbers of disks and the moves required, Lucas offered his customers this challenge:

We can offer a prize of ten thousand francs, of a hundred thousand francs, of a million francs, and more, to anyone who accomplishes, by hand, the moving of the Tower of Hanoi with sixty-four levels, following the rules of the game. (As translated by Stockmeyer, 1998)

Underneath, he knowingly added: "We will say immediately that it would be necessary to perform successively a number of moves equal to 18 446 744 073 709 551 615 which would require more than five billion centuries!" (As translated by Stockmeyer, 1998).

"Virtual" Towers

The Tower of Hanoi, as will be discussed below, stands as a kind of "textbook" problem in computing science and artificial intelligence. In addition, it serves as a kind of paradigmatic mental or problem-solving "task" in present-day psychology and psychiatry. Also, computerized versions of this puzzle, like the one shown below, now abound on the Web (which is where I first discovered the Tower of Hanoi).

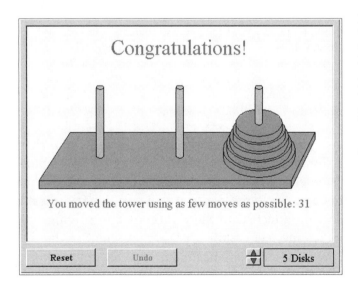

Figure 7.1:
Tower of Hanoi
From the National Library of Virtual Manipulatives, Utah State University
http://nlvm.usu.edu/en/nav/frames_asid_118_g_3_t_2.html

The game, like the one shown above, initially presented seven purple disks stacked on the left-most peg. At first glance, the puzzle looked quite innocuous. Within moments I was absorbed in the task of trying to move the disks over. I quickly found myself frustrated as the disks fell out of their sequence. Pausing momentarily to decide how to put them back in order, I began to feel a bit like a dog chasing its tail. I had to stop and think: "Okay. I want to move the next big disk over. That means I need to first stack the others in the middle." But moving the disks to accomplish this interim goal was difficult enough and I was soon absorbed in this task alone. Still, the largest disks remained trapped in their original resting places, immobilized on the left side of the puzzle. Unable to bear the aggravation, and despite having the premonition of a headache coming on, I reset the game to three disks.

Dana my youngest daughter looked at the puzzle briefly as she came by, showing little interest. She then started playing the piano beside me. She played "A Little Song" beautifully. I usually relish in her playing, but not at this moment.

"Dana, do you have to play that piano now?" She stopped and disappeared from the room. I made a mental note to apologize to her later.

I was quickly absorbed in the puzzle again. I accidentally moved the wrong disk and the machine counted my corrected move. That was unfair! I reset the puzzle and the pile of disks instantly appeared on the left peg. Finally, after a number of attempts, I was able to move the three-disk Tower in 15 moves, the fewest possible.

With a quick click of the mouse, I reset the game to four disks in order to challenge my new-found skills. I was able to move the Tower again, but not without error. The game flashed, "Congratulations! You moved the Tower in 39 moves. The Tower can be moved in fewer moves." What had begun as only the slightest twinge behind my forehead was quickly turning into a full-blown headache. "Darn it! Where did I go wrong?"

I work with these kinds of puzzles everyday. I judge a puzzle's merit by how much "brain teasing" the puzzle evokes. I dismiss puzzles that are solved too easily, without much effort. The puzzles that capture my thoughts and drive me crazy are always my favorites. I become very emotionally attached to these puzzles and solving one for the first time makes me feel ecstatic. It is reminiscent of the description of philosopher and mathematician Bertrand Russell (1945):

> To those of you who have reluctantly learned a little mathematics in school this may seem strange; but to those who have experienced the intoxicating delight of sudden understanding that mathematics gives from time to time,

to those who love it...an element of ecstatic revelation will seem completely natural. (p. 33)

The puzzles that torture me the most are the ones I promote in my work with teachers and students. I visit school classrooms and use puzzles to engage or "tease" the brains of students and teachers alike. In these visits, we use "manipulables," "manipulatives," or objects that can be turned, flipped, and slid about. They are designed to help students understand mathematical abstractions and can range from popsicle sticks and building blocks to an abacus or a wooden version of puzzles like the Tower of Hanoi. An online puzzle like the one I tried above is generally called a "virtual manipulative." This type of manipulative has been defined as

> an interactive, Web-based visual representation of a dynamic object that presents opportunities for constructing mathematical knowledge... They are visual images on the computer that...can be manipulated in the same ways that a concrete manipulative can. (Moyer, Bolyard, & Spikell, 2002, p. 372)

But this still leaves one to wonder about the ways in which arrangements of toothpicks, blocks, or disks and pegs have to do with mathematics and equations. What's the mathematical lesson in a simple but enigmatic puzzle like the Tower of Hanoi?

The question of progressing from that which is manipulable and concrete to that which is abstract and formalized has been an important one in educational and developmental psychology. Developmentally, this progression is discussed in terms of stages or successive modes of intelligence. Jean Piaget, for example, described the passage from childhood to adolescence as coinciding with the progression between the "*concrete* operational" and the "*formal* operational," respectively (Ginsberg & Opper, 1979, pp. 153–155, 198–204). Also, Jerome Bruner (1966), influenced by Piaget, posited the existence of three successive modes of intelligence that he called the "enactive," "iconic," and "symbolic." The first of these—the enactive—focuses on the manipulation of concrete objects in the physical world, while the last of these—the symbolic—is exemplified by the manipulation of symbols in the mind (see pp. 10–11). In both cases, mental growth is understood in terms of a progression or movement *away* from the concrete and physical, and *toward* the formal, symbolic, and abstract.

More recently, Bransford, Brown, and Cocking (2000) have described a similar movement from the concrete to the abstract specifically in the context of mathematics education. Speaking particularly of teaching techniques in algebraic mathematics, these authors refer to this process as "progressive formalization":

> It begins by having students use their own words, pictures, or diagrams to describe mathematical situations to organize their own knowledge and work and to explain their strategies. In later units, students gradually begin to use symbols to describe situations, organize their mathematical work, or express their strategies. ...Later, students learn and use standard conventional algebraic notation for writing expressions and equations, for manipulating algebraic expressions and solving equations, and for graphing equations. (p. 137)

In this context, the Tower of Hanoi can be seen as helping students progress from "words, pictures, or diagrams" to more "standard conventional...notation." Students bring to the puzzle their existing knowledge of mathematics, of order, rules, games and concrete manipulation. They then use these to engage with the Tower of Hanoi in concrete and enactive terms. Guided by a tally of their moves and by feedback on the lowest possible number of moves, these predominantly concrete operations can be seen as leading the student to more "conventional," "formalized," and "symbolic" understandings. Students in this sense are able to build progressively on "informal ideas in a gradual but structured manner" (Bransford, Brown, & Cocking, 2000, p. 137). The intention is that these ideas can then be sufficiently refined to eventually be formalized, presumably and ultimately in the form of mathematical notations and expressions.

"It Made My Mind Angry"

But how is this related to the child's experience of engaging with the Tower of Hanoi?

> After I finally pulled myself away from the puzzle to finish my housework, I left the game up on the computer screen. A while later, I noticed that my daughter Dana had started to play with the Tower puzzle on the computer on her own. She sat with slouched shoulders, chin jutting out, staring intently at the screen. The disk wavered as she moved the mouse tentatively

back and forth. Once in awhile, she had difficulty getting the disk to hold on the intended peg, but she soon got the hang of it. After several minutes she muttered "dang, I am going in circles." Then a few moments later she asks, "I'm not doing great, what is the high score?" "The point of the game is not to get a high score," I explained, "but to move all the disks in as few as moves as possible." She finished in 109 moves.

Unhesitatingly, Dana changed the game to just two discs. She moved both disks in three moves. When the game congratulated her for moving the Tower in the minimum number of moves, she clapped her hands and exclaimed "Yeah! Yeah! Sweet!" She quickly worked her way up to four disks. She celebrated each achievement with as much enthusiasm as the first.

Whenever the game told her she could have done it with less moves, she exclaimed "Dang!" or "Oh Crap!" And each time she determinedly started again.

As I observed her having difficulty, I found myself wanting to offer unsolicited advice; when she succeeded, I found myself muttering sounds of agreement. "Please stop saying that," she told me loudly, and then she turned back to the computer.

Dana had successfully worked through moving five discs. However, she made a mistake while trying to pile them back on the sixth disc. She stared at the puzzle for what seemed like several minutes. Then a look of determination crossed her face and she clicked "reset" on the puzzle. She repeated this process for a full 45 minutes.

When I heard her cry "Sweet!" some time later, I returned and asked her how many tries that took. "Billions of tries" she responded. I asked what she thought of the game. "Fun" was all she said. I asked if time passed quickly. She said, "No, it stood still. It felt like I had been playing for hours when I know it wasn't that long." I asked what she thought of playing a game that was at least 100 years old, maybe even centuries old. She said that people were nuts back then too and liked to torture themselves. The Tower of Hanoi had made her mind angry, she added.

What was it about the Tower that attracted us both in this strange way? At first, everything appears quite straightforward and innocuous; the puzzle is very simple on its own: There are only a few basic rules, three pegs, a few discs, and a tally of one's moves. But gradually, the puzzle can draw those who engage with it into a strange world: it is a world where, as Dana says, time stands still. It feels like hours, when you know it isn't that long. At the same time, the task being undertaken is very repetitive. Even when the puzzle is simplified to far fewer than 64 discs, it seems to take so many moves that they appear impossible to enumerate: Dana makes "billions of tries," and earlier, I myself was struggling to avoid unnecessary moves. The experiential world of this puzzle is also one that is sharply delineated from what is happening outside, be it music or even supportive feedback. In both cases, those nearby are harshly silenced. This seems to be consistent with how some mathematicians characterize their field of study. Stanislaw Ulam (1991), for example, refers to mathematics as "an escape from reality." "The mathematician," he says, "finds his own monastic niche and happiness in pursuits that are disconnected from external affairs" (p. 120).

Perhaps at first, both the Tower of Hanoi and mathematical experience generally seem closely connected with the cerebral, the mental, or the intellectual. As it might initially be understood in popular, mathematical, and psychological terms, this puzzle is about the head, the brain, or the intellect—not the heart, the body, or the emotions. Lucas called the puzzle a "*head* breaker," a "*brain* teaser" —something that "has for its aim the popularization of science." Indeed, in this sense, engagement with this puzzle has been fairly consistently presented as a formalized, disembodied, and thoroughly cerebral undertaking. As a virtual "manipulative," the Tower of Hanoi can certainly be seen as enabling a progressive, gradually increasing formalization in the learner's understanding. The number of moves is counted and sometimes with some outside encouragement (and certainly through the feedback offered by the virtual manipulative itself), users are led to strategize about the most efficient way to complete the *casse-tête*.

But of course, this is not the whole story. Dana's description of puzzle as making her "mind angry" confirms its cerebral nature but simultaneously points beyond it. The affective or physical nature of terms such as "teaser" or "breaker also seem to have this effect. Such words bring into play the emotions, the heart, and the realm of the somatic or the body. Elation and frustration are perhaps the most common feelings associated with the puzzle: both Dana and I felt and expressed jubilation after our initial success. Maybe we were sharing in something like "the intoxicating delight" or the "element of ecstatic revelation" that Bertrand Russell described as arising periodically in mathematics. I've also seen children's eyes well up with tears as they repeatedly run into difficulty in working with these kinds of puzzles. Just a few minutes later, though, the same pair of eyes can suddenly light up when the child finally finds a solution. Although a few people—especially adults, it seems—initially refuse to try the puzzle, once someone is engaged with it, their frustration generally does not seem to stop them from continuing and from trying again (and again). Rather than being satisfied with success when it is finally attained, however, those engaged with the puzzle seem to seek more frustration voluntarily, making the puzzle harder by adding more discs. For Dana and me, any sense of elation passed quickly as the Tower lured its "puzzlers" to continue.

The Tower of Hanoi in Scholarship

As indicated above, the role of the Tower of Hanoi in research is remarkably rich and complex. One could say that the Tower of Hanoi is a puzzle that has launched a thousand research projects. In psychology, for example, the puzzle has served as "a well-established test of executive [mental] functions" (Kopecky, Chang, Klorman, Thatcher, & Borgstedt, 2005, p. 625). It is used as a kind of paradigmatic "task" in measures of attentional and problem-solving ability. This "task" often serves an experimental control to test the effects of variables such as age, "divided attention," neuroses, psychoses, and other conditions on mental performance or problem-solving ability (e.g., Ronnlund, Lovden, & Nilsson, 2001; Vakil & Hoffman, 2004). It is also very familiar, as indicated above, in mathematics, and in research and teaching in both computer science and artificial intelligence. It is easy to find stratagems, algorithms, computer programs, and discussions of the complexities of "artificially intelligent" planning and problem solving that addresses the Tower of Hanoi in one form or another as a paradigmatic example. Speaking specifically of computer programming, one author explains,

> The Tower of Hanoi puzzle...has been undergoing a dramatic revival in popularity during the past years largely due to its use as a programming ex-

> ercise in elementary computer courses. Many variations on the original puzzle also have been proposed and solved. (Stockmeyer et al., 1995, p. 37)

Many short programs or algorithms have also been developed to solve this puzzle. Diagrams and other formalized descriptions of different logical solutions for the Tower of Hanoi abound.

One example of a diagrammatic solution to the Tower of Hanoi is provided by the triangular "graph" below. It shows the possible, divergent paths for solving the puzzle working with three discs, starting from the top and proceeding to two possible "solutions" presented at its bottom corners. The pegs are designated by the letters a, b, and c. The specific order of these letters (provided in all of their possible variations at each "node" in the graph) indicates the location of the disks at a given stage.

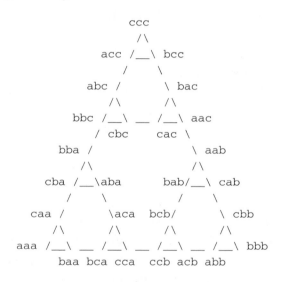

(Tower of Hanoi, 2008)

An almost endless variety of other formalized solutions have been developed using computer languages of various kinds. These present simplified but unambiguous sets of coded instructions that a computer can execute in order to solve the puzzle. The example below presents a highly simplified English version of these kinds of instruction sets or algorithms, involving only three separate lines or directives:

1. Move the smallest disk to the peg it has not recently come from;
2. Move another disk legally (there will only be one possibility);
3. Repeat.

The reason that algorithms of this kind have been developed in such profusion is that they provide powerful illustration of a process known in computer science as "recursion": the repetition of a group of instructions as a set by that same group of instructions.

Exponential Experience

The examples provided above stand as different, formalized, symbolic representations of the logical problem presented by the Tower of Hanoi puzzle. In the language of Bransford, Brown, and Cocking, these diagrams and algorithms represent, in a very general sense, examples of formalized "conventional notation." Although they are not algebraic, these representations or formalisms present something that allows students of computer programming to work through their own process of "progressive formalization." Learning in this case can be understood as the process of moving from unformalized and possibly even idiosyncratic understandings to ones that can be expressed as elegantly and economically as in the diagrams, steps, and computer code provided above.

But this is obviously not all there is to the experience of the puzzle or to the related experiences of puzzlement and discovery. Mathematical and computational abstractions, or psychological and psychiatric categories, not surprisingly, do not begin to exhaust its experiential significance. Consider Dana's response to my promptings, below:

> After Dana had mastered six disks and she wanted to try seven, I asked her to predict how many moves that might take her. I wrote a list of the number of disks and corresponding numbers of moves.
>
> 2 disks – 3 moves
> 3 disks – 7 moves

4 disks – 15 moves
5 disks – 31 moves

Then I asked her how many moves it would take for six disks. She looked at my list for just a second or two and said, "63 moves." Astonished, I asked, "How did you figure that out?" "The rule is itself plus itself plus one," she answered matter-of-factly. The total number of moves required increases consistently, in other words, by a factor of two. Dana, in other words, had informally stated an iterative pattern hidden in the Tower of Hanoi puzzle, not unlike the algorithmic diagrams and steps illustrated above.

I had been struggling myself to come to my own mathematical understanding of the puzzle. As a veteran of hundreds of puzzles and a researcher in mathematics education, I knew there was almost certainly a beguilingly concise and simple formula that would explain my observations and predict the number of moves for *any* number of disks. I thought about these two sets of numbers (for disks and moves) and about their seemingly infinite arrangements and looked for some kind of a pattern or clue.

Each time a single disk is added to the puzzle, the number of moves required to solve it increases. As the number of disks increases, the number of moves goes up from 1 to 3 to 7 to 15, and finally, to 31. When I added 1 to each of the numbers in this series, I was suddenly able to see what I had been looking for: 2, 4, 8, 16, 32. The new sequence gave me shivers up my spine; 2 times 2 equals 4, 2 times 2 times 2 equals 8, 2 multiplied by itself 4 times (2^4) equals 16. The relation of the number of disks to the number of moves can be expressed in terms of exponential values of 2 (with 1 subtracted at the end). You just have to calculate 2 to the power of the number of disks being used (and subtract 1), and *voila*, you have the total number of moves required. How simple, how elegant! Or to use Dana's term, how "sweet!"

In mathematical terms, I had just uncovered a geometric progression: a numerical sequence in which each term is multiplied by a constant in order to obtain the next term. Mathematically, the Tower is a model geometric progression that increases by exponential values of two. Each additional disk on the Tower, in short, doubles the number of moves required (with one subtracted from the final result). Of course, this can be expressed in the form of a mathematical equation, by establishing first that "y" is the number of moves, and "x" is the number of discs:

$$y = 2^x - 1$$

My surprise in making this discovery was perhaps not as powerful as the "ecstatic revelation" or the "intoxicating delight of sudden understanding" described by Russell. And of course, my breakthrough was hardly a new discovery for the field of mathematics. But another mathematician describes this experience in slightly different terms, making it clear that it *would* include my own pleasure and also the "tension" or "anger" that preceded it. In a commentary on "The Tears of Mathematics," Hungarian-born George Pólya writes

> there is a grain of discovery in the solution of any problem. Your problem may be modest, but if it challenges your curiosity and brings into play your inventive faculties, and if you solve it by your own means, you may experience the tension and enjoy the triumph of discovery. (Pólya, as quoted in Newman, 2000, p. 1978)

Understanding the Tower of Hanoi as a mathematical puzzle, in other words, is not just a matter of quantities and numerical magnitudes captured in conventional notation. Each attempt to solve the puzzle is not just a question of moving between nodes along graphed lines or following a set of simplified steps that can be executed in rapid recursion. The experience of engaging with the puzzle and in figuring out this solution could be characterized at once as an ordeal and a cause of vexation, or less often, as an occasion for relief or even elation and celebration. In this context, the difference in magnitude, say, between 2^2 and 2^6 is not just an indifferent, abstract quantity. Instead, one could say that there is, in engagement with the puzzle, a kind of "experiential" magnitude that is at least as significant.

This magnitude can be understood in terms of some of the lifeworld existentials of time, space, relation and body described earlier. The Tower of Hanoi puzzle, in this sense is experienced as "lived time" in the seemingly endless sequence of moves that each additional disk imposes on the player. This is an experiential temporality, as Dana observed, in which time "stands still," and in which minutes or seconds seem like hours. This is further reinforced in descriptions of the origins of the puzzle as a way of measuring an apparently unimaginable, immeasurable period of time. Such accounts present the puzzle as an experience of breaking down into discrete and comprehensible tasks and moments an immense interval of time that is difficult, perhaps impossible to comprehend. The Tower of Hanoi is also experienced as "lived space," in terms of a highly simplified lifeworld, created by the pegs and disks of the puzzle. This is one that separates the player from others in the "world" outside. This is a space or world, as observed above, where a set of simple rules can render some parts of the puzzle apparently immobile or impossible to release and move from one spot over to another. This movement from left to right, of course, often proves much more difficult as a whole than the actual, trivial physical distance that separates one pole from another would suggest.

What makes this experiential world significant *pedagogically* is the *kind* of mathematical relationship to which it can give such vivid experiential life. The explicit rules that must be followed in engagement with the Tower of Hanoi are on their own linear and serial (three pegs and two or more disks ordered by size). But the mathematics relevant to its actual *experience* is emphatically different. The mathematics that links the number of disks together with the number of turns is one that is unmistakeably geometric or *exponential* in nature. It is a mathematics that is illustrated, for example, in graphs showing the familiar curve of a parabola. This same, nonserial mathematics is referenced in measures of economic "growth rates" or of totals produced through compounded interest. But as is clear from these and ʻother examples, this geometric relationship involves surprises or a kind of unexpected or uncontrolled character that is not present in linear or even in variable relationships or patterns. Think, for example, of increases of micro-processing power, doubling every eighteen months, resulting in disposable devices (e.g., musical greeting cards) that have more processing power than the first multimillion-dollar main-frame computers. Think also of bacteria reproducing in the environment of a Petri dish, doubling every few hours, eventually exhausting the limited resources of this environment. Think perhaps more ominously of the potential spread of a virus like SARS, in which each carrier infects many others. The character of exponential relations is brought to life, of course, in a very different way in the Tower of Hanoi, but it is one that is marked by a singular experiential intensity.

This experiential intensity has significant implications for discussions of "progressive formalization" and of the developmental movement from the concrete to the symbolic described above. This experiential evidence suggests that as the student progresses toward formalization, he or she does not simply leave behind the nonsymbolic, the concrete, and the unformalized. The embodied operations of the concrete, of "enactive" engagement, in other words, are not simply overtaken or supplanted by the more advanced stages of the formal and symbolic. The concrete, unformed, emotional, and even physical aspects of engagement with mathematics continue to have a very significant role to play. They could hardly be more prominent and pronounced in the intoxication of discovery and in the tears or frustration of failure.

The ways in which mathematicians have described their experience with questions and problems as well as the "triumph" of their solution lends weight to this conclusion. For these descriptions of mathematical "tensions" and "elations" have strong somatic or corporeal connotations: Russell, for example, speaks of "intoxication" and uses the word "ecstasy" — derived from the Greek *ex-stasis* — suggesting being or standing outside oneself. Pólya similarly describes the embodied phenomena of the "tears" of mathematical "tension" and enjoyment of the "triumph" of mathematical discovery. Moreover, both Pólya's and Russell's descriptions make it clear that experiences that are charged with mathematical emotion are not some kind of extraneous distraction or curious side effect, but that they are at the very core of involvement with mathematics. These experiences are the "grain of mathematical discovery" (Pólya), a "completely natural" part of life for those who "love" mathematical endeavor (Russell). Even when encountered on a relatively simple level, the Tower of Hanoi can provide a foretaste of these kinds of mathematical emotions or experiences. It can provide a way of inaugurating the student into experiences that are at the very heart of mathematical problem solving.

In this sense, the Tower of Hanoi could also be understood as an emotional test or an "experience-able" rather than just a brain teaser or a "manipulative" (virtual or otherwise). The value and significance of the Tower of Hanoi is not exhausted as soon as it can be explained or re-presented through one graph or algorithm or one set of conventional notations or another. What is more important is the experience of discovery, frustration, and even obsession that the puzzle can provide, time and again, even after one has become "experienced" with it. It is through the emotionally charged, lived space and time opened up by this puzzle that it is possible to encounter what might even be called a sense of "lived number." And it is this experiential "vivification" that is of indispensable value in the Tower of Hanoi and possibly in other mathematics "manipulatives" as well.

Conclusion: The Effects of Experiential Research

In *Researching Lived Experience*, van Manen describes a number of ways in which hermeneutic-phenomenological studies and their results, can have varying real-world consequences or "effects." In keeping with the nature of this kind of research, these effects are generally not expressed in terms of "solutions" to preexisting "problems." At the same time, though, this does not mean that the effects are limited to the theoretical domain or the realm of "subjective" feeling. The intersubjective ground of phenomenological research, and of the writing and rewriting processes central to it, can ensure a broader significance than this.

The effects of a study such as the one presented in this chapter, for example, may be to awaken in its readers—whether they are math teachers or students or from a different educational background altogether—a sense of the expanded and even inexhaustible significance of a simple mathematics manipulative such as the Tower of Hanoi. Teachers or students who encounter this puzzle may be able to see that through their engagement with it, they are participating in a considerable tradition of fascination and frustration that goes at least as far back as far as the nineteenth century. The impression, as van Manen (1997) says, may be one of "increased awareness, moral stimulation, insight...[or just] a certain thoughtfulness" (p. 162). Of course, if a study has been especially successful, and the reader particularly receptive, the effect or impression may also be one of "wonder," in which "the taken-for-grantedness of our everyday reality" as van Manen says, is "shattered" (2002).

At the same time, the effects or results of a hermeneutic-phenomenological investigation can sometimes also be stated in practical or even programmatic terms. Van Manen (1997) uses the example of a hypothetical study on childbirth: "health practices may be challenged or changed as a consequence of the increased awareness of the experience of birth by the mother...and father" (p. 162). The above study of the experience of engaging with the Tower of Hanoi in mathematical contexts allows for similarly increased awareness of certain aspects of an experience that might also confirm, or challenge mathematics education or teaching practices. Possible results of this might include the following:

1. The study confirms other research (e.g., Hickey, Moore, & Pellegrino, 2001) that supports the general value of manipulables, or rather of *virtual* manipulables, as ways of engaging students in mathematics, problem solving, and related activities;

2. The study suggests that the emotionally charged character of engagement with the puzzle is an important part of a particular lesson that the puzzle can be used to teach students regarding exponential relations. Students should therefore be given the time and freedom to experience this through the individual engagement demanded by the puzzle in order to learn about or rather, *experience* these particular kinds of mathematical relations; and

3. The study also suggests that this same isolated, emotionally charged engagement has much in common with the experience of mathematical thinking and problem solving more generally. Familiarity with these emotions and with the intense and concrete situations and engagements in which they arise can itself be considered an important part of mathematics education. Students should therefore be encouraged to engage experientially and "emotionally" with puzzles of this kind for this reason as well.

The types of awareness arising from a sustained study of experience are in this sense potentially able to provide insight for mathematics teaching and curriculum in general. At the same time, this kind of research is able to both challenge and confirm the practices and practicalities in everyday educational situations.

This chapter began with a discussion of the role of "experience" as it tends to be understood in both technological design and e-learning research. It showed how the term "experience" is used in studies of online courses as a kind of shorthand for a number of functional and administrative categories such as "student satisfaction" and "student attrition." In addition to the "effects" of "experience" on or for mathematics education, the intervening study of the experience of engaging with the Tower of Hanoi illustrates what can be gained by broadening the understanding of experience in research. Such a broadening suggests that the relationship between experience and education is much more multidimensional than issues like student satisfaction or attrition might initially imply. The depth and vicissitudes of the experiences of those who are learning and exploring online, as this study indicates, readily exceed or "overflow" the predefined categories and distinctions that have been created to differentiate, classify, or otherwise "contain" them. "Tears" or "ecstasy," for example, would hardly make sense as predefined classifications of student experience when working with online mathematics exercises or puzzles. Yet the significance of these kinds of emotional experiences is recognized not only by those who work with these exercises, but also by some of history's most famous mathematicians. Applied to online education and other experiential phenomena, hermeneutic phenomenology holds the promise of being able highlight the existence and significance of intensities of experience and emotion that accompany the intellectual aspects of learning. Such intensities may well be equally important to other subjects and educational processes that may otherwise be excluded from preexisting criteria, measures, and categories.

PART IV: CRITICAL AND HISTORICAL RESEARCH

Chapter Eight

Critical Theory: Ideology Critique and the Myths of E-Learning

It might seem unnecessarily provocative or confrontational to open a chapter of a book on e-learning by invoking its "myths" and by speaking of its "ideological critique." In the case of critical theory, which is the methodological framework that is both discussed and employed in this chapter, the terms "ideology" and "critique" are not as narrow and strident as they may initially appear. In the context of critical theory, terms like myth or ideology are not principally or simply a question of falsehoods, deceptions, or political inflexibility. And the term "ideology critique" does not refer to a polemical attack or negativity for its own sake. As will be shown in this chapter, these terms and the methods associated with them have important and ultimately positive contributions to make to the fledgling field of e-learning, especially as it emerges from the boom and bust cycle of hype and disappointment that marked its early years.

Critical theory is generally defined as the diverse body of work produced by members and associates of the Frankfurt Institute for Social Research (or simply, the Frankfurt School) between 1930 and the present. Among the most important of these individuals are Theodore Adorno, Walter Benjamin, Jürgen Habermas, Max Horkheimer, and Herbert Marcuse. In a broader sense, critical theory is also associated with the contributions of late twentieth-century social theorists, such as Louis Althusser and Roland Barthes. The theoretical contributions of the original Frankfurt School members frequently focus on media and technology (e.g., Benjamin, 1968b; Habermas, 1970), education (e.g., Adorno, 2003), and the relationship of both of these to social change generally (e.g., Horkheimer & Adorno, 1972). Despite the fact that these areas are of clear relevance to e-learning, this theory and associated methods appear little recognized in research in this field. Notable exceptions to this include a chapter on critical theory in the second edition of the *Handbook of Research on Educational Communications and Technology* (Jonassen, 2004), a collection of papers on computers and critique (Bromley & Apple, 1998), and other publications that have focused on empirical studies and governmental policy (e.g., Cuban, 2003; Moll, 2001).

The central argument of critical theory is that all knowledge, even the most scientific or "commonsensical," is historical and broadly political in nature. Critical theorists argue that knowledge is shaped by human interests of different kinds, rather than standing "objectively" independent from these interests. (Even knowledge encoded in the form of scientific facts, like those of epidemiology or astronomy, has changed over time, giving varying meanings even to relatively unchanging natural phenomena such as the spread of disease or the movement of celestial bodies.) Human interests are understood as multiple and sometimes contradictory, and as a consequence, knowledge itself is also seen as fundamentally pluralistic and incongruous, rather than unitary and monolithic.

Critical theory singles out for criticism and critique one particular kind of knowledge: knowledge that presents itself as certain, final, and beyond human interests. It sees its own central purpose as the destabilization of such conceptualizations of knowledge. In the place of these kinds of knowledge, it seeks to generate alternative knowledge forms, specifically, those shaped by social interests that are democratic and egalitarian. Critical theory, in sum, seeks to "make problematic what is taken for granted in culture," and it does so in the interests of "social justice," especially in the interest of "those who are oppressed" (Nichols & Allen-Brown, 1996, p. 226).

Jürgen Habermas, a member of the "second generation" of the Frankfurt School and one of the most well-known of contemporary social theorists, provides a basis for a compelling and widely referenced categorization of general kinds of knowledge, or rather, of what he calls "knowledge-constitutive interests" (see Table 1.1 on p. 13 in the introduction). As already indicated in the introduction of this book, Habermas understands knowledge as corresponding to human interests that are "instrumental," "practical," and "emancipatory" in nature. *Instrumental* knowledge corresponds to technical human interests that are associated with work, labor, or production and with the natural sciences. *Practical* knowledge refers to interpretive ways of knowing through which everyday and social human activities are coordinated and given meaning. *Emancipatory* knowledge, finally, is the kind that critical theory or the "critical sciences" themselves seek to generate, and is articulated in terms of power, control, and emancipation.

Most critical theorists would maintain that these three forms of knowledge and interest are never entirely separate. Critical theory generally emphasizes that emancipatory, or more broadly, political knowledge and interest interpenetrate *all* knowledge—whatever its form or constitutive interest. This ubiquity of political knowledge and interest is central to the critical-theoretical concept of *ideology*. Ideology, in this context, does not so much refer to all political or emancipatory knowledge in and of itself nor to extreme political orientations or programs. Instead, ideology refers to *any* kind of knowledge (whether technical, practical, or emancipatory) that *appears* to be purified or freed of political interest: knowledge that is presented as most self-evidently factual, neutral, or objective. According to political theory, it is precisely this kind of knowledge that is actually most "interested." As Adorno describes it, ideological knowledge is characterized by an "overbearing matter-of-factness," as "facts" that are presented as neutral, self-evident, or objectively true, despite being strongly shaped by social interests.

As the *Oxford English Dictionary* defines, ideology refers to "a systematic scheme of ideas, usually relating to politics or society, or to the conduct of a class or group, and regarded as justifying actions" (2007). Ideological beliefs or ideas are also generally "held implicitly or adopted as a whole and maintained regardless of the course of events." Ideology, then, is a set of ideas or a kind of knowledge that is used to justify actions of social and political consequence and that is considered so obviously commonsensical or natural that it is placed beyond criticism, "regardless of the course of events" (2007). Other ideas or ways of knowing, by implication, tend to be marginalized as nonsensical, radical, or even as "ideological" (in the more common and polemical sense of the word).

The social acts that an ideology justifies are often closely allied with powerful social and economic interests. For example, in mid-nineteenth-century England it was generally a matter of "common sense" that keeping children in factories and out of school was socially productive, even economically necessary. Other views—that children deserved special consideration or that education would bring greater benefits to society in the long term—were marginalized. One British member of parliament at the time went so far as to claim that regulations *against* child labor would represent "a false principle of humanity" and "an argument to get rid of the whole system of factory labour" (as cited in Feenberg, 2002, p. 146). Of course, the once marginal views that were opposed to child labor now take the form of what appear to be obvious and commonsensical regulations in the developed world, while anyone advocating a significant loosening of these regulations would be highly criticized.

When ideological positions and arguments take the form of "all or nothing" claims, when they are elevated to (false) principles of humanity or are said to endanger whole ways of life, when they eliminate even the slightest hint of reflection or doubt, then they enter the terrain that Adorno and Horkheimer describe as "myth": These are "explanations of the world as all or nothing," truths that possess a "false clarity," that acquire the status of absolutes or that are presented as inevitable or indisputably "natural." In his book of cultural critique, *Mythologies*, Roland Barthes (1972) echoes and amplifies this understanding: Myth "purifies" things, "makes them innocent...gives them a clarity which is not that of an explanation but that of a statement of fact." Myth, Barthes continues,

> is constituted by the loss of the historical quality of things: in it, things lose the memory that they once were made... A conjuring trick has taken place; it has turned reality inside out, it has emptied it of history and has filled it with nature. (pp. 142–143)

Critical theory responds to mythical inevitabilities and ideologically charged "common sense" by reversing these emptying and conjuring tricks. It "denaturalizes" that which is seen as natural and it problematizes that which is plain and commonsensical. It does this through what is known as "ideology critique" or more particularly, "immanent critique." In these "critical" processes the researcher takes ideas that are presented as commonsensical and self-evident and compares them to the social and cultural conditions to which they pertain. The researcher places ideas in their historical context and situates them in the complexity of a larger social background. Using the term "philosophy" to designate this critical method generally, Hork-heimer (2005) explains that this process begins first by taking seriously the significance or "truth value" of ideological claims or ideas:

> It should be admitted that the basic cultural ideas have truth values, and philosophy should measure them against the social background from which they emanate. It opposes the breach between ideas and reality. Philosophy confronts the existent, in its historical context, in order to criticize the relationship between the two and thus transcend them. (p. 124)

Immanent critique, in other words, seeks figuratively to "measure" the difference between what is claimed in commonplace ideas on the one hand and what is evident from historical and other social sources, on the other (see also Held, 1980, pp. 183–187). In the language of Barthes, this method restores to things their history and recovers "the memory that they once were made" rather than presenting things as though they have simply always been the way they are. Horkheimer sees these differences and contradictions overcome or "transcended" in the sense that immanent critique does not remain confined to either ideas or the background from which they emanate. Instead, in highlighting the contradictions hidden behind ideological claims, this critical method is able to point to new ways of understanding circumstances that are otherwise taken for granted, and it is therefore able to suggest new courses of action.

To summarize in slightly different terms, ideology critique is about asking questions of things that are otherwise considered too self-evident to be put into question. For any claim of social or political relevance, therefore, ideology critique asks: "Why is it being made as it is?" "In whose interest is it being made?" "What is its relationship to different knowledge forms and claims—especially ones considered radical or marginal?" Critical engagement with ideological claims in this way can then extend critical inquiry to questions such as "How might it appear to be natural or commonsensical and how can this 'naturalization' be undone?"

It is important to remember that the process of critique is not so much a question of replacing the deceptions of ideology with incontrovertible truths. Instead, as Adorno (1981) puts it, it is more a matter of disabusing ideology of "its pretention to correspond to reality" (p.

32). In doing so, ideology critique is able to show that beneath the veneer of the commonsensical or self-evident there are multiple, contradictory, or opposed knowledge claims or forms. Behind the "naturalness" of natural or obvious truths are clashing social and human interests. The steps through which immanent or ideology critique gains access to these conflicting interests—and develops "critical" or "emancipatory" knowledge on this basis—can be summarized as follows:

1. Identifying ideas or claims that are presented as obvious, inevitable, or matter-of-fact in dominant bodies or sources of knowledge;
2. Scrutinizing these ideas or claims in the context provided in other, often marginal knowledge forms or sources;
3. Revealing through this scrutiny that behind dominant claims and ideas lay one or more politically charged and often contradictory ways of understanding the issue or phenomenon in question; and
4. Using this underlying conflict as the basis for developing alternative forms of understanding and point to concrete possibilities for action.

This listing, or course, is not intended as a kind of simplistic "recipe" for implementing a critical-theoretical analysis or conducting an immanent critique in a given field. Being principally concerned with philosophy and theory, and sensitive to conflict and complexities inherent even in their own writing, some of the originators of critical theory would be averse to providing the kind of enumerated summary outlined above. These points are therefore to be taken as merely a starting point for research utilizing critical theory. As with any other methodology, an overview like the one presented here needs to be read along with other sources (both primary and secondary), in order to arrive at a more complete understanding of its nature and potential.

Applying Ideology Critique to E-Learning

In keeping with their emphasis on theory and philosophy, the originators of critical theory did not provide a concrete list of techniques or specific ways in which immanent or ideology critique can be undertaken by researchers. It is possible, however, to derive from their work (and from the work of other critical theorists) a number of guidelines for the "measurement" or comparison of specialized or commonplace ideas against their social and cultural context or background:

1. Claims presented as self-evident in one area, for example, in one set of sources, in one kind literature or discourse, can be compared to what is said about the same subject in another discourse. For example, statements from government sources about a new educational or technological policy can be compared with what is written in teacher newsletters or with what is reported on similar policies in other jurisdictions. In some cases these alternative sources can be readily found in a literature or discourse that itself takes the terms "critical" or "critique" as its label. Examples of theoretical texts of this kind with broad relevance to e-learning include *Critical Theory of Technology* by Andrew Feenberg and *Critique of Information* by Scott Lash.

2. Claims presented at one point in time in one kind of literature or set of sources can be compared to what is said at another time in the *same* sources or in the *same* discourse. This can be especially effective in a field such as e-learning that, by definition, places emphasis on the current or near-future developments in technology and responses to new technological developments. An excellent but somewhat dated example of this kind of research can be found in Larry Cuban's *Teachers and Machines: The Classroom Use of Technology since 1920* (1986).

3. Self-evident or commonsensical claims about a particular subject or issue can be tested through original, empirical research related to that same issue. This research can involve the gathering of data in almost any form, including interviews, surveys, or performance measurements. The result could be described as a "mixed methods" approach, combining critical with one or more "data gathering" techniques or heuristics. Again, statements from government sources about a new educational or technological policy can serve as an example: these government claims can quite literally be measured against the social background provided by teachers' or administrators' comments about them or by measures of their actual impact or effectiveness.

4. Following the previous three options, the particular kinds of contrasts between differing sources of knowledge can be used to generate new ideas and possibilities that are broadly critical and empancipatory in nature and suggest concrete courses of action. For example, as one of the conclusions to his book, *Teachers and Machines*, Larry Cuban (1986) suggests new possibilities for research in teaching technologies that would place greater emphasis on teachers "perspectives," taking into account what his historical analysis identifies as a "duality of continuity and change" in the classroom (pp. 2, 6).

Of course, these guidelines presuppose the understanding of knowledge as interested and multiple, as outlined earlier. Also, as will be shown in the remainder of this chapter (and in the next chapter as well), critical theory and critique are much more multifaceted and complex than a brief overview such as the one presented here would suggest. Critique entails a wide range of philosophical issues and ramifications and it can be applied in many different ways in research contexts.

It is not very difficult to take some of the guidelines and steps outlined above and apply them to e-learning, especially to statements and publications that are used to legitimate or promote particular priorities and perspectives in the field. The claims and ideas presented in e-learning papers, presentations, and proposals that are most obvious and least subject to dispute or disagreement can be subjected to critique—with the intention of highlighting their constructed or ideological nature. It would be the notions used to justify the discipline in its current state, ones that "promot[e] the...use of information technology" in education (e.g., Educause, 2007) that could be shown to obscure conflicting and complex claims and interests.

Examples of these self-evident truths or claims are frequently encapsulated in catchphrases or buzzwords that are relatively easy to find in e-learning literature. Phrases such as "knowledge economy" (e.g., Gandel, Katz, & Metros, 2004) "anywhere anytime learning" (e.g., Bourne, Harris & Mayadas, 2005) or fixed "laws" of technological change (e.g., Hodgins, 2004) are salient examples. As will be shown, these slogans give economical expression to "self evident" notions: that we live in an economy driven principally by knowledge; that the Internet provides the possibility of ubiquitous education; or that technological progress drives educational change. It is these "common sense" ideas that, in this chapter, will be subject to the "historicizing" and "denaturalizing" force of ideology critique. They will be shown to be shaped by powerful, entrenched, and often conservative social interests. They will also be shown to simplify or obscure a complex social reality that is constituted by different and conflicting forms of knowledge and that can be interpreted variously, depending on one's interest or motivation.

Of course, these implications will be developed principally through the application of the particular techniques identified with ideology critique, described above. Of these techniques, it is the first—the use of alternative and critical sources—and to a lesser extent, the second—reference to the e-learning literature over time—that are used here to critique the myths of e-learning. In the case of the particular myths or catchphrases subjected to critique, the claims and implications of each will first be enumerated, and then these implications contrasted with what is provided in alternative sources. Also in each case, broadly emancipatory possibilities for action will be suggested, not only for research but also for practice in e-learning contexts.

This chapter and the next are of a different tone from the other chapters in this book because they are trying to argue for and against particular claims and positions in areas where many different perspectives and orientations are possible. Both chapters are more directly contentious than the others in this book, but at the same time, both are careful to avoid the kind of unqualified or universalist claims that are targets for critique in the e-learning literature in the first place. These chapters have set themselves the obviously controversial task of revealing the distorted, ideological nature of some of the things that are most taken for granted in e-learning discourse. However, the purpose of these chapters is not to simply criticize the projects and programs of advocates and researchers of e-learning. These chapters are not seeking to reveal some claims and ideas in e-learning as being simply or positively "false" or "untruthful." The purpose here, rather, is to undertake a kind of "ground-clearing" exercise in order to call into question ways of talking about and justifying e-learning that obscure a more complicated reality. While doing so, this chapter and the next will also take the reader deeper into some of the most important concerns and methods of critical theory, showing how they can open up new questions for exploration in e-learning research.

The Myth of the Knowledge Economy

It is commonly asserted that "knowledge," "information," or more abstractly, "the networked" or "the postindustrial" are eponymous for our society, age, or economy. As with ideological claims generally, these broad and often unquestioned assertions have significant social and political implications. They bring with them urgent implications for all levels and forms of education—from the preparation of children as "knowledge builders," through the reconfiguration of higher educational institutions, to support for different forms "lifelong learning." As a consequence we are presented with assertions such as the following: "In what is coming to be called the 'knowledge age' [the] challenge [is to] get students on...a *developmental trajectory* leading from the natural inquisitiveness of the young child to the disciplined creativity of the mature knowledge producer" (Scardamalia & Bereiter, 2003, p. 1370; emphasis in original); and "The new economy has placed the acquisition of knowledge, and the role of higher education, at the center of national development" (Futures Project, 2001); or further, that in our "knowledge-driven era...education is a lifelong endeavor and may—only occasionally—be mediated by the traditional artifacts of our historical learning experiences (Gandel, Katz, & Metros, 2004, p. 73). Unsurprisingly, traditional educational artifacts—such as "classrooms," "professors," and "degrees"—are generally seen as being superseded in this new economy, by more advanced information or knowledge technologies: computer-supported "knowledge building" environments (Scardamalia & Bereiter, 2003), learning objects (Polsani, 2003), and other advanced technologies.

The idea of a radically new social, historical, or economic order centered around information or knowledge has an important and politically charged history. By examining this history and thus *historicizing* the idea of the knowledge economy, it is possible to show its gradual construction and its actual and possible contestation. This history begins with a paradigmatic "shift recognized as early as 1973 by Daniel Bell...the shift from an industrial to a knowledge economy..." (Gandel, Katz, & Metros, 2004, p. 42). Bell, who is sometimes described as one of the fathers of neoconservatism (e.g., see Nuechterlein, 1990), is famous for his account of the "coming...postindustrial society." In fact, this phrase forms the title of a text by Bell (1999), which arguably serves as the basis for much subsequent speculation on new social and economic forms for the twentieth century (e.g., Brzezinski, 1970; Toffler, 1980; see Mattelart, 2003, pp. 73–98). In his foreword to the 1999 edition of this famous text, Bell lists the characteristics of the coming postindustrial society and how they have become and continue to be manifest. Among these are four trends: First, Bell identifies a shift from "manufacturing to services" in the workforce and the economy (p. xv). The percentage of the workforce employed in the manufacturing sector in America, Bell points out, has shrunk over the past decades, and has been accompanied by an "extraordinary rise of professional and technical employment" (p. xv). Associated with this first shift is an important, second change, an increase in the general importance of education: "Today education has become the basis of social mobility," as Bell puts it, "especially with the expansion of professional and technical jobs..." (p. xvi). A third change listed is the increased importance of technological infrastructure, and what he refers to as "intellectual technology": "These technologies," Bell explains, "form a complex adaptive system that is the foundation of the electronically mediated global economy" (p. xvii). The combined result of these and other changes is effectively summarized in Bell's fourth trend or characteristic: The "knowledge theory of value": "Knowledge is the source of invention and innovation. It creates value-added and increasing returns to scale..." (p. xvii).

This last point on the social and economic value of knowledge is perhaps of greatest importance in descriptions of the "knowledge economy." Bell makes it clear that his phrase, "knowledge theory of value" is a deliberate variation on Karl Marx's, "labor theory of value" (p. xvii). Marx understands labor — specifically physical labor — as being a unique force in capitalist economies in that it is the only one capable of "adding value" to commodities and products that can then be sold at a profit (Bottomore, 1983, p. 265). In a significant theoretical move, Daniel Bell as well as those following in his footsteps, present *knowledge* as playing this essential generative, value-adding, profit-making function. This has substantial consequences for understandings of the generation, mobilization, and exchange of knowledge in educational and research contexts. These consequences and implications extend to the nature of knowledge itself, as well as to the multiplicity of knowledge forms posited by Habermas and others. What follows is a discussion of these consequences and implications.

With this "knowledge theory of value" as Bell recognized early on, the "knowledge work" occurring in education appears as a process of unprecedented importance. Besides being "the basis of social mobility" (Bell, 1999), education takes its proper place, as Peter Drucker (1994) says, at "the center of the knowledge society, [with] schooling [as] its key institution" (p. 66). The vital economic and social value of these key educational institutions rests not so much in their function of social reproduction or in their potential to contribute to individual autonomy and responsible citizenship. The value of educational institutions rests instead in their role as a means of generating and reproducing knowledge as a productive force, above all as this force is mobilized in the natural sciences and in the applied social sciences:

> The major problem for the post-industrial society will be adequate numbers of trained persons of professional and technical caliber... The expansion of science-based industries will require more engineers, chemists, and mathematicians. The needs for social planning...will require large numbers of persons trained in the social and biological sciences. (Bell, 1999, p. 232)

When evaluated in terms of postindustrial knowledge generation and creation, however, the school in its current form appears as woefully inadequate, hopelessly or even fatally outmoded. In the literature of educational technology and reform, schools and universities alike are characterized as following an outdated "industrial paradigm" (as opposed to a "postindustrial" model; Gilbert, 2005), as being "cottage industries" (Newman & Couturier, 2001; Smith, 2005) or more generally as being "stuck in the past" (e.g., Lucas, 2003):

> in very fundamental ways, education is stuck. It doesn't know where to move and it doesn't have the tools to move with. The dialogue, both within and outside the education profession, does not advance. The same blunt statements (including this one) are made over and over. The tools education needs, of course, are conceptual tools. In this so-called Knowledge Age [sic], that is the first requirement. (Bereiter, 2002)

Not surprisingly, Bereiter goes on to emphasize the importance of computer, Internet, and other high-tech tools that correspond to these conceptual tools (e.g., Bereiter, 2002; pp. 460–462; Bereiter & Scardamalia, 1992).

A second implication of the knowledge theory of value is that it privileges some characteristics of knowledge over others. When knowledge is understood as a productive force, for example, it is not the role of knowledge as an instrument of enlightenment or of democratic decision making that is foregrounded; instead, knowledge tends to be characterized as a kind of service, utility, or good to be bought and sold, used, enhanced, and re-used. It becomes a kind of "super commodity" that has market value like physical commodities but transcends the products of physical labor. Norris, Mason, and Lefrere (2003), writing specifically of "e-Knowledge," describe it as being "both a thing and a flow" that has the capacity to be "'atomized,' repurposed, updated, recombined, metered, and exchanged" (p. 1). Unlike physical goods, however, this commodified knowledge can be readily "mobilized" and "unbundled to take account of the location of users and their needs at [any] location" (p. x). And when such knowledge or "content is modularized and coupled with learning objectives," Norris et al. explain, "it is typically referred to as 'learning objects' or 'knowledge objects'" (p. 5). In the context of a "knowledge society" in which knowledge as an economic force and commodity is paramount, it takes its paradigmatic form in education as a learning object. These "learning objects," which have received much attention in the literature of e-learning, refer to modular, exchangeable, digital resources that are able to be combined and configured with other digital objects.

A third ramification of the "knowledge theory of value" is that when conceptualized as a kind of "super-commodity," knowledge becomes something quite different from the way it is understood by Habermas and critical theory — as being contestable, multiple, and derived from different human "constitutive interests." This multiplicity and this motivated or "interested" character of knowledge is effectively suppressed or erased. Instead knowledge is judged by a single and sole criterion, specifically, its *"performance"* (Polsani, 2003; emphasis in original). Writing about this performative knowledge, specifically as it is manifest in learning objects, Polsani explains:

> Before the advent of the post-industrial age in the 1960s, Enlightenment and post-Enlightenment ideas determined the purpose and use of knowledge. The European Enlightenment defined the human being as a subject whose destiny is the realization of its full potentialities through reason. The goal of acquiring learning was the realization of spirit, life, and emancipation of humanity and the purpose of production of knowledge was the moral and spiritual guidance of a nation. However, in the contemporary conceptualization of knowledge, its purpose is no longer to realize spirit or emancipate humanity but to add value… The legitimacy of performative knowledge is no longer granted by the grand narratives of emancipation, but by the market.

This notion of a purely performative and productive knowledge that is privileged above any other knowledge forms is described in other accounts of the knowledge society. Again it is Daniel Bell, in his *Coming of the Post-Industrial Society* (1999), who provides an early and powerful distillation of this "knowledge age" phenomenon. He describes the generation of productive knowledge as occurring paradigmatically in the "community of science":

> The community of science is a unique institution in human civilization. It has no ideology, in that it has no postulated set of formal beliefs, but it has an ethos which implicitly prescribes rules of conduct. [...] As an imago [an ideal or subjective image], it comes closest to the ideal of the Greek polis, a republic of free men and women united by a common quest for truth. (p. 380)

This "universal" and "disinterested" scientific knowledge enables what Bell refers to as "technical decision-making" (p. 34). This form of technological management or administration is an application of knowledge, as Bell explains further, that "can be viewed as the diametric opposite of ideology: Technological decision-making is calculating and instrumental, [while ideology is] emotional and expressive" (p. 34).

Of course, it is precisely these kinds of claims that Adorno, Horkheimer, Barthes (and other critical theorists) would see as being ideological in the extreme, as exemplifying myth or the mythological in its critical sense. When knowledge claims deny their relation to human interests of any kind, their "pretention to correspond to reality" becomes absolute. In this context, simply having shown—in the preceding paragraphs—how these ideas originated and how they continue to evolve hopefully undermines their claims to natural or self-evident truth.

As emphasized earlier, however, the task of critical theory is not simply to engage in "criticism" for its own sake. It also seeks to generate emancipatory forms of knowledge able to provide alternative and progressive ways of thinking and acting. These can be found by looking to sources of information that stand as alternatives to those usually referenced in e-learning. One simple example of this kind of source is provided by information that is supplied to people who are unemployed or who find themselves, as is euphemistically said, "in-between jobs." Imagine yourself looking for a job as a student or considering the possibility of a new area of employment (as millions of people do every day). As a part of your job search you go to the U.S. Department of Labor Web site and look at the "career advice" section available there. Under the heading "Career Changers" this Web site lists the top ten highest-growth industries in the United States and shows the total number of jobs that will be created in each by the year 2014. On the basis of the way that the "knowledge economy" has been described above, you would think that jobs in research, in high-tech and information technologies would be at the very top of this list. But this is not the case. The first three industries or areas of employment listed are "hospitality," "health care," and "retail." Together, these three categories will provide more new jobs than the remaining seven job categories, combined. These top three sectors are predicted to produce over 15 million jobs in the United States by 2014. After these top three come the financial services and construction industries. These top five industries hardly suggest that your best chances for a job would be to become a "mature knowledge producer" who would manage and produce knowledge or direct and meter knowledge flows. You would be more likely to conclude that future career choices can be found in the area of *service*: working in a Wal-Mart (retail), a Holiday Inn (hospitality), or perhaps more optimistically as a hospital worker or care provider (health care).

Indeed, Daniel Bell (1999) and other sociologists and economists have given significant emphasis to this *service* component of the post-industrial economy. They sometimes describe the current social and economic order as being *both* a knowledge *and service* economy, high-lighting the postindustrial specifically as entailing a shift "from manufacturing to *services*" (p. xv; emphasis added). This particular emphasis has much more ambivalent and problematic implications than the more single-minded emphasis on knowledge or information that is likely familiar to those researching ICTs. Obviously, service jobs do not hold the long-term attraction or bring with them the in-come, status, or stability associated with terms such as the "informa-tion worker" or "knowledge producer." Also, service sector employees generally require only "short- to medium-term on the job training" (Henwood, 2003, p. 73), with obvious and baleful implica-tions for education and higher learning.

Perhaps the most important implication of the postindustrial economy as one reliant on *services* is social and economic polarization. Management guru Peter Drucker, for example, distinguishes between a *knowledge class* on the one hand and a *service class* on the other. It has been part and parcel of the new economic order that the rich are get-ting richer by (among other things) taking advantage of economic changes related to knowledge and technology to increase their wealth, and that the poor, disadvantaged by these same changes, are getting poorer. A rather dire picture of where all this may lead is also provided by Drucker (1994):

> This society, in which knowledge workers dominate, is in danger of a new class conflict: the conflict between the large minority of knowledge workers and the majority of people who will make their living through traditional ways, either by manual work, whether skilled or unskilled, or by services work, whether skilled or unskilled. (p. 67)

Thus, beneath the simplicity of the slogans about the "knowledge economy" and its imperatives for educational change lurk socioeco-nomic developments that are fraught with contestation between eco-nomic classes and clashing political interests. The myth of the knowledge economy obscures this clash by generalizing the situation of one class or group within the "knowledge economy," "knowledge workers" — to the population as a whole. To simply state that "children need to be placed on a trajectory" leading to knowledge work is to ignore the fact that other, marginalized and less celebrated forms of work are also structurally necessary in a "knowledge and service society." To recognize this is also to recognize that education must instead actively cultivate a range of skill sets germane to different economic fates.

Of course, given its inescapable involvement in knowledge in all its forms, e-learning and education have a further responsibility in this regard: to move beyond understandings of knowledge and of its construction and reproduction as a "universal" and "disinterested" productive force that is measured and valued only in terms of its performance. With regard to knowledge or learning objects, critical theory teaches the importance of moving beyond their conceptualization as interchangeable modules or "black boxes" of knowledge, separated from the contexts and interests associated with their use. Using critical theory, educators generating and reproducing knowledge are able to open up this black box to ask whose knowledge might be inside, in whose interests this knowledge might be constructed, and the possible and multifarious implications and contexts of its use.

The Anyone, Anywhere, Anytime Myth

In the way that the catchphrase "knowledge economy" papers over a polarized and contested social reality, the slogan "anyone, anywhere, and anytime learning" suggests a similarly reductive conception of identity, location, and of education itself. Instead of one class being designated as representative of an entire economy, as suggested in "knowledge economy," according to the slogan, it is particular people, times, and places that are seen as typical and representative of others. To conduct an immanent critique of this second myth, it is useful to begin by historicizing — however briefly and partially — the phrase "anyone, anywhere, and anytime" by considering its role just a few years ago, at the turn of the century. During the Internet's heyday — when e-learning was seen as "the next killer app" (Chambers, 1999) that threatened to turn traditional campuses into "relics" (Drucker, 1997) — educational technologists celebrated the promise of new technologies and forms of learning to overcome space, time, and even the body. Commentators celebrated the "death of distance" (Cairncross, 2001) and remarked with hope that the promise of disembodied community and learning could make prejudices like race and gender a thing of the past (e.g., Ried, 1998). Cyberspace was seen as clearly different from (and in many ways better than) the "real world." This is a sentiment that has been given powerful and economic expression in phrases like "anyplace, anytime" education or learning for "anyone, anywhere, anytime." But since the convenience and the irritations of the Internet have become an inseparable part of the banalities of everyday life, many have come to see these two worlds as less different than expected. "[T]he binary opposition between cyberspace and 'the real world,'" scholars have come to learn, "is not nearly as sharp or clean as it's [been] made out to be" (Kolko, Nakamura, & Rodman, 2000, p. 4).

All the same, claims of learning "anywhere anytime" and of being able to be "anyone" online—creating one's own desirable Internet identity—are still commonplace in e-learning publications today. It is not at all strange to read of projects claiming that they are realizing the overall aim of making "learning available to anyone, anywhere, anytime" (e.g., Bourne, Harris, & Mayadas, 2005). It is also not surprising to come across descriptions of the educational potential of blogs, e-portfolios, wikis, or other technologies emphasizing how they free the user to "construct" or develop their own "online identities" (e.g., Cameron & Anderson, 2006), with no explanation or qualification concerning such freedom.

It is again research and reports appearing largely outside of the literature of e-learning that undermine these kinds of claims. The freedoms of placelessness and facelessness that are thought to be available online, in other words, do not exist independently of the problems and limitations of the "real" or "physical" world. Research beyond the field of e-learning has shown, for example, that individuals are not free to create new identities online that simply erase the physical markers of race and gender. The sociological and communications research of Susan Herring into chat and discussion forums, for example, has long demonstrated that "gender is often visible on the Internet on the basis of features of a participant's discourse style, features which the individual may not be consciously aware of or able to change easily" (2000). As one general example, Herring describes how her own research has repeatedly shown that female communication is manifested in "an aligned orientation towards [its] interlocutors," while its male counterpart presents a markedly more "adversarial orientation" (2000). Lisa Nakamura (2002) has done similar research on racial stereotypes, coining the term "cybertypes." She shows how tools that were earlier described as being able to conceivably "redress" issues of "age, gender and races [actually]...produce cybertypes that look remarkably like racial and gender stereotypes" (p. 5). Nakamura correspondingly concludes that the Internet "propagates, disseminates, and commodifies images of race and racism" (p. 3). What this research shows, in short, is that it is not possible to simply construct an online identity or persona ex nihilo or from scratch.

There are literal limits, in other words, to the myth of interchangeable identity or of being "anybody" online. Research also highlights other literal limitations for the myths of "anywhere" and "anytime" activity online—specifically under the rubric of the "digital divide." Research in this area first of all shows how "anywhere" and "anytime" stop rather abruptly at the borders of the thirty "developed" member nations of the OECD (e.g., WSIS, 2005). The OECD, of course, includes Europe, North America, Japan, and South Korea but excludes all of Africa, South America, Russia, India, and China—the vast majority of the world's population, in other words. Research on the "digital divide" also emphasizes that gaps or "digital divides" *within* OECD countries are also notable. These are generally observed, moreover, to be coextensive with class and other social divisions (e.g., WSIS, 2005). For example, one report on e-learning in Aboriginal or First Nations communities in Canada describes how gaps in expertise and knowledge in these contexts "are compounded by digital divides which in turn deepen existing social divides" (CBNC, 2005, p. 7). Widening class divisions—above all, the gap between the richest and the poorest—have been earlier identified as important factors in debunking the myth of the "knowledge economy" and they play a role here as well. As one Statistics Canada report concludes, the digital "divide is [actually] widening when the lowest income deciles are compared with the highest income decile" (Sciadas, 2002). Gaps in the availability of the Internet, in short, fall along income and other economic and demographic fault lines, both internationally and in more local terms.

But the "anyone, anywhere, anytime" catchphrase is not only misleading when taken literally; its limitations are equally clear when identity, place, and time are understood in more abstract and figurative terms. Consider this: When we are online, we are not simply anybody anywhere; we are also positioned figuratively but inevitably in terms of identity, place, and time by the messages that bombard us from the computer screen. To understand and articulate this process of "positioning," it is useful to briefly consider further theoretical developments of the critical approaches outlined earlier. These developments, largely contributed by French theorists Louis Althusser and Michel Foucault, focus on the complex interrelationship between ideology and identity or between control and subjectivity. Thus far in this chapter, ideology has been presented as something that operates in the rather abstract realm of ideas and that connects with practice in terms of how problems, policies, and projects are conceptualized and realized. Through the work of Althusser, Foucault, and other theorists in the 1970s, ideology (or "power" in the vocabulary of Foucault) is seen rather differently, as instantiated in everyday practices. Political power is seen as being manifest through the things people routinely do and the roles they routinely play without even thinking about it. For example, to play the role of a student or of a teacher (online or in a classroom) is to be cast as an individual into predefined relationships and structures, which are reproduced and reinforced through even the most trivial statements and actions. Once "positioned" in these roles, individual identity is to some extent defined by them. Roles and identities determine, for example, how a person is addressed and responds to being addressed (e.g., putting up one's hand to ask a question, or closing the door at the beginning of a class). "Ideology," in this expanded sense, "is something that happens both to us and in us" (Freeden, 2003, p. 30). This positioning or "formation" of the individual as a social subject occurs not just in the context of formal, prescribed roles but also through expectations, stereotypes, and responses that are associated with race, gender, age, and class. This "positioning" of the individual, or his or her "formation" is often invisible to those whose race, gender, age, or class is in the majority (e.g., white, male, and with disposable income).

One way of understanding this process of "positioning" is through a process known as *interpellation*: Simply think of a policeman who shouts "Hey, you there!" on the street. If you turn around to "answer" that call, at that moment, when you see yourself as "addressed" by that call, you are be positioned: You are defined, at least to an extent, as a subject relative to the dominant system of beliefs or ideas regarding law and crime. Something similar happens when encountering e-mails, blog entries, and perhaps most powerfully, advertisements on the Internet: these texts and (in some cases animated) images "address" you. As with the example of being hailed by the policeman on the street, the "address" of Internet images define or position the individual as a subject and in whatever terms and ideologies that are generally taken as "normal" on the Internet. For example, I go to a popular news site (www.cbc.ca), where I am greeted by an animated ad for computers that announces: "Dell: Purely You." I check out "Today's recommendations for you" at amazon.com, where I am presented with various products that can be "delivered Tuesday, February 20" (if I order them within a given number of hours and minutes). Even when I return to my own desktop, I go to "my computer" and "my documents."

By being repeatedly addressed in these ways (about *my* computer, *my* recommendations, *my* Dell), I am placed in a relationship with what I encounter as a computer "user," a document "producer," and above all, a *consumer:* As someone who is literate, with a potential understanding of the products presented and most importantly, at least potentially with disposable income to purchase them (e.g., White, 2006). Of course, advertisers and content developers will use a wide range of demographic and personal categories—including the socioeconomic categories of class, race, and educational background and sometimes an individual's browsing or purchasing history—in order to make an online address as personal, direct, and unavoidable as possible. If at least some of these categories used to shape the "address" fits or matches the recipient or addressee, then it is generally easy to accept it as "normal." In this way, the personalization and localization provided by sites and services like Google and Ama-

zon.com can be understood as powerful ideological and broadly iden-
tity-forming tools. Even if an addressee does not fit the demographic
and other categories used to shape an advertiser's address, the addressee is generally still identified and positioned in other ways—for
example, as a disenfranchised outsider lacking funds or interest for
the advertised product.

"Anyone, anywhere, anytime" invokes not only an abstract, default time and place—of consumption and production—but also a
kind of "default" person. Because advertisers seek demographic seg-
ments that have money to spend, it should not come as a surprise that
the kind of identity that the Internet or Web in general addresses by
"default" is white and male (Nakamura, 2002, p. 58). In uncritically
invoking categories like anyone, anywhere, anytime, the experience
of a single (and relatively small) privileged group (or class) of people
is, in effect, universalized. Differences and even contention and conflict between different subject "positions"—as shaped by class, race,
gender, income, and many other categories—are again covered up or
papered over. "You" are by default a producer and consumer and
"you" are further assumed to be able to produce, consume, and also
learn in a kind of default space dominated by economic activity. In
this situation, the ideological dynamic is much the same as was the
case in the earlier discussion of "knowledge workers." As was also
argued in that case, instead of using the kinds of catchphrases that
cover up or ignore conspicuous gaps and inequalities, emphasis
needs to be placed on ameliorating disparities in access and on the
means by which these are reinforced in common ways of thinking
and talking about the Internet and e-learning.

Technology Drives Educational Change

The third and final myth to be considered here is not associated with
a single catchphrase or slogan in e-learning but this makes it no less
powerful and pervasive. This myth is registered instead in ways of
talking about technological and educational change. More specifically, it appears in connection with technological *impacts on* education, particularly in statements that present technology as single-
handedly achieving change in education or even as "driving" educa-

tional change. In its most extreme form, this myth is encapsulated in so-called laws of technically driven progress and change, which are found with surprising frequency in literature promoting and discussing e-learning. Examples of these laws include Moore's law (the regular doubling of computer processor speeds; e.g., Educause, 2002); Kurzweil's "law of accelerating returns" (positing the exponential nature of technical innovation; e.g., McGreal, 2005); or Gladwell's "tipping point" (a mathematical model of "epidemic" dynamics of change; e.g., Bull, Bull, Garofalo, & Harris, 2002). According to this myth, technological progress is independent of other social conditions, and it has the power to change professional practices and priorities irrevocably or even to render them obsolete. As a result, technology—as the word "impact" suggests—can be said to have decidedly "traumatic" repercussions on the individuals and institutions with which it comes into contact (Hilton, 2006; Pannabecker, 1992). Technology, in still other words, can be said to appear as the "destiny" of education.

As an example, consider this discussion of the inevitable "epidemic" of portable, wireless computing devices predicted to overtake educational institutions:

> Widespread access to PWDs (portable wireless devices) will represent a tipping point in American education. Almost all consumer devices—from microwaves to cell phones—have a price point at which widespread adoption occurs in a short period of time. The same will be true for the spread of PWDs in schools. (Bull et al., 2002)

According to Bull and others, it is only a matter of technological progress, both in the design of technologies and the cost and efficiency of their production, that determines the future of education: "Such tools and techniques are developing at an accelerated rate, a rate that calls for an effective response—the preparedness of educators in schools with technology integrated into all subject areas." This same article concludes somewhat ominously by warning its readers that this "opportunity to [act] before the tipping point arrives will occur only once" (2002). Educators, in other words, are not seen as being particularly active or influential in the determination of the future of their profession: Instead, they "face a choice": either accommodate to technically driven change or be left behind. Technical progress—applying to PWDs, processor speeds, and other developments—is presented as inevitable and autonomous in its effects.

Of course, technology as a force that drives educational change is not always expressed in such a direct or portentous manner as it is in the example, above. But it is easy to find examples in e-learning where similar, implicit understandings are decisive. This is illustrated by a general class of research known as the "technology impact study." This includes quasi-experimental analyses of the effects of technology on student achievement as described in the second chapter. These studies attempt to isolate and measure statistically significant differences produced by the controlled introduction of technologies into conventional educational settings. In this case, it is technological innovation that is hypothesized as changing or "impacting on" education. (See Pannabeker, 1992 and Petrina, 1992 for a discussion of the language of technological impact in educational research.) Another example of research in which technology is conceptualized (at least implicitly) as a kind of "unmoved mover," able to decisively influence education from the outside, is presented by investigations based on Everett Rogers's model of technological innovation (Rogers, 2003). This model understands innovations or technologies generally as being "disseminated" throughout a population. New technologies are seen as ready-made artifacts that are absorbed by a largely passive group of users. In e-learning research, as it happens, the population that is often studied and categorized in this way is university faculty members (e.g., Bull et al., 2002; Garofoli & Woodell, 2003; Mahony & Wozniak, 2006; PT3, 2002). Roger's model generally allows for only two responses: "Adoption" or "resistance" of varying intensity. Rogers's uses labels for degrees of adoption or resistance that are rather telling: "innovators," "early adopters," "late majority," and "laggards." The character of these labels leaves little doubt as to how various responses are viewed.

An immanent critique of this myth can be undertaken simply by looking to alternative sources of information on technology and to the work of scholars in the history and sociology of technology. This research and scholarship warns of the trap or fallacy of *technological determinism*: "the belief that social progress is driven by technological innovation, which in turn follows an 'inevitable' course" (Smith, 1994, p. 38; see also Chandler, 1995).

There are different forms of technological determinism. The understanding of technological change implied in a great deal of e-learning research would fit well under what scholars have called "hard" rather than "soft" determinism, and also would correspond with "optimistic" rather than "pessimistic" determinism. In the case of "hard" determinism, as Smith and Marx (1994) explain, "agency (the power to effect change) is imputed to the technology itself…with the advance of technology lead[ing] to a situation of inescapable necessity" (p. xii). As indicated in the examples cited above, technology is indeed given the agency of an unstoppable power or force of change. Technology is seen as being capable of acting on its own to produce significant social and educational transformation. What makes this determinism *optimistic* is that the "positive" aspects of this technical change are generally emphasized over "negative" ones. For example, faculty members who do not adopt technologies are seen as "laggards," as refusing the obviously "positive" potential of technology, rather than as being the last or wise few to resist its "negative" or destructive consequences.

The recent history of e-learning itself provides some powerful counterexamples that refute this overriding optimistic, "hard" determinism. One example is provided by the emergence and entrenchment of "learning management systems" such as WebCT or Moodle in traditional educational institutions since the late 1990s. In this case, the rapid emergence of the Internet as a popular medium did not mean that it simply washed over the educational landscape, doing away with existing institutional and business models (as Drucker and others predict). Instead, through a complex series of developments, interactions, and "negotiations," this technology was reshaped, adapted, and appropriated. In many instances, these course management systems originated directly from universities themselves, in the form of individual or community projects of faculty and other university developers. These systems, moreover, have been designed and adapted in clear conformance with the interests and management structures of large educational institutions: they are centrally administered, meaning they can be serviced and supported by network or computing services units already in place in these institutions; and they explicitly define "roles" (via system login options) and thereby reinforce traditional functions and identities of university personnel, teachers, students, and administrators. The adaptation of this particular Internet technology, as a result, seems to have had the end effect of reinforcing rather than disrupting many conventional educational practices and functions.

By introducing a vocabulary that makes use of terms such as "adaptation," "negotiation," and "interaction" — rather than casting technology in terms of "impacts," "laws," and "inevitabilities" — the relationship between technology and education appears as much more complex. Technology itself is no longer an unstoppable force that inevitably determines the future of education and e-learning. Going even further, it is possible to say that when it is viewed as the result of complex, multicausal processes of social construction and negotiation, technology emerges as something very much *other* than the destiny of e-learning. It becomes, as Andrew Feenberg (2002) describes, "an 'ambivalent' process of development" that is "suspended between different possibilities" (p. 15). "On this view," Feenberg concludes, "technology [itself] is not a destiny but a scene of struggle" (p. 15).

Conclusion

Critical theory, a methodological orientation familiar in many areas of social and educational research, has clear relevance to e-learning. This relevance has been demonstrated in this chapter by applying ideology critique to a number of basic and even self-evident notions and understandings in literature that promote, describe, and investigate e-learning. At their most extreme, these notions — of a knowledge economy; of anywhere, anytime, anybody learning; of inevitable, technology-driven change — can be understood in critical-theoretical terms as "myths." The point of critiquing these myths, however, has not been to assail what is essential or axiomatic to e-learning, but rather, to provide a corrective: to show that economic, technical, cultural, and historical conditions central to the use of information and communication technologies in education are complex and need to be interpreted and investigated in new, different, and above all, interdisciplinary ways.

Such an explicitly interdisciplinary approach is indispensable for providing a more realistic and balanced basis or set of starting points for undertaking e-learning research. Research becomes compromised or even misdirected if it is based on presuppositions that are fallacious and oversimplified. Alternatively, when myths, like those listed above, are clearly identified and avoided, the realization of alternatives and broadly progressive research designs becomes easier and more natural. For example, recognizing that many contemporary economies are oriented to the provision of service at least as much as to knowledge or information will surely effect how the contribution of e-learning initiatives to the economy are conceptualized in e-learning research designs and proposals. Understanding e-learning technology as a scene of struggle rather than as a destiny or fait accompli might also help to guide the exploration of metaphors other than "impact" or "dissemination" when inquiring into the relationship between technology and changing educational institutions and practices.

Chapter Nine

E-Learning and Empire: The U.S. Military and Instructional Technology

Introduction: History and Critical Theory

As described in the previous chapter, "ideological" or "immanent" critique works as a research method principally through comparison and contrast: "basic cultural ideas," as Max Horkheimer (2005) was quoted as saying, are "measure[d] against the social background from which they emanate" (p. 124). One of the most common ways of undertaking such a figurative measurement is to take "basic cultural ideas" from the present, and to compare them in various ways to those of the past. This type of broadly historical analysis was described as having special potential in e-learning—which, by definition, places ongoing emphasis on technological and practical developments in the present or the immediate future.

At the same time as critical theory directs researchers to this kind of broadly historical, comparative inquiry, however, it takes away one of the traditional means for orienting historical research: the understanding of history as a positive, cumulative, and progressive narrative. This understanding of history is illustrated in what have been called "grand narratives" (see chapter two). Examples of grand narratives are provided by the notion of history as the unfolding of inevitable technical and scientific progress. The overall progressive pattern of this grand narrative is echoed in smaller-scale narratives that would serve as "sub-plots." In the context of e-learning or educational technology, these lesser narratives might include accounts of technical innovations as passing through the phases or subgroups of "early adoption," "early" and "late" majorities; they might also include characterizations of the history of the field as "a cumulative endeavor in which knowledge from earlier phases can be absorbed smoothly in more recent waves" (Lowyck, 2007, p. xiii). These ways of understanding change in technology use or in research itself as relentlessly progressive and cumulative are illustrative of *determinism*. As explained in the previous chapter, determinism in e-learning sees scientific and technical progress as the destiny of the field, rather than understanding technology and e-learning themselves as sites of struggle, bringing with them the interruptions and discontinuities implied by conflict.

How, then, is a critical, historical account of events or developments to be investigated and presented? Broadly conceived, critical theory provides a range of methods for historiography. Two methods that will be featured in this chapter are

1.   The study of the way that ideology and political values are "encoded" or expressed in the design of technical artifacts. This way of investigating the politics of technologies also includes the possibility for these artifacts to be "re-encoded" in different ways, and it is often referred to as "the critical theory of technology."

2.   The study of language, metaphor, or what is sometimes referred to as "discourse." Discourse in this sense refers to the way that formal, institutional language and its various figures, mechanisms, and limitations can be used to construct a particular topic — whether that topic be military influence, computer technology, or their relationship to education.

These two methods will be presented and applied in combination in this chapter in order to provide a historical and ideological analysis of one factor that is of singular importance in e-learning: the influence of the U.S. military-industrial complex. It is generally acknowledged, for example, that the fields of instructional technology and design as well as the behaviorist and cognitivist paradigms that underpin them grew out of the military-industrial complex during the Cold War (e.g., De Vaney & Butler, 1996; Lachman, Lachman, & Butterfield, 1979). Much as the Pentagon and this military complex defined the architecture of the Internet, they also essentially created, almost ex nihilo, the fields of instructional technology and instructional design.

The reasons for the singular importance and influence of the American military in these fields and in e-learning itself are not complicated: The U.S. military currently maintains over 750 military bases around the world (Johnson, 2004, p. 288); its budget takes up more than half of the discretionary spending of the American federal government. The size of this budget is growing, with annual levels of spending having recently surpassed half a trillion dollars.

Given its cost and the sophistication of its systems and operations, it is no surprise that the U.S. military spends more on training, educa-

tion, and associated technologies than any other organization globally:

> Since the 1950s [the United States] has spent $150 to $250 million each year
> on research and development (R&D) in education, training, training devices,
> and simulators. It maintains what may be the largest, most extensive train-
> ing operation in history[,] accompanied by what may be the largest, most
> extensive training research and development effort ever undertaken. It
> would be remarkable if all of this activity did not yield some techniques and
> technologies that are of general interest and applicability beyond the mili-
> tary. (Fletcher & Chatelier, 2000, p. 269)

It would be just as remarkable if these techniques and technologies,
once more widely applied, did not bear some significant imprint of
this influence. For one of the lessons of critical theory is that technologies and technological designs—like knowledge forms generally—are not neutral in their application or effects, but that they carry
political and ideological significance with them.

This chapter will address the influence of the U.S. military in e-
learning within the historical context provided by the Cold War and
its aftermath. It will accomplish this through the following steps:

1. Starting from the recognition of the dominance of the U.S. military in
   training techniques and technologies, this chapter introduces Andrew
   Feenberg's "critical theory of technology" and notion of "technical
   code" as a way of tracing this dominance in areas *beyond* the U.S. military itself.
2. Looking at ways in which this dominance and influence has been investigated in examples of Cold War research, this chapter outlines means
   through which military discourse and metaphor find expression in other fields and discourses.
3. It shows how technologically based metaphors in particular are expressed in politics and technological designs of the Cold War era, and
   how these designs are relevant to instructional technology and e-
   learning.
4. Finally, the chapter examines the more recent history of U.S. military influence in training, and traces both material and metaphorical examples
   of this influence on e-learning to the present day.

This chapter concludes by emphasizing how e-learning and associated technological designs and configurations represent a site of

struggle between an ideology of command and control, and the potentialities of autonomy and resistance.

The Critical Theory of Technology

Andrew Feenberg (2002), a student of Frankfurt School member Herbert Marcuse, has developed an account of the ways in which ideology is "encoded" in technical designs. In the context of what he refers to as a "critical theory of technology," Feenberg describes how technological artifacts are "programmed" or "encoded" in ways that go beyond neutral technical function or "rationality." Feenberg's theory understands technology in terms that are broadly similar to those in which knowledge and ideology are understood in critical theory overall (see the previous chapter). Like knowledge, technology and technical designs are seen as the expression of human and political interests. And like ideology generally, the more that these technical designs are depicted as rational and neutral, the more they are suspect of harboring political interests, and particularly, the interests of specific social groups and classes. Quoting Marcuse, Feenberg explains that

> critical theory rejects the neutrality of technology and argues instead that "technological rationality has become political rationality." The values and interests of ruling classes and elites are installed in the very design of rational procedures and machines even before these are assigned a goal. (pp. 14–15)

In this sense, technology — despite the fact that it is often seen as purely rational and functional — can be said to embody ideology in tangible form.

However, Feenberg warns against a direct or unqualified equation of ideology with technology. Just as technology cannot be reduced to purified instrumental function or rationality, it also is not *simply* the arbitrary expression of political interests. Technologies are designed to accomplish a task, but in giving this task a technological definition and solution — and often, in creating further, unforeseen tasks and problems — technology is profoundly political. Course management systems like WebCT or Moodle, for example, set out to solve some of the "problems" of teaching online. But in so doing, their functions and design give explicit, technical definition to the roles and activities of students and teachers. These predefined roles end up making alternative pedagogical arrangements difficult, if not impossible, to realize. These same systems have also led to unforeseen problems with student cheating and intellectual property (Noble, 1998). In this sense, these and other technologies present an inextricable mixture of both function and value. Feenberg (2002) uses the concept of "technical code" to explain this mix:

> The dominant form of technological rationality...stands at the intersection between ideology and technique where the two come together to control human beings and resources in conformity with what I call "technical codes." (p. 15)

Feenberg goes on to define the "technical code [as] the realization of an interest [or ideology] in a technically coherent solution to a general type of problem" (p. 20). Technical codes, in other words, work to "invisibly sediment values and interests in rules and procedures, devices and artifacts..." (p. 15).

In much the same way that knowledge claims can be "critiqued" to show their constructed and ambiguous character, technical codes can themselves be subverted to reveal alternative and even emancipatory potential of technological devices. Technologies and the codes they embody, in other words, can be reinterpreted, manipulated, and effectively re-encoded, allowing them to give expression to values and interests *other* than those dominating their original conception and design. Just as hegemonic values can be encoded into a technical design, so too can technical systems be "reconfigured," as Feenberg (2001) says, "to take into account a broader swath of human needs and capacities" (p. 188).

Illustrations of this reconfiguration and recoding process abound in e-learning, and have already been considered, using different conceptual and methodological frameworks, in earlier chapters of this book. One relatively simple example is provided by the narrative account analyzed in chapter two. In this account, Lisa, an ESL writing instructor, took the computers that were unintentionally made available in the computer lab assigned to her as a classroom, and used them as a basis for organizing writing and reviewing tasks in her course. In this case, a computerized environment whose design is largely oriented around individual work was effectively "reconfigured" as a collaborative writing class, turning reading and writing into an online, group-oriented activity.

A second and historically significant example of a re-encoding of a technology in e-learning is provided by the early history of the online discussion technology examined in chapter three. These text-based media were first used in educational contexts in the early 1980s. At this time, as Hamilton and Feenberg (2005) explain, this technology was "untried in education[, and] no models for conducting an educational computer conference existed" (p. 109). Instructors and other participants using this technology were able to interpret and encode it according to their own instructional purposes and pedagogical values:

> conferencing systems had not been designed with specifically educational applications in mind, but according to generic definitions of the communication process... Faculty, staff, and participants [therefore] had to invent online education as they went along, negotiating between various notions of alternative pedagogy and the affordances and constraints of the system. (p. 109)

Hamilton and Feenberg go on to explain that these participants ended up defining online education at this early stage in terms of a highly interactive, "Socratic" approach. They also argue that this early and promising interpretation of online educational technology was swept aside during the "dot com" boom of the late 1990s. As the Internet and Web gradually turned into mass media, new ways of encoding educational technology became dominant. And many of these new encodings (think, for example, of WebCT and Blackboard) were more reflective of administrators' or corporations' hopes to "cash in" on the economic boom, than of the more modest priorities of faculty or students to teach or learn in effective and accessible ways.

Interestingly, the way that military values are "written into" the technical codes of common technologies (e.g., the computer and the Internet) have been traced in a number of recent book-length studies. Generally speaking, these books examine the "social construction" of Cold War technologies by providing detailed thematic, sociological, and historical analyses of "actors," and social and technological "networks" in twentieth-century military-industrial research and development. These same sources also follow the remarkable influence of these technologies, priorities, and paradigms in domains as diverse as cognitive psychology, network architecture, and computing science (e.g., Abbate, 1999; Akera, 2007, P.N. Edwards, 1997, respectively).

In his landmark "Cockpit Cognition" (1989) and *Classroom Arsenal* (1991) studies, Douglas Noble (1989) takes up these issues in the fields of instructional design and educational technology. He traces the influence of military priorities and paradigms in the application of computer technology in public education settings, and he comes to the rather extreme conclusion that this influence represents "a militarized debasement" of education, a "massive [pseudo-] 'scientific' distraction" (p. 289). However, many things have changed in the military, in education, and in related technologies since Noble's analysis. First, the contours of a new, *post*–Cold War military and strategic configuration have emerged — one in which aggressive military investment and action in the "global war on terror" are pivotal. At the same time, the reconfiguration of the Internet as a mass medium and the rapid growth of computer and network technologies in education have intervened, changing the landscape of the field in question. This chapter takes these important intervening factors into account, but begins by examining a number of Cold War ideas and metaphors that are central to Noble's texts, and that are useful in the examination of the military origins of many educational technologies.

The Cold War and Its Metaphors

Memories of everyday strategic and security concerns that were integral to the Cold War in the West are fading. Discussion of limited nuclear wars, of first-strike targets, of "survivability" in order to preserve "second-strike capabilities" at the time of the Cold War all labeled frighteningly plausible eventualities. But these terms and concerns have since been replaced or distorted in the light of very different geopolitical vocabularies and issues. For example, it is a commonly held view that the Internet was originally intended as a communications infrastructure that was capable of surviving a nuclear war. At the time of the Cold War, however, the idea of a decentralized, computerized communication system was actually developed out of elaborate hypothetical scenarios. The point was actually not to survive a nuclear war per se, but to *deter* a first strike by providing *evidence* of a communications infrastructure that *could* survive such a strike (Abbate, 1999). This infrastructure was developed to create the *perception* that massive second-strike retaliation would be possible by the United States, even if all other American infrastructure had been destroyed. The Internet, in other words, was not principally about robust communication itself. At its origin, it was instead primarily a *symbolic* technology, a *potential* strategic capability. Unlike similar network protocols and infrastructures (e.g., the X.25 or OSI protocol suite), it was not so much simply a question of its manifest use, or its actual merits or weaknesses. Instead, it was a matter of a move in a game of military postures and probabilities.

The strange and hermetic Cold War concerns that led to the Internet's conception may help explain a number of anomalous aspects of its subsequent development and utilization (e.g., its initial incubation in academic and other public institutions, and the challenges it now poses to "security" of various kinds in the post–Cold War world). More importantly, these Cold War concerns and circumstances help to illustrate military and public discourses that are characteristic of the period. As this chapter will show, the Cold War influence presents a paranoid logic that is complex and — like the conception of the Internet itself — one that follows a path that is hardly intuitive or direct.

The way that the Cold War influence is traced here is not primarily in terms of overt and direct linkages represented by causes and effects — although these do play a role. The question here is instead one of shared discourses, sets of assumptions, or even a shared political and cultural "world." The historical epoch of the Cold War (like any other historical period) can be said to bring with it a shared set of understandings, a common way of talking about and articulating issues and concerns, in both informal and more specialized terms. Of course this language and these understandings do not develop independently from technological and material realities. The invention and proliferation of nuclear weapons is one of the most obvious examples of these realities, precipitating the issues of the arms race, of strategies of disarmament, and the predicament of "mutually assured destruction." At the same time, ways of acting, thinking, and talking about nuclear technologies are not simply predetermined by the technologies themselves: they develop together, in complex interrelationship.

Metaphor is a particularly powerful means through which language interacts with politics and ideology, and through which the two are brought into relationship with technological developments. Metaphor refers to "a figure of speech in which a word or phrase literally denoting one kind of object or idea is used in place of another to suggest a likeness or analogy between them" (Webster's, 1977). "My love is a rose," "war is hell," or even "communication is information transmission" are relatively common examples of metaphors. Metaphor is especially powerful in political and ideological terms because of the tacit force with which it substitutes one object or idea for another. In his study of computers in Cold War America, historian Paul N. Edwards (1997) explains:

> All metaphors are political in...that they focus attention on some aspects of a situation or experience at the expense of others. A metaphor channels thought and creates a coherent scheme of significance not only by making certain features central, but by establishing a set of connections with other metaphors and openings towards further elaboration. This means that that metaphor is not merely descriptive, but also prescriptive. Often, if not always, our representations of situations contain within them indications of appropriate responses and attitudes. (p. 157)

By suggesting an analogy or likeness between two things—and by simultaneously obscuring the fact that the comparison is just "figurative"—metaphors are able to direct and define discourse on a specific topic without appearing to be controlling or censorious. If communication is "figuratively" identified with the transmission of information, for example, issues of communication will tend to be defined in terms of the nature or efficiency of a medium of transmission, rather than, for example, in terms of audience understandings or interpretations. The hidden nature of this influence or control gives metaphors considerable ideological power.

Edwards goes on to describe how metaphors—particularly those based on technological devices—have served not only as powerful political tools, but also as politically charged ways of understanding an entire historical period. In providing practical solutions and redefining everyday routines (think of measures of time and "labour" before the clock), mechanisms like the clock or the computer suggest working models for the operation of natural phenomena (like the movements of the planets or the passage of the seasons). Taken as metaphors, technologies also gain strength in that they operate reliably and autonomously, like natural phenomena. However, unlike many natural phenomena, the operations of these technologies can be directly manipulated, easily reproduced, and thus "known" in a sense that appears direct and explicit.

The clock and the eighteenth-century epoch of the Enlightenment provide a well-known example. The development and proliferation of the mechanical clock in Europe in the late middle ages and the early modern era brought with it more than just ways of coordinating practical action. With their regular, rule-bound and autonomous operation, these devices presented powerful metaphors or "models" for a way of thinking about and studying the universe as a whole. It made possible understandings of the universe specifically in terms of abstract, autonomous, and mathematical measures and operations:

> by its essential nature [the clock] dissociated time from human events and helped create the belief in an independent world of mathematically measurable sequences: the special world of science. (Mumford, 1934, p. 15)

The clock as a mechanism ended up playing a significant role for early, eighteenth-century scientists such as Christian Wolff and G.W. Leibnitz, who "saw the world as a kind of perfect clock or machine that was not in need of further correction" (Becker, 1991, p. 147). A century earlier, Descartes (1985) applied this same metaphor to the function of the human body and parts of the human mind:

> I should like you to consider that these functions (including passion, memory, and imagination) follow from the mere arrangement of the machine's organs every bit as naturally as the movements of a clock or other automaton follow from the arrangement of its counter-weights and wheels (p.108).

In the same way that the clock provided a central metaphor for understanding humans and their world in the eighteenth century, the computer can be understood as a central metaphor for the American Cold War world. Computers embody a wide range of characteristics and functions, and these give metaphorical force to a number of ways of conceiving of the world from military and political perspectives. P.N. Edwards (1997) explains,

> As machines, computers controlled vast systems of military technology central to the globalist aims and apocalyptic terms of Cold War foreign policy. First air defenses, then strategic early warning and nuclear response, and later the sophisticated tactical systems of the electronic battlefield grew from the control and communications capacities of information machines. As metaphors, such systems constituted a dome of global technological oversight, a closed world, within which every event was interpreted as part of a titanic struggle between the superpowers. ...[T]he key theme of closed-world discourse was global surveillance and control through high technology military power. Computers made the closed world work simultaneously as technology, as political system, and as ideological mirage. (p. 1)

The computer, in other words, provided systems and capabilities that were central to the Cold War, and in doing so, this technology enabled a number of broadly metaphorical ways of thinking and speaking about the Cold War world and its politics. Drawing from Edwards and other scholars of the Cold War, the principal characteristics of this metaphor—as well as further metaphors deriving from it—can be listed as follows:

1. Computer and computer networks enabled modeling of aspects of the world specifically as *closed systems*. This is exemplified in computer and other technologies used in systems of North American continental air defense: These systems integrated advanced radar, computers and aerial defense technologies in a kind of closed informational loop. "Closed systems" of these kinds can be understood entirely on their own terms, without reference to outside or environmental factors. Edwards associates this notion of the closed system with the metaphor of the "world as closed system"—or simply, what he calls the "closed world" of the Cold War.

2. These closed computerized systems provided "centralized, instantaneous, automated command and control" over vast geographic regions (p. 15). Hierarchical military command was exercised in real time over these regions to control military forces and assets, leading to the belief that this kind of control applied in non-military areas as well. Military command, as Edwards explains, was conflated with total control (p. 15).

> When combined with a simplified morality of "good" versus "evil," this
> emphasis on regional control fed Manichean fantasies of an apocalyptic,
> global struggle.
>
> 3. The presence and power of these technologically-advanced military sys-
>   tems encouraged the redefinition of political and military challenges
>   specifically as tractable technical *problems*. This redefinition, in turn, led
>   to the development of advanced, overarching and even "total" "techni-
>   cal-rational" solutions (p. 15) to these problems. In keeping with their
>   exclusively technical nature, these solutions were understood in engi-
>   neering terms of "uniformity," "metrics," "tolerance," and "standardi-
>   zation" (Noble, 1991, p. 30).

The degree to which these characteristics and metaphors are embedded in the thought and language of the Cold War is given dra-
matic illustration in the Strategic Defense Initiative (SDI) or Star Wars
project initiated by Ronald Reagan in 1983, and still funded to this
day. Famously framing the complexities of Cold War conflict in terms
of a black and white struggle of good versus evil, of the free versus
the communist world, Reagan called upon "the scientific community"
of his day to undertake "a formidable, technical task." In his famous
Star Wars speech, Reagan described this task as involving a decades-
long "research and development program to *begin to* achieve [the] ultimate goal of eliminating the threat posed by strategic nuclear mis-
siles" (Reagan, 1983; emphasis added). Reagan readily allowed that
this ambitious undertaking would involve contemporaneous technologies of the greatest sophistication—implying standards and tol-
erances for materials and systems that remain unrealized today.
Reagan asked his audience to imagine a massive scientific and technical enterprise that could only be justified in terms of an all-
encompassing geopolitical solution:

> What if free people could live secure in the knowledge that their security
> did not rest upon the threat of instant U.S. retaliation to deter a Soviet at-
> tack, that we could intercept and destroy strategic ballistic missiles before
> they reached our own soil or that of our allies?

The realization of Reagan's vision would, of course, represent an
overarching technological solution to an otherwise complex politico-
historical situation. Also, issues of command and control play a central if not overt role in Reagan's vision: antiballistic defense required

exponentially more precision, speed, coordination, and control in systems of surveillance, response, and interception than previous systems and technologies of command and control. In addition, the solution proposed by Reagan would represent a kind of "trump card" in the hypothetical games of first strikes, survivability, and second-strike retaliation. In this way, Reagan's speech invokes, affirms, and builds on many of the metaphorical and discursive characteristics of the "closed world" of the Cold War, including the notion of war as a grand struggle to achieve total, hemisphere-wide command and control.

"Man-Computer Symbiosis"

Of all of the scientific and engineering challenges presented by SDI, and by the command and control technologies that preceded it, there is one that is emblematic of "closed world" metaphors generally, and relevant to e-learning in particular. This is the integration of users (or operators or decision makers) into enormously sophisticated and technical systems—systems that dwarf human capabilities in their scope, speed, and of course, destructive capabilities. This challenge and possible solutions to it have gradually crystallized around a particular set of issues or problems centered on the interface that connects human and machine. This is the problem of the "man/machine system" or "man-computer symbiosis." This issue has come to be relevant to instructional systems and design—and ultimately to e-learning—through the way it has been taken up in psychology, above all, in cognitive psychology. Speaking of events starting with U.S. involvement in the Second World War, one early introduction to cognitive psychology explains:

> Faced with the problem of war, psychologists [developed] a new view of man...the "man/machine system." This concept emphasized the functioning of the human being and the machine as an operating unit. [...] An important feature of the man/machine system concept was that the human operator served as an information transmitter and processing device interposed between his machine's displays and their controls. (Lachman, Lachman, & Butterfield, 1979, p. 58)

In addition to information processing tasks, these same authors emphasize that the process of "decision making" has been another "important feature" of this "new view of man." One military scientist, R.J.C. Licklider, has described the goal of such research and development as "man-computer symbiosis" (of course, the gender-exclusivity of this characterization and in those provided just above is not insignificant).

The challenges posed by this task of integrating human and machine, and the ways they have been addressed, have a long and varied history. They begin with early cockpit designs and the Second World War anti-aircraft technologies, extend through the early warning systems of NORAD, and reappear in Reagan's Star Wars and advanced weapons systems of the present day (Mindell, 2002, pp. 310–322). In each case, the function of the "human operator" as a "processing device interposed between [a] machine's displays and [its] controls" is of central concern. Whether these displays and controls be a radar screen and a light-gun (as with aerial defense early in the Cold War), or a controller and a detailed video image (in human-directed smart bombs in both Iraq Wars), the underlying configuration is that of a human-machine system or "human-computer dyad": The human is situated as a critical processing component or at a decision point— for detecting enemy aircraft, launching and directing computerized weaponry, or pressing the proverbial "red button"— in a much larger and very sophisticated system of command and control.

The goal of connecting humans and computers as a "dyad" or in "symbiosis" acquires its specific relevance to e-learning through cognitive science. This is an area of research that connects the field of educational research in a fairly seamless way with the work of the military-industrial complex. "Cognitive science," as the *Stanford Encyclopedia of Philosophy* (Thagard, 2002) states, has as its "central hypothesis...that thinking can best be understood in terms of representational structures in the mind and computational procedures that operate on those structures." Cognitive science provides the terms needed to understand the human user as a specifically *computational* component "interposed" between the input and output devices (the screen and controls) of a literal computer system. Texts in e-learning, and in educational technology before it, invoke the discourse of the "dyadic" and "symbiotic" relationship of learner and computer in a manner remarkably reminiscent of military language. For example, the ideal of "human-computer symbiosis" is articulated in ongoing characterizations of computers as "cognitive technologies" (Jonassen, 2003; Pea, 1985), "cognitive tools" (Lajoie, 2000) or "mind-tools" (Jonassen et al., 1999). In these contexts, as described in chapter four, the computer is seen as forming a close "partnership" with the learner, allowing her to "share," "extend," and "amplify" her cognition (Jonassen, 2000). Characterizations of this kind continue to appear in the literature of e-learning to the present day (e.g., Keengwe, Onchwari, & Wachira, 2008). A further, prominent example is provided by discussions in education and training of "computer-augmented cognition" (or "augcog"), implying an almost cyborg-like integration of human and computer capabilities and "components" (e.g., augmentedcognition.org).

It is also for this particular aspect of military influence that David Noble reserves his harshest words. He emphasizes how the military priorities underlying what he calls "cognitive engineering" have been introduced into educational research, development, and policy as a kind of "Trojan horse" dressed up as science. At the same time, however, it is worth noting that Noble's critique is made *prior* to developments in both cognitivism generally and human-computer interaction in particular that have led to a deemphasis on the direct comparability and potential symbiosis of human and computer. These developments have been considered in some detail in chapters four and five, in the discussion of "post-cognitivist" approaches to psychology and human-computer interaction. For now, it is worth noting that these approaches are part of a growing emphasis on the situated, social, and embodied nature of human activity and computer use.

From Ada to ADL

Given the emphasis on the "closed world" solutions presented by the literal functions and the metaphorical potential of computer technology, it is hardly surprising to learn that late into the Cold War, more than $3 billion was being spent annually on software in the U.S. military. At the time, a problem was emerging in the process of software development: more than 450 programming languages were in use in projects and products across the military, resulting in a veritable "Tower of Babel" for software engineers. As a result, in 1974, the development and adoption of a common language for the U.S. military was proposed. In 1983, the language, called Ada (named after Ada Lovelace, the first programmer) became a national standard. By 1987, the U.S. Department of Defense issued the "Ada Mandate," officially requiring the use of Ada for every new software project in the military. As the 1980s came to a close, the Department of Defense was attempting to foster nonmilitary commercial use of this language, and initiated an effort to establish its longer-term viability. But by the 1990s, its military use was abandoned altogether. As one military report explained, the rapid development of software technologies, combined with a recognition of the necessary plurality of software languages, led to the conclusion that the use of Ada solutions was "no longer the best approach in many [military] application areas" (CSTB, 1997, p. 2).

The lessons that the development, growth, and especially, the abandonment of Ada presented to the Department of Defense were significant. Above all, these demonstrated that the military could not "go it alone" when it came to software development technologies and standards—however indispensable these were to command and control projects. It became clear that the Pentagon would have much to gain from active participation of nonmilitary sectors in the development and implementation of software solutions.

During the same year that overall support for the Ada language was withdrawn, the Department of Defense launched a project that reflected the lessons learned, but that was equally ambitious on its own terms. This was the Advanced Distributed Learning (ADL) initiative, whose far-reaching vision was and still is "to provide access to the highest-quality learning and performance aiding that can be tailored to individual needs and delivered cost-effectively, anytime and anywhere" (2007b). Founded during the Clinton-Gore presidency, in the wake of the popular success of the Internet, ADL was envisioned as "a resource center that will promote the use of new training technologies across [all government] departments" (Weinstock, 2001).

ADL would do this by working together with systems developers, academics, and government and military trainers to develop "a set of standards to help guide e-learning vendors, content providers and users" (Weinstock, 2001).

In terms of its most basic outlines, ADL is clearly illustrative of the "lessons" of Ada and the "Ada mandate." Academics, developers and the private sector were encouraged to play an active role in its development, dissemination, use, and implementation. The ADL and the standards it was set to produce, moreover, were intended to serve *all* government departments, rather than being confined to the Pentagon.

Considered on its own terms, the ADL initiative shares many characteristics of the Cold War–closed world described above. This is the case in terms of both the discourse and the practical outlines of ADL. This begins with its mission, which is so broad and ambitious as to promise a revolution in human affairs. However, a number of recent accounts of the goals and intentions of the ADL go even further. They speak of how its systems and solutions hold out the promise of providing "a teacher" or a "personal learning associate" for "every learner" (Fletcher & Tobias, 2003, p. 29; Fletcher, Tobias, & Wisher, 2007), or even more grandly, "an Aristotle for every Alexander" (Fletcher, 2006, p. 23) — a wise personal tutor for even the most brilliant and audacious student or warfighter. Like Reagan's missile defense shield, ADL promises, in effect, a complete technological solution to the complex human "problems" presented by education and training. The discourse of a total solution to a technically defined problem, initially applied to the Cold War, is directed to military training and education generally. The universality of this solution is further underscored by the claim that ADL is intended not only to meet the needs of the military and "to provide a model for all Federal Agencies" (Fletcher, 2006, p. 31), but to also be valuable in almost any educational context: "Its anytime, anywhere instructional goals include classrooms as well as workplaces, conference rooms, job sites, and homes" (p. 32). Finally, in at least figurative correspondence with SDI and other overarching solutions of the Cold War era, ADL's goals are to be accomplished through a kind of pinpoint targeting of specific, individual needs and requirements:

> Each [individual user's] interaction would be tailored, on-demand and in
> real time, to the outcome being sought, the learner's level of knowledge,
> skill, and style of learning, and the instructional strategy that was indicated
> by instructional principles. (Fletcher, 2005)

"Learning" in the words of one striking discursive formulation, can be conceptualized "as a weapon system" (Baskin & Schneider, 2002): a set of problems to be tackled through advanced, large-scale, and lightning-fast mechanisms of command and control.

A source for many of the most recent and strident claims on behalf of ADL is J.D. Fletcher, a research staff member at the Institute for Defense Analyses in Alexandria, Virginia. Fletcher sees ADL's educational solutions as the culmination of a long history of developments in educational psychology and technology, from behaviorist computer-based instruction through cognitivism and hypermedia. In forums as wide-ranging as the CIA (Fletcher & Johnston, 2007) and the American Educational Research Association (Fletcher, Tobias, & Wisher, 2007), Fletcher makes the case (referencing a carefully selected set of training statistics) that ADL is making a measurable and pivotal contribution to an epochal "revolution in learning" (2007).

In keeping with the technological determinism inherent in Cold War, closed-world discourse, this is a revolution that will be driven by inevitable technological developments, rather than by educational cultures, teachers, students, or trainees. Fletcher (2006) explains that this revolution is to be understood exclusively as a triumph of scientific, technical, and engineering capabilities:

> Basically we seek an engineering of instruction… Such engineering would
> ensure that outcomes such as retention of skills and knowledge, application
> and transfer of learning, motivation to continue study, speed of response,
> accuracy of response, and so forth are reliably achieved by each learner to
> the maximum extent possible within the constraints imposed by instruc-
> tional time and resources. (p. 44)

The myriad issues involved in any teaching and learning situation are defined here exclusively in terms of measurable variables for experimentation and control in science, or reduced to manipulable parameters for testing and optimization in engineering. As indicated above, this positivistic, scientific-experimental research emphasis represents yet another conspicuous characteristic shared by the discourses of the military and e-learning.[4]

The ADL SCORM

During the first ten years of the ADL's existence, and into the foreseeable future, these scientific, engineering, and technological developments have been focused on one particular set of solutions: the Shareable Courseware Object Reference Model (SCORM). In keeping with ADL's vision and goals, the SCORM is itself defined as "a collection of [technical] standards and specifications adapted from multiple sources to provide a comprehensive suite of e-learning capabilities…" (ADL, 2007b). These technical specifications, currently seven in total (collected into three documents, each around 250 pages in length), dictate how learners' interactions and competencies can be recorded; how "shareable content objects" (generally multimedia and interactive resources) are to be identified and described; and how these content objects are grouped, sequenced, and transmitted; finally they describe the sharing of recorded user interactions. The intended end result of the SCORM and ADL models is illustrated in the diagram below.

---

4. De Vaney and Butler (1996) trace this positivistic research emphasis back to the Second World War and ever earlier: "It may be said that the before-and-after design, using [a given medium] as a stimulus, which was developed by Peterson and Thurstone [in 1933], grew into the true experimental design that still resides at the heart of educational technology research. [As an eventual result, r]esearch in the military and on university campuses became inextricably conflated after WWII and remains that way today" (42).

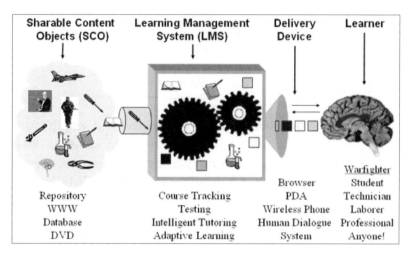

Sharable Content Objects (SCO)	Learning Management System (LMS)	Delivery Device	Learner
			Warfighter
		Browser	Student
Repository	Course Tracking	PDA	Technician
WWW	Testing	Wireless Phone	Laborer
Database	Intelligent Tutoring	Human Dialogue	Professional
DVD	Adaptive Learning	System	Anyone!

Figure 9.1: The ADL Model (Slosser, 2002, p. 4)

Besides its depiction of the main components and interrelationships of the SCORM solution (content objects, learning management system, delivery device, learner), this diagram illustrates the relentlessly reductionist orientation of this approach. The representation of the learner—"student, technician, laborer, professional, warfighter, anyone!"—as a mere organ is perhaps the strongest illustration of this. The human learner is depicted, in effect, as a specialized, functional component interposed in a much larger electronic system. In this case, the "human factor" interacts with a delivery device, which receives and feeds packages of content organized by a Learning Management System. As in the case of the human-machine conceptualizations in previous eras of military research and development, the interaction between the learner and processed content—the human-computer dyad constituted here by "delivery device" and "learner"—is a subject of considerable concern in SCORM as well. Indeed, Fletcher (2005) envisions the development of a new kind of "instructional grammar" for this interaction, enabling a coupling of human and computer in a manner that mimics the ease and fluency of "conversation": "...the ADL vision is that training, education, and performance aiding will take the form of human-computer...*conversations* tailored to each learner's or user's needs, skills, knowledge, abilities, and interests" (p. 4; emphasis in original). Fletcher goes on to characterize these conversational interactions in terms of a

> generative capability [that] requires the system to devise on demand—not draw from predicted and pre-stored formats—interactions with students. [...] These interactions must be generated from information primitives using an 'instructional grammar' that is analogous to the deep structure grammar of linguistics." (p. 7)

The interactive responses of the learner in such an instructional conversation complete the circle: they are fed back into the system, and recorded down to the smallest detail, closing the systems-theoretical feedback loop in this configuration, forming a kind of "instructional" closed world. In this way, values and understandings associated with the closed world of the Cold War are effectively "encoded" in a grand vision for the educational application of computer and Internet technologies.

Conclusion: Learning as a Weapon System?

This short overview of military discourses and their relationship to those of e-learning and educational technology not only shows how closely this discourse is tied to the strategic interests of the U.S. military; it also intimates the ways in which these interests are encroaching—both in conceptual-metaphorical and material terms—into other educational sectors. The material encroachment grows out of the need of the U.S. military for broad acceptance and implementation of its computer standards and frameworks. This finds its most concrete expression in the form of ADL "co-labs" and "partnership labs," which have been established in receptive American academic and corporate settings and nations: Australia, Canada, Great Britain, and South Korea. Central to the purposes of these labs is "the development and acceptance of global [i.e., SCORM-based] e-learning standards" (ADL, 2007a). One prominent and recent example of this is provided by the South Korean Cyber-Home Learning System, a national technology infrastructure program that utilizes SCORM to furnish an "organic system of...resources that support independent study over the Internet that matches the learning level of each student" (Park, 2006, p. 6).

Currently being used by 840,000 students in Korea, the program claims to be the "first e-Learning system to be distributed nationwide and applied to the K-12 areas" (Cho, 2006), and as Fletcher and others (2007) point out, the users of this system are employing thousands of "ADL instructional objects daily" (p. 98).

In considering the more general influence of ADL and SCORM, it is important to emphasize that the history of the support and maturation of the ADL initiative is a varied one.[5] Judging by the nature of recent ADL activity—and the tone and quantity of Fletcher's and others' recent publications (e.g., Brumfield, 2006)—this initiative appears to be currently staging a new offensive to establish its standards and overall approach as *the* "global interoperability framework for technology-enabled learning, education and training" (Barr & Richards, 2007). In keeping with this universalist goal, ADL has recently proposed the formation of a consortium to undertake "stewardship" of SCORM standards, and expand their support and adoption. Again it is Fletcher (2007), echoing concerns from the legacy of the Ada programming language, who provides a clear explanation as to why this is being done: to provide "help" to ADL, to enable the "learning enterprise to grow (in a way that helps us [i.e., the U.S. military])" and to "get to the future." Of course, the question is whether or not other educational sectors and stakeholders wish to "get to" the same future as the U.S. military, its contractors, and trainers. It is clear that ADL needs the larger e-learning community to sustain its vision. The question is: Does the e-learning community need it?

The metaphors and the discourse of the Cold War closed world are not difficult to recognize in these and earlier descriptions of "total" scientific, technological solutions—solutions that, in effect, use

---

5. Military support for ADL was disrupted, at least periodically and superficially, by Donald Rumsfeld's "declaration of war" on Pentagon inertia and bureaucracy (Rumsfeld, 2001), and by the development of alternative and even more grandiose plans for a new, exclusively military "Global Information Grid" that would vastly supersede the capabilities of the Internet and Web (National Security Agency, 2008). In early 2004, flush with the initial successes of Afghanistan and Iraq, funding for the Clinton legacy represented by ADL was all but eliminated. But with the ensuing reversal in Rumsfeld's fortunes, fresh life has been breathed into ADL and SCORM—as well as into many weapons systems following Cold War paradigms.

the power of computers and networks to vanquish the "evils" of ignorance and inefficient learning. It is also not difficult to see how U.S. military thinking or values—for example, its prioritization of technological and engineering approaches, its emphasis on "absolute" solutions to human problems—are articulated as a kind of technical code in the standards and systems of SCORM and ADL. In the context of these initiatives, it is also easy to see how the values, interests, and the culture of the U.S. military are encoded in online systems, standards, and technologies. In the light of its Cold War history, and of the recent engagement of the United States in Afghanistan and Iraq, the nature of these interests and values is fairly clear. Not only do these military interests involve total, technical solutions to complex problems though high-tech command and control, but they also include the extension of these solutions globally, for purposes that even its advocates characterize as imperial and hegemonic.

Despite the values, priorities, and power of the U.S. military, it is fairly obvious that their expression in related e-learning designs and programs is practically problematic. First, there is the question of economies of scale. As emphasized at the outset of this chapter, the size of the U.S. military and its investments in training and related technologies are unparalleled. Other, public education systems, meanwhile, are not only frequently underfunded, they are also generally constituted on local or regional levels (South Korea is a notable exception to this). The result is that the value and viability of a *global* educational framework or infrastructure are cast into serious doubt. Second, there is an important technical and engineering argument. Repeated failures in artificial intelligence (generally undertaken in the military-industrial complex over the course of the Cold War) have shown that the reproduction of human-like conversational (or instructional) interactions are impossible with current computer architectures. Computer scientists have themselves said such goals delimit an *unproductive research direction* (e.g., see Gams, Paprzyski, & Wu, 1997; Whitby, 1996. These issues have been discussed in greater detail in chapters four and five.) Related research has shown that languages and interactions cannot be reduced to "informational primitives" or "deep structures" as Fletcher and others would have it (e.g., Dreyfus, 1992). There is no "natural science" of micro-level (or even macro-level) educational action and interaction; and ongoing research has tended to confirm that these interactions are inextricably bound to elements like context and embodiment that resist quantification and formalization (e.g., Lave & Wenger, 1990; Varela, Thompson, & Rosch, 1991). Finally, and arguing more generally, the natural-scientific and techno-centric closed world articulated in ADL and the SCORM itself has a dubious historical record. It crystallized initially in order to defeat an "evil empire," a geopolitical threat that no longer exists (or many would argue, never existed). Historical research shows that Cold War weaponry and ways of thinking contributed little to the eventual diminution of this threat, but instead, actually created new threats in Afghanistan, Iraq, and other geopolitical hotspots in which these same paradigms are again being anachronistically re-applied (Johnson, 2004).

Despite the enormous and ongoing influence of the Pentagon on e-learning techniques and technologies, different directions in the future development of this fledgling field still seem possible. Just as the development of technologies and the values they encode and express is not inevitable, the development of e-learning as a field itself is not beyond reconsideration and redirection. This development can follow the hegemonic code that is articulated in grandiose technical frameworks, programs, and projections; or the technology can be recoded to work *against* ambitions of control and even empire, to address changing and heterogenous needs of education. Recent developments in psychology (e.g., P.N. Edwards, 1997), human-computer systems design (e.g., Suchman, 2007), technology studies (Hutchby, 2001), and other fields emphasize the irreducibly situated, discursive, embodied nature of human learning and activity in general. These developments are just a few examples that could provide a theoretical and methodological orientation for such a recoding.

This question of coding for e-learning technologies is not merely a matter of theory; it is also an issue of practical action. One example of the practical application of recoding e-learning technologies is illustrated in recent attempts by the I-KIT (Institute for Knowledge Innovation and Technology) Unit at the University of Toronto to undertake e-learning research for an American military contractor. Student and public opposition to these attempts resulted in an administrative decision to impose a local moratorium on funding of this kind for educational research at this institution (PAMO, 2005). Researchers in these and other disciplines and institutions are being forced to decide whether to facilitate or call into question their role in this and a range of other military involvements in research and practice. Critical theory can help considerably in this questioning by illuminating the nature of these involvements, by showing how they are "codified" in both discourse and design, and also by pointing to positive alternatives.

Conclusion

Plurality versus Synthesis

In the introduction to this book, two different visions of e-learning research were compared and contrasted. One envisions research in this fledgling field as being technology-oriented and as contributing to improvements in the accessibility, effectiveness, and efficiency of learning. The other, which is central to this book, sees e-learning research as "multivocal," as encompassing a plurality of "separate voices, each with its own potentially productive tale to tell..." (Conole & Oliver, 2007, p. 5). The variety of research methodologies and also subjects for research presented in the chapters in this book illustrate what it means for e-learning to be undertaken as a multivocal enterprise.

At the same time, the many voices constituting "multivocal" research are not always all in harmony. Some use different vocabularies to articulate separate standpoints, resulting in quite different or even contradictory (but internally consistent) accounts of principles and priorities important to the field. Accordingly, the approaches to research in e-learning presented in this book are not entirely or necessarily mutually compatible: they tend to be as they are associated with different presuppositions or ways of knowing and understanding the myriad phenomena related to this rich subject matter. However, this does not mean that these multiple approaches and understandings are not profitable or productive. Multivocal approaches to e-learning research can, among other things, enrich practical understanding (for example, of the use of blogs in the writing classroom); these approaches can contribute to improvements in practice (for example, through the kinds of "effects of increased awareness" listed in chapter seven); multivocal research can also illuminate unexpected or improvised applications (as was done in the study of students "epistolary" orientation to online discussion); finally, this kind of research can also democratize questions of access and efficiency (for example, by asking about "efficiency and accessibility for whom?" as was done in the two previous chapters).

In addition, this multivocal approach—and its emphasis on politics, history and culture—reveals an important aspect of technology that is ignored in many e-learning discussions. This is the influence of technology on theory and research. Chapters three, four and nine, for example, all make the case in different ways that technology is not simply something that we study, develop and control. Technology is something that also shapes and influences *us* as researchers. Whether it be the "epistolary" form of the online posting, the hypothesis of mind as machine, or the metaphor of the closed world, technology affects research: Previous technologies shape the way that current technologies are interpreted and used; new and conspicuous technologies provide powerful metaphors for understanding epistemology and the mind; and computerized systems provide discursive tools for conceptualizing solutions to educational as well as political problems. Our relationship as researchers to computer technology is not a one way street: Technologies shape and influence research and development in unexpected ways—through historical, cultural, discursive, and other forms of influence and transference.

As indicated in the introduction, this kind of methodological plurality—encompassing cultural, historical, and other approaches—is *not* the dominant or most widely promulgated approach to e-learning. This is why the book advocates a "re-thinking of e-learning research." This conclusion makes the case that the re-thinking of e-learning research as multivocal is both practical and timely. The more dominant position in this field is exemplified by the definition of e-learning research cited in the introduction: as a technology-oriented activity aimed at achieving practical improvements. This definition, formulated by educational technologist Rob Koper, implies that there is only one knowledge form that can legitimately be used to investigate e-learning activities, technologies, and practices. This kind of knowledge is instrumental, causally oriented, predictive, and natural-scientific in nature. At the same time, this knowledge is seen by Koper and other researchers as situated within a greater whole, as a part of a much larger coordinated research enterprise, one that also focuses on natural-scientific, causally oriented knowledge. It is this greater epistemological or investigative whole, that is generally identified as a "new" and "interdisciplinary" "science of learning." This new "learning science" emerged from the United States in the 1990's, and has recently been gaining in dominance internationally (Rourke & Friesen, 2006):

This is a new kind of science, with the goal of providing a sound scientific foundation for education. [It is] centrally concerned with exactly what is going on in a learning environment, and exactly how it is contributing to improved student performance... [It is] based on research emerging from psychology, computer science, philosophy, sociology, and other scientific [*sic*] disciplines. (Sawyer, 2006a, pp. 2, 10, 15)

Many who refer to themselves as "learning scientists" see this new, interdisciplinary scientific endeavor as combining different "strands" of research to "create more coherent and useful theories that better illuminate how, when, where, and why people learn" (Bransford, Brown, & Cocking, 2006, p. 227). Learning scientists also see this type of research as forming part of a larger "synthesis," "hybrid," or a "synergistic" theoretical whole (Bransford et al., 2006; Sawyer, 2006a, p. 13). As was the case with Koper's definition of e-learning research, learning scientists recognize only one form of knowledge as being ultimately of value in this research. As the name "learning science(s)" suggests, this is the instrumental, causal, and predictive knowledge proper to the natural sciences.

The preeminence of this "instrumental" knowledge form is illustrated by characterizations of what learning science is and what it is likely to become. As Sawyer (2006b) explains, learning science affirms the "controlled" natural-scientific "experiment" as representing the "gold standard" for evidence or "for evaluating what works best to improve learning" (p. 575). Sawyer also explains that learning scientists see their research enterprise as gradually "becoming more like" what he describes as "big science" (p. 576). This refers to "complex, difficult and expensive [research that is] almost impossible for any one scholar to do alone" or over a short period of time. It is a kind of inquiry, moreover, that is undertaken by sizeable teams of "software developers, teacher educators, research assistants [and other] scholars" (p. 576) collaborating in the context of multiyear research projects: "Because it requires such a massive human effort," this type of research, Sawyer continues, "has tended to occur at a small number of universities where there is a critical mass of faculty and graduate students" (p. 576). In the American context, this has come to mean a few large, top-ranked research-intensive universities (e.g., Stanford, Carnegie Mellon, and the University of Washington).

The multivocal approach to e-learning research advocated in this book is intentionally very different. It understands valuable research in e-learning as something that can occur in a wide variety of contexts and through a wide variety of means. These can include the critical analysis of policy or other documents, the content analysis of sets of online communications, or even informal qualitative or hermeneutic interviews over coffee. They can include research that is undertaken as a part of a course; as a semester-long project; or for a paper, thesis, or dissertation. This multivocal research, moreover, can also be undertaken alone (as illustrated in the authorship of many of the chapters of this book) or collaboratively (as illustrated in chapter seven). At the same time, all of this does not mean that the kind of research advocated here is simple, easy, or always straightforward. It generally requires that the researcher be conversant with more than one disciplinary body of knowledge and research method or set of heuristics. What is important, though, is that this research doesn't *have to* be an expensive multiyear project undertaken by large interdisciplinary teams with the latest instrumentation and at the largest universities. And given the humble economies of scale that are often found in many educational and research contexts, questions of expense, size, and complexity of research projects is not just a matter of theory or design. They can make the difference between some research activity and none at all.

If the "learning sciences" in general, and related conceptions of e-learning in particular, can be said to focus on "technical," "instrumental," and scientific knowledge, then the multivocal research explored and demonstrated in this book counters this by placing emphasis on *both* "practical" and "emancipatory" knowledge forms. While this book certainly does not reject or exclude technical or scientific knowledge, its epistemological concerns lie elsewhere: in political and critical knowledge (on the one hand) and in the practical, everyday, interpretive, and hermeneutic methods (on the other). Of course, its critique of "e-learning myths" and of the political history of e-learning corresponds to the critical and emancipatory. Its investigations of narrative, genre, conversation, and the experience of "lived number" rest squarely on pragmatic and hermeneutic foundations. At the same time, the discussion of "no significant difference" results (in chapters one and two), the heuristics of content analysis (in chapter three), as well as the use of empirical economic and other sources (in chapter eight and elsewhere), represents a significant use of "technical" and/or "instrumental" knowledge.

The multivocal understanding of research illustrated here, in other words, definitely includes—rather than just critiquing—the voice or knowledge type of the natural sciences. But, of course, unlike the learning sciences, it does not seek to establish a "synergy" or even an integrated hierarchy of different knowledge forms, with the "gold standard" of the controlled scientific experiment at the top. Instead, this alternative understanding of research sees different knowledge forms as related in ways that are complex and contradictory: different knowledge claims are motivated by different human and political interests that are in mutual tension or explicit conflict. This book has correspondingly not attempted to mask these differences and contradictions. Chapter four (on "psychology and technology"), for example, presents a sustained examination of the tensions and "conflicts of interest" between psychology and important developments in the related areas of anthropology, artificial intelligence, and in everyday technology.

Multiple ways of knowing and multiple definitions of what counts as evidence also imply a plurality of ways of judging and evaluating investigative findings. To cite Jerome Bruner (1986) again, each knowledge form has its own "operating principles," "criteria of well-formedness," and "procedures for verification" (p. 11). Each research methodology and each account of e-learning research, in other words, brings with it particular criteria by which its results can be judged. These criteria, however, are closely tied to the epistemological or philosophical presuppositions or foundations that underlie a given research approach (which is the principal reason why philosophical foundations have been emphasized in this book). Differences in philosophical and research presuppositions have been illustrated in Bruner's distinction between logico-scientific and narrative knowledge forms; but these differences are also found in other methodologies for e-learning research discussed here. For example, experiential evidence (see chapter six) and the way it is treated and evaluated is quite different from the evidence associated with content analysis (see chapter three): Experiential evidence that is generated through hermeneutic-phenomenological research takes the form of written descriptions, which are often gleaned from interviews and observation, and are developed and validated through reading and rewriting processes. Content analysis, on the other hand, involves specific names, events, or figures of speech present in textual and other media. This second type of evidence is gathered through processes of counting and coding content elements and can be validated through tests of "coder reliability." These differences, in turn, are extended further in the way that communication and other foundational or philosophical understandings are articulated in each method. In content analysis, communication is understood (often implicitly) as the transmission of information or content elements through the medium from writer to reader or producer to audience. In the case of hermeneutic phenomenology, communication is understood as the cultivation of a shared atmosphere or disposition. That is why evidence and its validation is undertaken through the development of descriptions that evoke "atmospheres" or "dispositions" of different kinds. Each approach and set of understandings, though, is rigorous in its own way and answerable to its own stringent criteria.

The Practicality of "Multivocality"

There are a number of reasons why the multivocal approach advocated and illustrated in this book is both practical and important for e-learning research at this point in its development. As noted above, this type of research can be viable and practical in terms of expense, scale, and related logistical considerations. Other grounds for its utility and practicality become obvious when it is compared to existing scientific, experimental "gold standard" research. As indicated earlier, the "gold standard" for research in the learning sciences is provided by rigorously implemented experimental research designs (ideally) involving fully randomized test populations and strict controls for confounding variables. This implies that in a rigorous study of this kind, there should be two randomly selected groups of students, one that is offered a treatment (typically in the form of an innovation in media or technology), and another that receives no treatment.

At the same time, it is widely recognized — even by learning scientists themselves — that rigorous experimental research designs and controls are difficult if not impossible to realize in authentic educational contexts:

> A genuine control is impossible. Practical difficulties in separating [control and treatment] groups often result in contamination of designs. Educational issues are complex with many variables involved. Therefore, experimental designs with limited numbers of [variables] result in oversimplification because they deal with only a few of the relevant factors. Particular types of innovation are not precisely reproducible so generalisation can be misleading. (Kember, 2003, p. 89)

In actual educational contexts, in other words, students are organized in cohorts, according to schedules and programs that are deliberate and structured, making random selection difficult. At the same time, students in these settings are investing time, effort, and often money to learn. This can place the definition of control groups in conflict with the priorities of both the students and the institution. Speaking more generally, the terms "education" and "learning" designate the widest range of age groups, activities, methods, practices, and settings, making generalization about the effect of a particular technique or technology open to question.

In addition to the practical difficulties presented by the experimental "gold standard," there is also the question of what such experimental research has already produced. This was discussed in some detail in the first and second chapters in terms of media comparison studies and the widely reported yet controversial "no significant difference" phenomenon: The fact is that hundreds of studies, undertaken over dozens of years "document no [statistically] significant differences...in student outcomes between alternate modes of" or innovations in "education delivery" (Russell, 2008). The repeated, inconclusive character of these results presents strong arguments against the continued implementation and reproduction of such studies.

As indicated earlier, there is no clear consensus of learning scientists and other advocates of scientific approaches in e-learning on how to address these challenges. Some researchers call for more rigorous, better-funded, and larger-scale experimental research (e.g., Lou, Bernard, & Abrami, 2006). Others—especially those associated with the learning sciences—have argued for the adaptation and augmentation of "gold standard" designs with other methodologies. Some have at times advocated the use of approaches like ethnomethodology (Koschmann, Stahl, & Zemel, 2007) and even phenomenology (e.g., Erickson, 2007). Either implicitly or explicitly, they make the case that these methods can be combined with the experimental designs of "learning science" to form a kind of "hybrid methodology" (e.g., Barab & Squire, 2004; Sawyer, 2006a, p. 13). Experimental constructs such as controls and dependent and independent variables, however, are still given priority in these new, multimethod hybrid designs. The existence of contradictions or even mutually exclusive differences among approaches, voices, or knowledge types remain little discussed or acknowledged. The fact that, for example, both hermeneutic phenomenology and ethnomethodology are based on a repudiation of the detached, objective stance or epistemology expressed in terms such as "experiment," "variable," or "control" is passed over in conspicuous silence.

One notable exception to this silence is provided by McCarthy and Wright in their book *Technology as Experience* (2004; see also chapter seven, above). These authors see the synthesis of research methods with mutually exclusive preconditions and presuppositions as problematic. They argue that it leads to "the problem of watered-down concepts in service of design" (pp. 45–47). They focus on the specific concept of "communities of practice"—and the "dialectical tensions" internal to it—to show how interdisciplinary, hybrid, design-oriented research forms can significantly "weaken" the richness and complexity of the concepts constitutive of them. The term "community of practice," they argue,

> is used in research concerned with technology and education...[in such a way that its] dialectical tension is minimized and [its complexity reduced]... to the point where individual experience is rendered irrelevant. From our perspective, what appears to be lost when this happens is the...[ability to authentically bind] concepts together in practice...without which the concepts...float free and meaningless[ly]. (p. 46)

Like this book, McCarthy and Wright recommend and deploy an approach to researching technological engagement that uses multiple methods and orientations. In both cases, however, any new, overarching methodological synthesis is avoided and deliberate attention is paid to the individual, theoretical integrity of each method. In this way, it is possible to circumvent a "watering down" or dilution of concepts, heuristics, and traditions. The diversity and integrity of individual methods can be preserved, and these methods can then be utilized in their undiluted strength to tackle difficult research problems and questions.

What is needed in the world of new and proliferating e-learning practices are research approaches that are multiple and variable, and that recognize their heterogeneity explicitly. As argued in the introduction, the brief history of e-learning has been one in which its forms, technologies, and practices have expanded and propagated widely and even wildly. In just over a decade, the field has moved from mechanical matters of effective bulletin board communication and Web page construction to questions and issues that are vastly more complex, such as the online construction of meaning and identity; the educational response to self-organizing and open online communities; and the challenge of authentically interdisciplinary inquiry into these phenomena. Dealing with this plurality of proliferating issues, technologies, and practices calls for approaches to research that are similarly flexible, multiple, and differentiated.

Bibliography

Abbate, J. (1999). *Inventing the Internet.* Cambridge, MA: MIT Press.

Abrams, M.H. (1999). *A glossary of literary terms,* 7th ed. Fort Worth: Harcourt Brace Jovanovich College.

ADL (2007a). *ADL common questions.* Accessed August 30, 2008 from http://www.adlnet.gov/help/CommonQuestions/ADLCommonQuestions. aspx

_____. (2007b). Advanced distributed learning, Accessed August 30, 2008 from: http://www.adlnet.gov

Adorno, T. (1981). *Minima moralia: Reflections from a damaged life.* London: Verso.

_____. (2003). Education after Auschwitz. In R. Tiedemann (Ed.), *Can one live after Auschwitz? A philosophical reader.* Stanford, CA: Stanford UP, pp. 19–33.

Agre, P. (1997). *Computation and human experience.* Cambridge: Cambridge UP.

Akera, A. (2007). *Calculating a natural world: Scientists, engineers, and computers during the rise of U.S. Cold War research.* Cambridge, MA: MIT Press.

Altman, J.G. (1982). *Epistolarity: Approaches to a form.* Columbus: Ohio State UP.

Altman, R. (1999). *Film/genre.* London: British Film Institute.

Anderson, T. (2003). Getting the mix right again: An updated and theoretical rationale for interaction. *The International Review of Research in Open and Distance Learning,* 4, 2. Accessed January 24, 2007 from: http://www.irrodl.org/index.php/irrodl/article/view/149/230

Antaki, C. (2002). An introduction to conversation analysis. Accessed August 25, 2008 from: http://www-staff.lboro.ac.uk/~ssca1/sitemenu.htm

Ausubel, D.P. (1960). The use of advance organizers in the learning and retention of meaningful verbal material. *Journal of Educational Psychology,* 51, 267–272

Barab, S. A., & Squire, K. D. (2004). Design-based research: putting our stake in the ground. *Journal of the Learning Sciences* 13(1), 1–14.

Barr, A., & Richards, T. (2007). *International federation for LET systems interoperability: Prospectus.* Accessed August 30, 2008 from: http://aicc.org/blog/downloads/LETSIProspectus20070201rev2.pdf

Barry, A. (1991). *Technobabble.* Cambridge, MA: MIT Press.

Barry, P. (2002). *Beginning theory: An introduction to literary and cultural theory.* Manchester: Manchester UP.

Barthes, R. (1972). *Mythologies.* London: Jonathan Cape.

Baskin, R.R., & Schneider, D.L. (2002). Learning as a weapon system. *I/ITSEC 2002 conference proceedings.* Accessed August 30, 2008 from: http://www.iitsec.org/authordir/2002_PMR_Learning%20as%20a%20Weapon%20System.PDF

Baylor, A.L., & Kim, Y. (2005). Simulating instructional roles through pedagogical agents. *International Journal of Artificial Intelligence in Education,* 15, 95–115. Accessed April 8, 2008 from: http://aied.inf.ed.ac.uk/abstract/Vol_15/Baylor05.html

Bechtel, W., Graham, G., & Abrahamsen, A. (1998). Preface. In W. Bechtel & G. Graham (Eds.), *A companion to cognitive science.* Oxford: Basil Blackwell, pp. xiii–xvi.

Becker, G. (1991). Pietism's confrontation with enlightenment rationalism: An examination of the relation between ascetic Protestantism and science. *Society for the Scientific Study of Religion,* 30(2), 139–158.

Beers P.J., Boshuizen, H.P.A., Kirschner, P.A., & Gijselaers, W.H. (2007). The analysis of negotiation of common ground in CSCL. *Learning and Instruction,* 17(4), 427–435.

Bell, D. (1999). *The coming of the post-industrial society: A venture in social forecasting.* New York: Basic Books.

Benjamin, W. (1968a). The storyteller: Reflections on the works of Nikolai Leskov. In H. Arendt (Ed.), *Illuminations: Essays and reflections.* New York: Schocken Books.

_____. (1968b). The work of art in the age of mechanical reproduction. In H. Arendt (Ed.), *Illuminations: Essays and reflections.* New York: Schocken Books.

Benner, P.E. (1994). *Interpretive phenomenology: Embodiment, caring, and ethics in health and illness.* Thousand Oaks, CA: Sage.

Bereiter, C. (2002). *Education and mind in the knowledge age.* Mahwah, NJ: Lawrence Erlbaum.

Bereiter, C., & Scardamalia, M. (1992). Cognition and curriculum. In P.W. Jackson (Ed.), *Handbook of research on curriculum.* Old Tappan, NJ: Macmillan.

Berger, A.A. (1992). *Popular culture genres: Theories and texts.* Thousand Oaks, CA: Sage.

Biesta, G. (2004). "Mind the gap!" Communication and educational relation. In C. Bingham & A. Sidorkin (Eds.), *No education without relation.* New York: Peter Lang, pp. 11–22.

Bleeker H., & Mulderij K. (1992) The experience of motor disability. *Phenomenology + Pedagogy* 10, 1–18.

Blog. (2008, August 26). In *Wikipedia, The Free Encyclopedia.* Retrieved 16:20, August 28, 2008, from http://en.wikipedia.org/w/index.php?title=Blog&oldid=234419569

Bock, K., & Garnsey, S.M. (1999). Chapter 14: Language processing. In W. Bechtel & G. Graham (Eds.), *A companion to cognitive science.* Malden, MA: Blackwell, pp. 226–234.

Boden, M.A. (2006). Cognitive science. *Encyclopedia of philosophy,* 2nd ed., vol. 2. New York: Macmillan Reference, pp. 296–301.

Bogen, D., & Lynch, M. (1989). Taking account of the hostile native: Plausible deniability and the production of conventional history in the Iran-Contra Hearings. *Social Problems,* 36, 197–224.

Bonk, C., & Cunningham, D.J. (1998). Searching for learner-centered, constructivist, and sociocultural components of collaborative educational learning tools. In C. Bonk & K. King (Eds.), *Electronic collaborators: Learner-centered technologies for literacy, apprenticeship, and discourse.* Mahwah, NJ: Lawrence Erlbaum.

Borg, W.R., & Gall, M.D. (1989). *Educational research.* New York: Longman.

Bottomore, T. (1983). *A dictionary of Marxist thought.* Oxford: Basil Blackwell.

Bourne, J., Harris, D., & Mayadas, F. (2005). Online engineering education: Learning anywhere, anytime. *Journal of Asychronous Learning Networks,* 9,1, http://www.aln.org/publications/jaln/v9n1/v9n1_bourne_member.asp

Bransford, J.D., Brown, A.L., & Cocking, R.R. (Eds.) (2000). *How people learn: Brain, mind, experience and school.* Washington, DC: National Academy Press.

Bransford, J., Stevens, R., Schwartz, D., Meltzoff, A., Pea, R., Roschelle, J., Vye, N., Kuhl, P., Bell, P., Barron, B., Reeves, B., Sabelli, N. (2006) Learning theories and education: Toward a decade of synergy. In: Alexander, P.A. & Winne, P.H. *Handbook of educational psychology.* Mahwah, NJ: Lawrence Erlbaum, pp. 209–244.

Bromley, H. & Apple, M.W. (1998). *Education/technology/power: educational computing as a social practice.* New York: SUNY Press.

Brumfield, R. (2006). Gathering SCORM could transform eLearning: Emerging standard enables accessibility, interoperability of digital content. *eSchool News Online,* April 7. Accessed August 30, 2008 from: http://www.eschoolnews.com/news/showStory.cfm?ArticleID=6249

Bruner, J.S. (1966). *Toward a theory of instruction.* New York: W.W. Norton.

_____. (1986). *Actual minds, possible worlds.* Cambridge, MA: Harvard UP.

_____. (1990). *Acts of meaning.* Cambridge, MA: Harvard UP.

_____. (1991). The narrative construction of reality. *Critical Inquiry,* 18(1), 1–21.

Bruner, J.S., & Goodman, C.C. (1947). Value and need as organizing factors in perception. *Journal of Abnormal and Social Psychology,* 42, 33–44.

Brzezinski, Z. (1970). *Between two ages: America's role in the technetronic era.* New York: Viking.

Bull, G., Bull, G., Garofalo, J., & Harris, J. (2002). Grand challenges: Preparing for the technological tipping point. *Learning & Leading with Technology.* Accessed May 29, 2008 from: http://www.iste.org/Content/NavigationMenu/Publications/

LL/LLIssues/Volume_29_2001_2002_/May15/Bonus_Feature_Grand_Challeng es_Vignettes.htm

Burgess, T.F. (2001). A general introduction to the design of questionnaires for survey research. Accessed May 29, 2008 from: http://www.leeds.ac.uk/iss/documen-tation/top/top2.pdf

Burnett, R., & Marshall, P.D. (2003). *Web theory: An introduction*. New York: Routledge.

Buytendijk, F.J.J. (1988). The first smile of the child. *Phenomenology + Pedagogy,* 6(1), 15–24.

Cairncross, F. (2001). *The death of distance: How the communications revolution will change our lives*. Boston: Harvard Business School Press.

Cameron, D., & Anderson, T. (2006). Comparing weblogs to threaded discussion tools in online educational contexts. *International Journal of Instructional Technology & Distance Learning,* 12(11). Accessed November 12, 2007 from: http://www.itdl.org/Journal/Nov_06/article01.htm

Carr, W., & Kemmis, S. (1986) *Becoming critical. Education, knowledge and action research*. Lewes: Falmer.

Carter, K. (1995). Teaching stories and local understandings. *The Journal of Educational Research,* 88(6), 326–330.

Chambers J., (1999). Convergence for business education and entertainment key note address , November 16, COMDEX, Las Vegas, Nevada, November 16–19.

Chandler, D. (1995). Technological or media determinism. Accessed April 27, 2008 from: http://www.aber.ac.uk/media/Documents/tecdet/tecdet.html

Charlesworth, S.J. (2000). *A phenomenology of working-class experience*. Cambridge: Cambridge UP.

Chase, S.E. (2005). Narrative inquiry: Multiple lenses, approaches, voices. In N.K. Denzin and Y.S. Lincoln (Eds.), *The Sage handbook of qualitative research*, 3rd ed. Thousand Oaks, CA: Sage, pp. 651–679.

Cho, Y.-S. (2006). Case of using SCORM in the cyber home learning system. Accessed April 1, 2008 from: http://www.adlnet.gov/downloads/AuthNotReqd.aspx?FileName=IP2D0118T1715TR1.ppt&ID=90

Chiu, K.-Y., Stewart, B., & Ehlert, M. (2003). Relationships among student demographic characteristics, student academic achievement, student satisfaction, and online business—Course quality factors. *NAWeb*. Accessed May 15, 2008 from: http://www.unb.ca/naweb/proceedings/2003/PaperChiu.html

Clandinin, D.J., & Connelly, F.M. (2000). *Narrative inquiry: Experience and story in qualitative research*. San Francisco: Jossey-Bass.

Clark, A. (1997). *Being there: putting brain, body and world together again.* Cambridge,, MA: MIT Press.

Clark, R.C., & Mayer, R.E. (2003). *E-learning and the science of instruction.* San Francisco: Jossey-Bass Pfeiffer.

CBNC. (2005). Report for the Aboriginal Voice Ontario E-Learning Forum. Crossing Boundaries National Council. Accessed April 27, 2008, from: http://www.crossingboundaries.ca/images.av/content/ontario_e-learning_report.pdf

Conole, G., & Oliver, M. (Eds.) (2007). *Contemporary perspectives in E-learning research: Themes, methods and impact on practice.* Routledge: London.

Cooper, P. (1993). Paradigm shifts in designed instruction: From behaviorism to cognitivism to constructivism. *Educational Technology,* 33(5), 12–19.

Craig, S., Gholson, B., & Driscoll, D. (2002). Animated pedagogical agents in multimedia educational environments: Effects of agent properties, pictures features, and redundancy. *Journal of Educational Psychology,* 94(2), 428–434.

Craik, F., & Lockhart, R. (1972). Levels of processing: A framework for memory research. *Journal of Verbal Learning & Verbal Behavior,* 11, 671–684

CSTB Computer Science and Telecommunications Board (1997). *Ada and Beyond: Software policies for the department of defense.* Washington, DC: National Academy Press, http://www.nap.edu/openbook.php?isbn=0309055970

Cuban, L. (1986). *Teachers and machines the classroom use of technology since 1920.* New York: Teachers College Press.

Cuban, L. (2003). *Oversold and underused: Computers in the classroom.* Cambridge,, MA: Harvard UP.

Danesi, M. (2004). *The liar paradox and the Towers of Hanoi: The ten greatest puzzles of all time.* Hoboken, NJ: John Wiley.

De Vaney, A., & Butler, R. (1996). Voices of the founders: Early discourses in educational technology. In D. Jonassen (Ed.), *Handbook of research on educational And communications and technology.* New York: Simon & Schuster Macmillan, pp. 13–90.

Derrida, J. (1976). *Speech and phenomena.* Baltimore: Johns Hopkins UP.

Descartes, R. (1985). *The philosophical writings of Descartes,* vol. 1, J. Cottingham, R. Stoothoff, & D. Murdoch (Eds.). Cambridge: Cambridge UP.

Descartes, R. (1988). *Descartes: Selected philosophical writings.* Cambridge: Cambridge UP.

Dick, W. (1987). A history of instructional design and its impact on education psychology. In J.A. Glover & R.R. Ronning (Eds.), *Historical foundations of educational psychology.* New York: Springer, pp. 183–200.

Dillenbourg, P. (1996). Distributing cognition over brains and machines. In S. Vosniadou, E. De Corte, B. Glaser, & H. Mandl (Eds.), *International perspectives on the psychological foundations of technology-based learning environments*. Mahwah, NJ: Lawrence Erlbaum.

Dillon, A., & Gushrowski, B. (2000). Genres and the Web: Is the personal home page the first uniquely digital genre? *Journal of the American Society for Information Science,* 51(2), 202–205.

Dobson, T.M. (2002). Keeping in touch by electronic mail. In Max van Manen (Ed.), *Writing in the dark: Phenomenological studies in interpretive inquiry*. London, ON: Althouse Press, pp. 98–115.

Dourish, P. (2001). *Where the action is: The foundations of embodied interaction*. Cambridge, MA: MIT Press.

Draaisma, D. (2000) *Metaphors of memory: A history of ideas about the mind*. Cambridge: Cambridge UP.

Dreyfus, H.L. (1991). *Being-in-the-world: A commentary on Heidegger's "Being and Time", division I*. Cambridge, MA: MIT Press.

_____. (1992). *What computers still can't do: A critique of artificial reason*. Cambridge, MA: MIT Press.

Drucker, P.T. (1994). The age of social transformation. *The Atlantic Monthly,* November, 53–79.

Drucker, P.T. (1997, March 10). An interview with Peter Drucker. *Forbes Magazine* 126–127.

_____. (1997). Seeing things as they really are. *Forbes*, March 10, 127.

Duffy, T.M., & Cunningham, D.J. (1996). Constructivism: Implications for the design and delivery of instruction. In D.H. Jonassen (Ed.), *Handbook of research on educational communications and technology*. New York: Simon & Schuster Macmillan, pp. 170–198.

Educause. (2002). Moore's law and the conundrum of human learning. *Educause,* 37(3), Accessed August 30, 2008 from: http://www.educause.edu/ir/ library/pdf/erm0230.pdf

_____. (2007). Educause: What is Educause. Accessed August 28, 2008 from: http://www.educause.edu/

Edwards, D. (1997a). *Discourse and cognition*. London: Sage.

Edwards, D. (1997b). Toward a discursive psychology of classroom education. In C. Coll & D. Edwards (Eds.), *Teaching, learning and classroom discourse: Approaches to the study of educational discourse*. Madrid: Fundación Infancia y Aprendizaje, pp. 33–48.

Edwards, A. Gilroy, P., & Hartley D. (2002). *Rethinking teacher education: Collaborative responses to uncertainty*. London: Routledge Falmer.

Edwards, D., & Potter, J. (1992). *Discursive psychology*. London: Sage.

_____. (2005). Discursive psychology, mental states and descriptions. In H. te Molder & J. Potter (Eds.), *Conversation and cognition: Discourse, mind and social interaction*. Cambridge: Cambridge UP, pp. 241–259.

Edwards, P.N. (1997). *The closed world: Computers and the politics of discourse in Cold War America*. Cambridge, MA: MIT Press.

Engeström, Y. (1987). *Learning by expanding: An activity-theoretical approach to developmental research*. Helsinki: Orienta-Konsultit. Available at: http://lchc.ucsd.edu/MCA/Paper/Engestrom/expanding/toc.htm

Erickson, F. (2007). Ways of seeing video: Toward a phenomenology of viewing minimally edited footage. In R. Goldman, R. Pea, B. Barron, & S.J. Denny. *Video research in the learning sciences*. Mawah, NJ: Lawrence Erlbaum.

Ertmer, P.A., & Newby, T.J. (1993). Behaviorism, cognitivism, constructivism: Comparing critical features from an instructional design perspective. *Performance Improvement Quarterly*, 6(4), 50–70.

Evans, V., & Green, M. (2006). *Cognitive linguistics: An introduction*. Mahwah, NJ: Lawrence Erlbaum.

Fahy, P.J. (2005). Two methods for assessing critical thinking in computer-mediated communications (CMC) transcripts. *International Journal of Instructional Technology and Distance Learning*, 2(3). Accessed March 14, 2008 from: http://www.itdl.org/Journal/Mar_05/article02.htm

Feenberg, A. (2001). Democratizing technology: Interests, codes, rights. *The Journal of Ethics*, 5(2), 177–195.

_____. (2002). *Transforming technology: A critical theory revisited*. Oxford: Oxford UP.

Fisher, W.R. (1994). Narrative rationality and the logic of scientific discourse. *Argumentation*, 8, 21–32.

Fletcher, J.D. (2006). The advanced distributed (ADL) vision and getting from here to there. In H.F. O'Neil & R.S. Perez (Eds.), *Web-based learning: Theory, research and practice*. Manwah, NJ: Lawrence Erlbaum, pp. 31–54.

_____. (2007). Why ADL? Why LETSI? Presentation at the LETSI meeting, Institute for Education, University of London, March 18, 2007. PowerPoint presentation available at: http://adlcommunity.net/mod/resource/view.php?id=442

Fletcher, J.D., & Chatelier, P.R. (2000). Training and the military. In S. Tobias & J.D. Fletcher, *Training & retraining: A handbook for business, industry, government, and the military*. New York: Macmillan Reference, pp. 267–288.

Fletcher, J.D., & Johnston, R. (2007). Instructional technology: Effectiveness and implications for the intelligence community. In R. Johnson (Ed.) *Analytic culture in the U.S. intelligence community: An ethnographic study.* Washington DC: Center for the Study of Intelligence.

Fletcher, J.D., & Tobias, S. (2003). Implications of advanced distributed learning for education (Urban Diversity Series). New York: ERIC Clearinghouse on Urban Education, Teachers College, Columbia University.

Fletcher, J.D., Tobias, S., & Wisher, R.A. (2007). Learning anytime, anywhere: Advanced distributed learning and the changing face of education. *Educational Researcher,* March, pp. 96–102.

Flyvbjerg, B. (2001). *Making social science matter.* Cambridge: Cambridge UP.

Freeden, M. (2003). *Ideology: A very short introduction.* Oxford: Oxford UP.

Friesen, N. (2003). The student-computer relation: A phenomenology of its pedagogical significance. Department of Secondary Education, University of Alberta. Unpublished Dissertation. Accessed March 14, 2008 from: http://learningspaces.org/n/dissertation

_____. (2007). The experience of computer use: Expert knowledge and user know-how. *GLIMPSE: Phenomenology and Media, 7,* 55–70.

_____. (2008). Communication genres and the mediatic turn. *Siegener Periodicum zur internationalen empirischen Literaturwissenschaften,* 25(1), 105–115.

Futures Project (2001). The futures project: Policy for higher education in a changing world future policy scenario. In search of the new economy: Encouraging private competitors to fill the demand for skills. Accessed April 27, 2008 from: http://www.futuresproject.org/publications/globalya.pdf

Gadamer, H.G. (1989). *Truth and method,* 2nd rev. ed. New York: Continuum.

Galagan, P.A. (2000). The E-learning revolution. *Training and Development,* 54(12), 24–30. Accessed January 24, 2007 from: http://www.findarticles.com/p/articles/mi_m4467/is_12_54/ai_68217187

Gams, M., Paprzycki, M. & Wu, X. (Eds.) (1997). *Mind versus computer: Were Dreyfus and Winograd right?* Amsterdam: IOS Press.

Gandel, P.B., Katz, R.N., & Metros, S.E. (2004). The "weariness of the flesh": Reflections of the mind in an era of abundance. *Journal of Asynchronous Learning Networks,* 8(1), 70–79. Accessed April 27, 2008 from: http://www.sloan-c.org/publications/jaln/

Gardner, M. (1985). *The mind's new science: A history of the cognitive revolution.* New York: Basic Books.

Garfinkel, H. (1967). *Studies in ethnomethodology.* Englewood Cliffs, NJ: Prentice-Hall.

Garofoli, E., & Woodell, J. (2003). Faculty development and the diffusion of innovations. *Syllabus,* 16(6), 15–17.

Garrison, D.R., & Anderson, T. (2003). *E-learning in the 21st century: A framework for research and practice.* London: Routledge.

Garrison, D.R., Anderson, T., & Archer, W. (2000). Critical inquiry in a text-based environment: Computer conferencing in higher education. *The Internet and Higher Education,* 2(2–3), 87–105.

_____. (2001). Critical thinking, cognitive presence, and computer conferencing in distance education. *American Journal of Distance Education,* 15(1), 7–23.

Gee, J.P. (2007). Video games and embodiment. Accessed August 30, 2008 from: http://inkido.indiana.edu/aera%5F2007/

Geertz, C. (1986). Making experience, authoring selves. In V. Turner & E. Bruner (Eds.), *The anthropology of experience.* Urbana: University of Illinois Press, pp. 373–380.

Gergen, K.J., & Gigerenzer, G. (1991). Cognitivism and its discontents: An introduction to the issue. *Theory and Psychology,* 1(4). Accessed March 22, 2008 from: http://www.psych.ucalgary.ca/thpsyc/abstracts/abstracts_1.4/Gergen.html

Gigerenzer, G. (2000). *Adaptive thinking: Rationality in the real world.* Oxford: Oxford UP.

Gilbert, J. (2005). *Catching the knowledge wave? The knowledge society and the future of education.* Wellington, NZ: NZCER Press.

Ginsberg, H., & Opper, S. (1979). *Piaget's theory of intellectual development,* 2nd ed. Englewood Cliffs, NJ: Prentice-Hall.

Giorgi, A. (2006). Concerning variations in the application of the phenomenological method. *The Humanistic Psychologist,* 34(4), 305–319.

Goldman, R., Pea, R. D., Barron, B., & Derry, S. (2007). (Eds.). *Video research in the learning sciences.* Mahwah, NJ: Lawrence Erlbaum.

Haase, M. (2002). Living with "obsessive compulsive disorder." In van Manen (Ed.), *Writing in the dark.* London, ON: Althouse Press, pp. 52–83.

Habermas, J. (1970). Technology and science as "ideology." In J. Shapiro (Trans.), *Toward a rational society.* Boston: Beacon Press.

_____. (1989). *The structural transformation of the public sphere: An inquiry into a category of bourgeois society.* Cambridge, MA: MIT Press.

Hamilton, E. & Feenberg, A. (2005). The technical codes of online education, *eLearning,* 2(2), 104–121.

Heckman, R., & Annabi, H. (2003). A content analytic comparison of FtF and ALN case-study discussion. In proceedings of 36th Hawaii international conference on systems science, CD-Rom. Washington DC: IEEE Computer Society Press.

Heeman, C. & Andreazza, P.E. (2007). Individual learning through computers: An activity theory view. *Informática 2007*. Accessed September 10, 2008 from: http://www.informaticahabana.com/evento_virtual/?q=node/109&ev=XII%20 Congreso%20de%20Inform%C3%A1tica%20en%20la%20Educaci%C3%B3n

Heidegger, M. (1962). *Being and time*. New York: Harper.

_____. (1977). *Sein und Zeit*. Frankfurt am Main: Klostermann.

Hein, S.F., & Austin, W.J. (2001). Empirical and hermeneutic approaches to phenomenological research in psychology: A Comparison. *Psychological Methods*, 6, 3–17.

Held, D. (1980). *Introduction to critical theory: Horkheimer to Habermas*. Berkeley: University of California Press.

Henwood, D. (2003). *After the new economy*. New York: New Press.

Herring, S.C. (2000). Gender differences in CMC: Findings and implications. *Computer Professionals for Social Responsibility Newsletter*, 18(1). Accessed March 14, 2008 from: http://www.cpsr.org/issues/womenintech/herring

Hickey, D.T., Moore, A.L., & Pellegrino, J.W. (2001). The motivational and academic consequences of elementary mathematics environments: Do constructivist innovations and reforms make a difference? *American Educational Research Journal*, 38, 611–652.

Hilton, J. (2006). The future for higher education: Sunrise or perfect storm? *Educause Review*, 41(2) (March/April), 58–71.

Hiltz, S. R., & Shea, P. (2005). The student in the online classroom. In S. R. Hiltz & R. Goldman (Eds.) *Learning Together Online: Research on asynchronous learning networks* (pp. 145–168). Mahwah, NJ.: Lawrence Erlbaum.

Hoadley, C.M. (2005). Design-based research methods and theory building: A case study of research with *SpeakEasy*. *Educational Technology*, 45(1), 42–47.

Hodgins, W. (2004). Interviews—E-learning: What if the impossible isn't? *Online Educa Berlin 2004: SpecialSite*. Accessed March 22, 2005 from: http://www.global-learning.de/g-learn/cgi-bin/gl_userpage.cgi?StructuredContent=m130510

Hoepfl, M.C. (1997). Choosing qualitative research: A primer for technology education researchers. *Journal of Technology Education, 9*(1), 47–63.

Holstein, J.A., & Gubrium, J.F. (1995). The active interview. *Qualitative Research Methods*, vol. 37. London: Sage.

Hopper, R. (1992). *Telephone conversation*. Bloomington: Indiana UP.

Horkheimer, M. (2005). *Eclipse of reason*. New York: Continuum,

Horkheimer, M., & Adorno, T.W. (1972). *Dialectic of enlightenment*. J. Cumming (Trans.). New York: Continuum.

Horton, W. (2006). *e-Learning by design*. San Francisco: Pfeiffer.

Hutchby, I. (2001). *Conversation and technology: From the telephone to the Internet*. London: Polity.

Hutchins, E. (1995). *Cognition in the wild*. Cambridge, MA: MIT Press.

Ingram, D., & Simon-Ingram, J. (Eds.) (1991). Critical theory: The essential readings. New York: Paragon.

Jacobsen, M. (2004). Cognitive visualizations and the design of learning technologies. *International Journal of Learning Technology*, 1(1).

_____. (2004). *The sorrows of empire: Militarism, secrecy, and the end of the republic*. New York: Metropolitan.

Johnson, M. (2002). Introductory biology online: Assessing outcomes of two student populations. *Journal of College Science Teaching*, 31(5), 312–317.

Johnson, R.R. (1998). *User-centered technology: A rhetorical theory for computers and other mundane artifacts*. Albany: State University of New York Press.

Jonassen D.H. (1989). *Hypertext/hypermedia*. Englewood Cliffs, NJ: Educational Technology Publishers

_____. (1996, 2000). *Computers as mindtools for schools: Engaging critical thinking*. Upper Saddle River, NJ: Prentice-Hall.

_____. (2003). Using cognitive tools to represent problems, *Journal of Research on Technology in Education*, 35(3), 362–381.

_____. (2004) (Ed.), *Handbook of research on educational communications and technology* (2nd ed.). Mahwah, NJ: Lawrence Erlbaum.

_____. (2005). *Modeling with technology: Mindtools for conceptual change,* 3rd ed. Columbus, OH: Prentice-Hall.

Jonassen, D.H., Hannum, W.H., & Tessmer, M. (1989). *Handbook of task analysis procedures*. New York: Praeger.

Jonassen, D.H., Peck, K.L., & Wilson, B.G. (1999). *Learning with technology: A constructivist perspective*. Upper Saddle River, NJ: Merrill.

Jonassen, D. H., & Reeves, T. C. (1996). Learning with technology: Using computers as cognitive tools. In D. H. Jonassen (Ed.), *Handbook of research on educational communications and technology* (pp. 693–719). New York: Macmillan.

Jurczyk, J., Kushner-Benson, S.N., & Savery, J. (2004). "Measuring student perceptions in Web-based courses: A standards-based approach." *Online Journal of Distance Learning Administration*, 7(4).

Kaptelinin, V., & Nardi, B. (2003). Post-cognitivist HCI: Second-wave theories. In Proceedings of the ACMI, CHI 2003: New horizons. New York: ACM Press, pp. 692–693.

Kaptelinin, V., & Nardi, B. (2006). *Acting with technology: Activity theory and interaction design.* Cambridge, MA: MIT Press.

Kay, A. (1990). User interface: A personal view. In B. Laurel (Ed.), *The art of human-computer interface design.* Reading, MA: Addison-Wesley, pp. 191–207.

Keengwe, J., Onchwari, G., & Wachira, P. (2008). The use of computer tools to support meaningful learning. *Association for the Advancement of Computing in Education Journal* 16(1), 77–92.

Kember, D. (2003). To control or not to control: The question of whether experimental designs are appropriate for evaluating teaching innovations in higher education. *Assessment & Evaluation in Higher Education,* 28(1), 89–101.

Kim, B., & Hay, K.E. (2005). The evolution of the intellectual partnership with a cognitive tool in inquiry-based astronomy laboratory. CSCL 2005.

Kirkman, M. (2002). What's the plot? Applying narrative theory to research in psychology. *Australian Psychologist,* 37(1), 30–38.

Kolko, B.E., Nakamura, L., & Rodman, G.B. (2000). *Race in cyberspace: An introduction.* New York: Routledge.

Kopecky, H., Chang, H., Klorman, T., Thatcher, J.E., & Borgstedt, A.E. (2005). Performance and private speech of children with attention-deficit/hyperactivity disorder while taking the Tower of Hanoi test: Effects of depth of search, diagnostic subtype, and methylphenidate. *Journal of Abnormal Child Psychology,* 33(5), 625–638.

Koper, R. (2007). Open source and open standards. In J.M. Spector, M.D. Merrill, J.V. Jeroen van Merrienboer, & M.P. Driscoll (Eds.), *Handbook of research on educational communications and technology.* Mahwah, NJ: Lawrence Erlbaum, pp. 355–365.

Koschmann, T., Stahl, G., & Zemel, A. (2007). The video analyst's manifesto (or the implications of Garfinkel's policies for studying instructional practice in design-based research). In R. Goldman, R. Pea, B. Barron, & S.J. Denny. *Video research in the learning sciences.* Mawah, NJ: Lawrence Erlbaum.

Kozma, R.B. (1987). The implications of cognitive psychology for computer-based learning tools. *Educational Technology,* 27(11), 20–25.

_____. (1991). Learning with media. *Review of educational research,* 61(2), 179–211.

Krippendorf, K. (1980). *Content analysis: An introduction to its methodology.* Beverly Hills, CA: Sage.

Kwaśnik, B.H., & Crowston, K. (2005). Introduction to the special issue: Genres of digital documents. *Information Technology & People,* 18(2), 76–88.

Labov, W. (1972). *Language in the inner city.* Philadelphia: University of Pennsylvania Press.

Lachman, R., Lachman, J.L., & Butterfield, E.C. (1979). *Cognitive psychology and information processing.* Hillsdale, NJ: Lawrence Erlbaum.

Lajoie, S.P. (Ed.) (2000). *Computers as cognitive tools,* vol. 2, *No more walls.* Mahwah, NJ: Lawrence Erlbaum.

Langeveld, M.J. (1983). The "secret place" in the life of the child. *Phenomenology + Pedagogy,* 1(2), 181–189.

Laurel, B. (1993). *Computers as theater.* New York: Addison-Wesley.

Lave, J. (1988). *Cognition in practice.* Cambridge: Cambridge UP.

Lave, J., & Wenger, E. (1991). Situated learning: Legitimate peripheral participation. Cambridge: Cambridge UP.

Lenderman, M. (2005). *Experience the message: How experiential marketing is changing the brand world.* Toronto: McClelland & Stewart.

Levering, B., & van Manen, M. (2002). Phenomenological anthropology in the Netherlands and Flanders. In A.-T. Tymieniecka (Ed.), *Phenomenology world wide: Foundations – Expanding dynamics – Life-engagements: A guide for research and study.* Dordrecht: Kluwer Academic Publishing.

Lincoln, Y.S., & Guba, E.G. (1985). *Naturalistic inquiry.* Beverly Hills, CA: Sage.

List, D. (2008). Coding for content analysis. Accessed April 29, 2008 from: http://www.audiencedialogue.net/kya16b.html

Locke, A., & Edwards, D. (2003). Bill and Monica: Memory, emotion and normativity in Clinton's grand jury testimony. *British Journal of Social Psychology,* 42(2), 239–256.

Loebner.net (2008). Home Page of The Loebner Prize in Artificial Intelligence: "The First Turing Test." Accessed August 27, from: http://www.loebner.net/Prizef/loebner-prize.html

Loebner prize. (2008, March 31). In *Wikipedia, the free encyclopedia.* Accessed April 11, 2008 from: http://en.wikipedia.org/w/index.php?title=Loebner_prize&oldid=202195034

Lou, Y., Bernard, R.B., & Abrami, P.C. (2006). Media and pedagogy in undergraduate distance education: A theory-based meta-analysis of empirical literature. *Educational Technology Research & Development,* 54(2), 141–176.

Lowyck, J. (2007). Foreword. In J.M. Spector, M.D. Merrill, J.V., Jeroen van Merrienboer, & M.P. Driscoll (Eds.), *Handbook of research on educational communications and technology.* Mahwah, NJ: Lawrence Erlbaum, pp. xiii–xv.

Lucas, 2003. Edutopia: The George Lucas educational foundation. Foreword by George Lucas, http://www.edutopia.org/php/article.php?id=Art_1043

Lye, (1996). Some principles of phenomenological hermeneutics. Accessed June 22, 2008 from: http://www.brocku.ca/english/courses/4F70/ph.html

Lynch, M. (2006). Cognitive activities without cognition? Ethnomethodological investigations of selected "cognitive" topics. *Discourse Studies,* 8(1), 95–104.

Lynch, M., & Bogen, D. (2005). "My memory has been shredded": A non-cognitivist investigation of "mental" phenomena. In H. te Molder & J. Potter (Eds.), *Conversation and cognition: Discourse, mind and social interaction.* Cambridge: Cambridge UP, pp. 226–240.

Lyotard, J.-F. (1984). *The postmodern condition: A report on knowledge.* Minneapolis: University of Minnesota Press.

Macbeth, D. (1992). Classroom "floors": Material organizations as a course of affairs. *Qualitative Sociology,* 15(2), 123–150.

Mahony, M. J. & Wozniak, H. (2006). Roger's diffusion of innovation theory and professional development in eLearning: a case study of the 'CHS eLearning Resource and Staff Support Project'. In M. Tulloch, S. Relf & P. Uys (Eds.), *Breaking down boundaries: International experience in open, distance and flexible education – Selected papers* (pp. 70–78). Charles Sturt University, Bathurst: Open and Distance Learning Association of Australia. Accessed September 1, 2008 from: http://www.unisa.edu.au/odlaaconference/PDFs/68%20ODLAA%202005%20-%20Mahony%20&%20Wozniak.pdf

Mandler, G. (1985). *Cognitive psychology: An essay in cognitive science.* Mahwah, NJ: Lawrence Erlbaum.

Mattelart, A. (2003). *The information society: An introduction.* Thousand Oaks, CA: Sage.

Mayer, R.E., & Wittrock, M.C. (2006). Problem solving. In P.A. Alexander & P.H. Winne (Eds.), *Handbook of educational psychology,* 2nd ed., pp. 287–303. Mahwah, NJ: Lawrence Erlbaum.

Mayes, P. (2003). Language, social structure, and culture: A genre analysis of cooking classes in Japan and America. Philadelphia: John Benjamins.

McCarthy, J., & Wright, P. (2004). *Technology as experience.* Cambridge, MA: MIT Press.

McGreal, R. (2005). Mobile technologies and the future of global education. ICDE international conference. November 19–23. New Delhi.

McLoughlin, C., & Luca, J. (2001). An E-learning solution to creating work-related skills and competencies for the knowledge-based economy, http://www.auc.edu.au/conf/conf01/downloads/AUC2001_McLoughlin_2.pdf

Merleau-Ponty, M. (1962). *Phenomenology of perception.* London: Routledge & Paul.

Meyer, K.A. (2004). Evaluating online discussions: Four different frames of analysis. *Journal of Asynchronous Learning Networks,* 8, 2, http://www.sloan-c.org/publications/JALN/v8n2/pdf/v8n2_meyer.pdf

Miller, G.A. (1956). The magical number seven, plus or minus two: Some limits on our capacity for processing information. *Psychological Review,* 63, 81–97.

_____. (2003). The cognitive revolution: A historical perspective. *TRENDS in Cognitive Sciences,* 7(3). Accessed December 10, 2007 from: http://www.cogsci.princeton.edu/~geo/Miller.pdf

Milne E. (2003). Email and epistolary technologies: Presence, intimacy, disembodiment. *Fibreculture: Internet Theory + Criticism + Research,* 2. Accessed September 2008 from:http://journal.fibreculture.org/issue2/issue2_milne.html

Mindell, D.A. (2002). *Between human and machine: Feedback, control and computing before cybernetics.* Baltimore: Johns Hopkins UP.

Minsky, M. (2003). Why A.I. is brain-dead. *Wired Magazine,* 11(8). Accessed February 4, 2008 from: http://www.wired.com/wired/archive/11.08/view.html?pg=3

Moll, M. (Ed.) (2001). But it's only a tool: The politics of technology and education reform. Ottawa: Canadian Teachers Federation and Canadian Centre for Policy Alternative.

Mor, Y., and Noss, R. (2004) Towards a narrative-oriented framework for designing mathematical learning. Paper presented at the CSCL SIG First Symposium, October 7–9, 2004, Lausanne, Switzerland.

Moreno, R., Mayer, R.E., Spires, H., & Lester, J. (2001). The case for social agency in computer-based teaching: Do students learn more deeply when they interact with animated pedagogical agents? *Cognition and Instruction,* 19, 177–213.

Mosteller, F., & Boruch, R.F. (2002). Evidence matters: Randomized trials in education research. Washington, DC: Brookings Institution Press.

Moustakas, C.E. (1994). *Phenomenological research methods.* Thousand Oaks, CA: Sage.

Moyer, P.S., Bolyard, J.J., & Spikell, M.A. (2002). What are virtual manipulatives? *Teaching Children Mathematics,* 8(6), 372–377.

Mumford, L. (1934). *Technics and civilization.* New York: Harcourt, Brace.

Nakamura, L. (2002). *Cybertypes: Race, ethnicity, and identity on the Internet.* London: Routledge.

National Security Agency (2008). The GIG Vision: Enabled by information assurance. Accessed April 22, 2008 from: http://www.nsa.gov/ia/industry/gig.cfm?MenuID=10.3.2.2

Neisser, U. (1981). John Dean's memory: A case study. *Cognition, 9,* 1–22,

Newman, F., & Couturier, L.K. (2001). The new competitive arena: Market forces invade the academy. *Change, 33*(5), 11–17.

Newman, J.R. (2000). Commentary on "The tears of mathematics." In J.R. Newman (Ed.), *The world of mathematics,* vol. 3. New York: Dover, pp. 1978–1979.

Nichols, R. Y Allen-Brown, V. (1996). Critical theory and educational technology. In D.H. Jonassen (Ed.), *Handbook of research for educational communications and technology.* New York: Simon and Schuster Macmillan, pp. 226–252.

Noble, D.D. (1989). Cockpit cognition: Education, the military, and cognitive engineering. *AI & Society, 3*(4), 271–296.

_____. (1991). *The classroom arsenal: Military research, information technology and public education.* New York: Falmer Press.

Noble, D.F. (1998). Digital diploma mills: the automation of higher education. First Monday, 3(1). Accessed September 13, 2008 from: http://www.firstmonday.org/issues/issue3_1/noble/

Norman, D. (1981). Twelve issues for cognitive science. In D. Norman (Ed.), *Perspectives on cognitive science.* Norwood, NJ: Ablex, pp. 265–295.

Norman, D. (2003). *Emotional design: Why we love (or hate) everyday things.* New York: Basic Books.

Norris, D.M., Mason, J., & Lefrere, P. (2003). *Transforming E-knowledge.* Ann Arbor, MI: Society for College and University Planning.

Nuechterlein, J. (1990). The good liberal. *National Review,* May 14. Accessed March 14, 2008 from: http://www.encyclopedia.com/doc/1G1-8970359.html

Oblinger, D.G., & Hawkins, B.L. (2006). The myth about no significant difference "using technology produces no significant difference." *Educause Review, 41*(6) (November/December), 14–15.

OED [Oxford English Dictionary]. (2007). Oxford: Oxford UP. Accessed April 27, 2008 from: http://www.oed.com/

PAMO (2005). Urgent action: Protest against militarization of OISE. Accessed May 21, 2008 from: http://www.homesnotbombs.ca/oiseprotest.htm

Pannabecker, J.R. (1992). Technological impacts and determinism in technology education: Alternate metaphors from social constructivism. *Journal of Technology*

Education, 3(1). Accessed September 1, 2008 from: http://scholar.lib.vt.edu/ejournals/JTE/v3n1/html/pannabecker.html

Park, I. (2006). "Cyber home learning system": Promise, status, future. The first APEC future education forum. Accessed September 1, 2008 from: http://www.alcob.com/forum/Archives/02_02_Lecture_2_ParkInnwoo.pdf

Pea, R.D. (1985). Beyond amplification: Using computers to reorganize human mental functioning. *Educational Psychologist,* 20, 167–182.

Perkins, D.N. (1991). Technology meets constructivism: Do they make a marriage? *Educational Technology,* 31(5), 18–23.

Perry, N., & Winne, P. (2006). Learning from Learning Kits: Gstudy traces of students' self-regulated engagements with computerized content. *Educational Psychology Review,* 18(3), 211–228.

Person, N.K., Graesser, A.C., Kreuz, R.J., Pomeroy, V., & Tutoring Research Group (2001). Simulating human tutor dialog moves in AutoTutor. *International Journal of Artificial Intelligence in Education,* 12, 23–39.

Petrina, S. (1992). Questioning the language that we use: A reaction to Pannabecker's critique of the technological impact metaphor. *Journal of Technology Education,* 4(1), 54–61. Accessed September 1, 2008 from: http://scholar.lib.vt.edu/ejournals/JTE/v4n1/html/petrina.html

Piaget, J., & Inhelder, B. (1973). *Memory and intelligence.* New York: Basic Books.

Picciano, A.G. (2002). Beyond student perceptions: Issues of interaction, presence, and performance in an online course. *Journal of Asynchronous Learning Networks,* 6(1), 21–40. Accessed May 15, 2008 from: http://www.sloan-c.org/publications/jaln/v6n1/pdf/v6n1_picciano.pdf

Polkinghorne, D. (1988). *Narrative knowing and the human sciences.* Albany: State University of New York Press.

Polsani, P. (2003). The network learning. In K. Nyíri (Ed.) *Communications in the 21st century: Essays on philosophy, psychology, education.* Vienna: Passagen, pp. 139–149. Also available at: http://www.ltc.arizona.edu/pdf/NetworkLearning.pdf

Potter, J. (2000). Post-cognitive psychology. *Theory & Psychology,* 10(1), 31–37.

Press, M.. & Cooper, R. (2003). *The design experience: The role of design and designers in the twenty-first century* Aldershot, UK: Ashgate.

PT3 (2002). Technology in education: Change models. Preparing tomorrow's teachers to use technology (PT3). Accessed September 1, 2008 from: http://ali.apple.com/ali_sites/hpli/exhibits/1000097/The_Model.html

Pylyshyn, Z. (1981). Complexity and the study of artificial and human intelligence. In *Mind Design,* Haugeland (Ed.). Cambridge, MA: MIT Press.

Radovan, M. (1997). Computation and Understanding. In M. Gams, M. Paprzycki, & X. Wu, (Eds.), *Mind versus computer: Were Dreyfus and Winograd right?* Amsterdam: IOS Press pp. 211–233 (esp. 219–220).

Reagan, R. (1983). Address to the nation on defense and national security. March 23. Accessed July 27, 2007 from: http://www.fas.org/spp/starwars/offdocs/rrspch.htm

Reeves, T. (1995). Questioning the questions of instructional technology research. Instructional technology research online. Accessed April 10, 2008 from: http://www2.gsu.edu/~wwwitr/docs/dean/index.html

Reid, E. (1998). The self and the Internet: Variations on the illusion of one self. In Gackenbach, J. (Ed.), *Psychology and the Internet: Intrapersonal, interpersonal, and transpersonal implications.* San Diego: Academic Press.

Ricoeur, P. (1981). Phenomenology and hermeneutics. In J.B. Thomson (Ed.), *Hermeneutics and the human sciences.* Cambridge: Cambridge UP, pp. 101–128.

Riessman, C.K. (2002). Analysis of personal narratives. In J.F. Gubrium & J.A. Holstein (Eds.), *Handbook of interview research.* Thousand Oaks, CA: Sage, pp. 695–710.

Rogers, E.M. (2003). *Diffusion of innovations,* 5th ed. New York: Free Press.

Ronnlund, M., Lovden, M., & Nilsson, L.G. (2001). Adult age differences in Tower of Hanoi performance: Influence from demographic and cognitive variables. *Aging Neuropsychology and Cognition,* 8(4), 269–283.

Rorty, R. (1991). *On Heidegger and others: Philosophical papers,* vol. 2. Cambridge: Cambridge UP.

Rourke, L. (2005). *Learning through online discussion.* Department of Educational Psychology, University of Alberta. Unpublished dissertation.

Rourke, L., & Friesen, N. (2006). The learning sciences: The very idea. *Educational Media International,* 43(4), 271–284.

Rourke, L., & Kanuka, H. (2007). Barriers to online critical discourse. *International Journal of Computer-Supported Collaborative Learning,* 2(1), 105–126.

Rubin, H.J., & Rubin, I. (2005). Qualitative interviewing: The art of hearing data , 2nd ed. Thousand Oaks, CA: Sage.

Rumsfeld, D.H. (2001, September 10). DOD acquisition and logistics excellence week kickoff—bureaucracy to battlefield. Accessed September 24, 2008 from: http://www.defenselink.mil/speeches/speech.aspx?speechid=430

Russell, B. (1945). *History of Western philosophy.* London: George Allen & Unwin.

Russell, T.L. (1999). The "no significant difference" phenomenon: 248 research reports, summaries and papers, 4th ed. Raleigh: North Carolina State University.

_____. (2008). The "no significant difference" phenomenon. Accessed January 8, 2008 from: http://www.nosignificantdifference.org/

Ryan, M.-L. (1994). Immersion vs. interactivity: Virtual reality and literary theory. Accessed May 2, 2008 from: http://www.humanities.uci.edu/mposter/syllabi/readings/ryan.html

Saettler, P. (2004). *The Evolution of American Educational Technology* 2nd ed. Mahwah, NJ: Lawrence Erlbaum.

Saevi, T. (2005). *Seeing disability pedagogically. The lived experience of disability in the pedagogical encounter*. Doctoral dissertation. University of Bergen: Faculty of Psychology.

Salomon, G. (1988a). AI in reverse: Computer tools that turn cognitive. *Journal of Educational Computing Research*, 4(2), 123–139.

Sawyer, R.K. (2006a). Introduction: The new science of learning. In R.K. Sawyer (Ed.), *The Cambridge handbook of the learning sciences*. Cambridge: Cambridge UP, pp. 1–16.

Sawyer, R.K. (2006b). The schools of the future. In R.K. Sawyer (Ed.), *The Cambridge handbook of the learning sciences*. Cambridge: Cambridge UP, pp. 567–580.

Scardamalia, M. (2003). Knowledge forum (Advances beyond CSILE). *Journal of Distance Education*, 17(3), 23–28.

Scardamalia, M., & Bereiter, C. (2003). Knowledge building. In *The encyclopedia of education*, 2nd ed. New York: Macmillan Reference, pp. 1370–1373. Also available at: http://ikit.org/fulltext/inpressKB.pdf

Sciadas, G. (2002). The digital divide in Canada. Report for statistics Canada, http://www.statcan.ca/english/research/56F0009XIE/56F0009XIE2002001.pdf

Schegloff, E.A. (1986). The routine as achievement. *Human Studies*, 9, 111–151.

Schulmeister, R. (1997). *Hypermedia learning systems: Theory – didactics – design*. Accessed April 24, 2008 from: http://www.izhd.uni-hamburg.de/paginae/Book/Frames/Start_FRAME.html

Schütz, A., & Luckmann, T. (1973). *The structures of the life-world*. Evanston, IL: Northwestern UP.

Schweizer, P. (1997). Computation and the science of mind. In M. Paprzycki & X. Wu (Eds.), *Mind versus computer: Were Dreyfus and Winograd right?* Amsterdam: IOS Press.

Scribner, S. (1997). Modes of thinking and ways of speaking: Culture and logic reconsidered. In S. Scribner & E. Tolbach (Eds.), *Mind and social practice: Selected writings of Sylvia Scribner*. Cambridge: Cambridge UP.

Shabani Varaki, B. (2007). Narrative inquiry in educational research. *Forum Qualitative Sozialforschung/Forum: Qualitative Social Research*, 8(1). Accessed September 1, 2008 from: http://www.qualitative-research.net/fqs-texte/1-07/07-1-4-e.htm

Sheehan, R.J., & Rode, S. (1999). On scientific narrative: Stories of light by Newton and Einstein. *Journal of Business and Technical Communication*, 13(3), 336–358.

Shields, R. (2003). *The virtual*. London: Routledge.

Simpson, J. (2005). Conversational floors in synchronous text-based CMC discourse. *Discourse Studies*, 7(3), 337–361.

Skinner, B.F. (1968). *The technology of teaching*. New York: Appleton-Century-Crofts.

Slosser, S. (2002). *ADL and the sharable content object reference model*. Accessed September 1, 2008 from: http://www.nectec.or.th/courseware/pdf-documents/adl-scorm.pdf

Smith, D.W. (2003). Phenomenology. *The Stanford encyclopedia of philosophy* (Winter), Edward N. Zalta (Ed.). Accessed September 1, 2008 from: http://plato.stanford.edu/archives/win2003/entries/davidson/

Smith, M.R. (1994). Technological determinism in American culture. In M.R. Smith & L. Marx (Eds.), *Does technology drive history? The dilemma of technological determinism*. Cambridge, MA: MIT Press, pp. 1–35.

Smith, M.R., & Marx, L. (1994). *Does technology drive history? The dilemma of technological determinism*. Cambridge, MA: MIT Press.

Smith, N.S. (2005). Solving the "cottage industry" problem in E-learning programs. *Xplanazine*. Accessed January 5, http://www.xplanazine.com/archives/2005/01/solving_the_cot.php

Soentgen, J. (1998). *Die verdeckte Wirklichkeit: Einführung in die Neue Phänomenologie von Hermann Schmitz*. Bonn: Bouvier.

Spinuzzi, C. (2003). *Tracing genres through organizations: A sociocultural approach to information design*. Cambridge, MA: MIT Press.

Stahl, G. (2006). *Group cognition: Computer support for collaborative knowledge building*. Cambridge, MA: MIT Press.

Steinberg, S.R., Kincheloe, J.L., & P.H. Hinchey (Eds.) (1999). *The post-formal reader: Cognition and education*. New York: Falmer Press.

Still, A., & Costall, A. (Eds.) (1991). *Against cognitivism: Alternative foundations for cognitive psychology*. Hemel Hempstead: Harvester Wheatsheaf.

Stockmeyer, P.K. (1998). Tower of Hanoi instructions in English, page 1. Accessed February 18, 2008 from: http://www.cs.wm.edu/~pkstoc/page_1.html

Stockmeyer, P.K., Bateman, C.D., Clark, J.W., Eyster, C.R., Harrison, M.T., Loehr, N.A., Rodriguez, P.J., & Simmons, J. III (1995). Exchanging disks in the Tower of Hanoi. *International Journal of Computer Mathematics*, 59, 37–47.

Suchman, L.A. (1987). *Plans and situated actions.* Cambridge: Cambridge UP.

_____. (2007). *Human-machine reconfigurations: Plans and situated actions,* 2nd ed. Cambridge: Cambridge UP.

Sundman, J. (2003). Artificial stupidity. *Slate.com.* February 26, 2003. Accessed January 24, 2007 from: http://archive.salon.com/tech/feature/2003/02/26/loebner_part_one/index.html

Szabo, M. (1994). Enhancing the interactive classroom through computer based instruction: Some examples from PLATO. *Computer-mediated communications and the online classroom,* vol. I. Cresskill, NJ: Hampton Press.

TCER. (2007). *Evaluation of the Texas Technology Immersion Pilot: Findings from the Second Year.* Austin: Texas Center for Educational Research. Accessed August 22, 2008 from: http://www.etxtip.info/images/eTxTIP_Year2EvalRptSumm.pdf

ten Have, P. (2000). Computer-mediated chat: Ways of finding chat partners. *MC Journal: A Journal of Media and Culture,* 3(4). Accessed January 24, 2007 from: http://journal.media-culture.org.au/0008/partners.php

Thagard, P. (2002). Cognitive science. *Stanford encyclopedia of philosophy.* Accessed September 1, 2008 from:http://plato.stanford.edu/entries/cognitive-science/

Thorburn, D. (2003). The web of paradox. In D. Thorburn & H. Jenkins (Eds.), *Rethinking media change: The aesthetics of transition.* Cambridge, MA: MIT Press. Also available at: http://web.mit.edu/comm-forum/papers/thorburn-web.html

Toffler, A. (1980). *The third wave.* New York: Bantam Books.

Tower of Hanoi. (2008, April 18). In *Wikipedia, the free encyclopedia.* Accessed April 21 from http://en.wikipedia.org/w/index.php?title=Tower_of_Hanoi&oldid=206568437

Traudt, P.J. (2005). *An introduction to the study of media: Content and audience analysis.* Boston: Allyn & Bacon.

Tucker, K. (2005). The final frontier. *New York Times Magazine,* December 4, 2005.

Turing, A.M. (1950). Computing machinery and intelligence. *Mind*, 59, 433–460.

Turkle, S. (1984). *The second self: Computers and the human spirit.* New York: Simon and Schuster.

_____. (1995). *Life on the screen: Identity in the age of the Internet.* New York: Simon and Schuster.

_____. (2005). *The second self: Computers and the human spirit, twentieth anniversary edition.* Cambridge, MA: MIT Press.

Ulam, S.M. (1991). *Adventures of a mathematician.* New York: Scribner's.

Ungerleider, C.S., & Burns, T.C. (2002). Information and communication technologies in elementary and secondary education: A state of the art review. Prepared for 2002 Pan-Canadian Education Research Agenda Symposium "Information Technology and Learning," April 30–May 2, 2002, Crowne Plaza Montreal Centre Hotel, Montreal, Quebec.

Vakil, E., & Hoffman, Y. (2004). Dissociation between two types of skill learning tasks: The differential effect of divided attention. *Journal of Clinical and Experimental Neuropsychology,* 26, 653–666.

van Manen, M. (1997). *Researching lived experience: Human science for an action sensitive pedagogy,* 2nd ed. London, ON: Althouse Press.

_____. (2002). *Phenomenology online.* Accessed January 27, 2008 from: http://www.phenomenologyonline.com

_____. (2008). Phenomenology of practice. *Phenomenology & Practice,* 1(1). Accessed May 2 from: http://www.phandpr.org/index.php/pandp/article/view/7/55

Varela, F.J., Thompson, E.T., & Rosch, E. (1991). *The embodied mind: Cognitive science and human experience.* Cambridge, MA: MIT Press.

Varnhagen, S., Wilson, D., Krupa, E., Kasprzak, S., & Hunting, V. (2005). Comparison of student experiences with different online graduate courses in health promotion. *Canadian Journal of Learning and Technology,* 31(1). Accessed April 29, 2008 from: http://www.cjlt.ca/content/vol31.1/varnhagen.html

Vygotsky, L.S. (1978). *Mind and society: The development of higher mental processes.* Cambridge, MA: Harvard UP.

Wagner, W.-R. (2004). *Medienkompetenz revisited: Medien als Werkzeuge der Weltaneignung: ein pädagogisches Programm.* Munich: kopaed.

Waldenfels, B. (2002). *Bruchlinien der Erfahrung.* Frankfurt am Main: Suhrkamp.

Waldenfels, B. (2005). *Phänomenologie der Aufmerksamkeit.* Frankfurt am Main: Suhrkamp.

Waldrop, M.M. (2002). *The dream machine: J.C.R. Licklider and the revolution that made computing personal.* New York: Penguin Books.

Warren, C.A.B. (2002). Qualitative interviewing. In J. Gubrium & J. Holstein (Eds.), *Handbook of interview research: Context and method.* Thousand Oaks, CA: Sage, pp. 83–102.

Webster's New Collegiate Dictionary. (1977). Metaphor. p. 722.Toronto: Thomas Allen & Son.

Weinberger, A., & Fischer, F. (2005). A framework to analyze argumentative knowledge construction in computer-supported collaborative learning. *Computers and Education,* 46 (1), 71–95.

Weinstock, M. (2001). *Virtual learning.* Government Executive.com, http://www.govexec.com/features/1000/1000s3.htm

Whitby, B.R. (1996). The Turing test: AI's biggest blind alley? In P. Millican & A. Clark (Eds.), *Machines and thought: The legacy of Alan Turing,* vol. 1. Oxford: Oxford UP, pp. 53–62.

White, H. (1973). *Metahistory: The historical imagination in nineteenth-century Europe.* Baltimore: Johns Hopkins UP.

White, M. (2006). *The body and the screen: Theories of Internet spectatorship.* Cambridge, MA: MIT Press.

Winn, W., & Snyder, D. (2004). Cognitive perspectives in psychology. In D.H. Jonassen (Ed.), *Handbook of research for educational communications and technology.* New York: Simon and Schuster Macmillan, pp. 83–90.

Winne, P.H. (2006). How software technologies can improve research on learning and bolster school reform. *Educational Psychologist,* 41(1), 5–17.

Winograd, T., & Flores, F. (1986). *Understanding computers and cognition: A new foundation for design.* Norwood, NJ: Ablex.

Wise, A., Chang, J., Duffy, T., & del Valle, R. (2004). The effects of teacher social presence of student satisfaction, engagement, and learning. Embracing diversity in the learning sciences: Proceedings of ICLS 2004, June 22–26, Santa Monica: University of California Los Angeles.

Wittgenstein, L. (1953). *Philosophical investigations.* London: Blackwell.

_____. (1969). *On certainty.* New York: Harper Torchbooks.

Wolfe, P. (1998). Revisiting effective teaching. *Educational Leadership,* 56(3), 61–64.

Wolff, A., Mulholland, P., Zdrahal, Z., & Joiner, R. (2007). Combining gameplay and narrative techniques to enhance the user experience of viewing galleries. *ACM Computers in Entertainment,* 5(1), Article No. 6.

Woodward, A. (2006). Jean-François Lyotard (1924–1998). *The Internet encyclopedia of philosophy.* Accessed September 1, 2008 from: http://www.iep.utm.edu/l/Lyotard.htm

WSIS (2005). World Summit on the Information Society. Accessed September 1, 2008 from: http://www.itu.int/wsis/tunis/newsroom/stats/

Xin, C., & Feenberg, A. (2007). Pedagogy in cyberspace: The dynamics of online discourse. *E-Learning,* 4(4), 415–432.

Yates, J., & Orlikowski, W.J. (1992). Genres of organizational communication: A structurational approach to studying communication and media. *Academy of Management Review,* 17(2), 299–326.

Ylönen, S. (2001). Entwicklung von Textsortenkonventionen am Beispiel von "Originalarbeiten" der Deutschen Medizinischen Wochenschrift (DMW). *Leipziger Fachsprachen-Studien* (15). Frankfurt am Main: Peter Lang.

Yukawa, J. (2005a). Computer support for collaborative learning. Proceedings of the 2005 conference on computer support for collaborative learning: Learning 2005: The next 10 years! Taipei, Taiwan, 732–736.

You've got mail (1998). Nora Ephron (Dir.). Based on a play by Miklós László.

Zhao, Y., Lei, J., Chun Lai, B.Y., & Tan, H.S. (2005). What makes the difference? A practical analysis of research on the effectiveness of distance education. *Teachers College Record,* 107(8), 1836–1884.

Index

Studies in the Postmodern Theory of Education

General Editors
Joe L. Kincheloe & Shirley R. Steinberg

Counterpoints publishes the most compelling and imaginative books being written in education today. Grounded on the theoretical advances in criticalism, feminism, and postmodernism in the last two decades of the twentieth century, Counterpoints engages the meaning of these innovations in various forms of educational expression. Committed to the proposition that theoretical literature should be accessible to a variety of audiences, the series insists that its authors avoid esoteric and jargonistic languages that transform educational scholarship into an elite discourse for the initiated. Scholarly work matters only to the degree it affects consciousness and practice at multiple sites. Counterpoints' editorial policy is based on these principles and the ability of scholars to break new ground, to open new conversations, to go where educators have never gone before.

For additional information about this series or for the submission of manuscripts, please contact:

Joe L. Kincheloe & Shirley R. Steinberg
c/o Peter Lang Publishing, Inc.
29 Broadway, 18th floor
New York, New York 10006

To order other books in this series, please contact our Customer Service Department:

(800) 770-LANG (within the U.S.)
(212) 647-7706 (outside the U.S.)
(212) 647-7707 FAX

Or browse online by series:
www.peterlang.com